Beyond Empathy and Inclusion

Beyond Empathy and Inclusion

The Challenge of Listening in Democratic Deliberation

MARY F. SCUDDER

OXFORD
UNIVERSITY PRESS

OXFORD
UNIVERSITY PRESS

Oxford University Press is a department of the University of Oxford. It furthers
the University's objective of excellence in research, scholarship, and education
by publishing worldwide. Oxford is a registered trade mark of Oxford University
Press in the UK and certain other countries.

Published in the United States of America by Oxford University Press
198 Madison Avenue, New York, NY 10016, United States of America.

Library of Congress Cataloging-in-Publication Data
Names: Scudder, Mary F. (Molly), author.
Title: Beyond empathy and inclusion : the challenge of listening in
democratic deliberation / Mary F. Scudder.
Description: New York, NY : Oxford University Press, [2020] |
Includes bibliographical references and index. |
Contents: The challenge of listening—The insufficiency of
inclusion and the need for uptake—Empathy as a strategy and ideal of deliberation :
the promise and perils—A listening-centered approach to democratic deliberation—
Listening toward democracy—Listening for difference in democracy—
Democratic ideals in a non-ideal world.
Identifiers: LCCN 2020016027 (print) | LCCN 2020016028 (ebook) |
ISBN 9780197535455 (hardback) | ISBN 9780197757413 (paperback) |
ISBN 9780197535462 (updf) | ISBN 9780197535486 (online) |
ISBN 9780197535479 (epub)
Subjects: LCSH: Deliberative democracy. | Listening—Political aspects. |
Empathy—Political aspects. | Political participation.
Classification: LCC JC423 .S394 2020 (print) |
LCC JC423 (ebook) | DDC 323/.042—dc23
LC record available at https://lccn.loc.gov/2020016027
LC ebook record available at https://lccn.loc.gov/2020016028

Paperback printed by Integrated Books International, United States of America

For Kyle and Lola

Contents

Acknowledgments

The ideas and arguments presented in this book have developed over the course of many years and across many jurisdictions. Naturally, I have amassed a great number of intellectual debts along the way. I am happy to acknowledge them here. The book grew out of the dissertation I completed in the Department of Politics at the University of Virginia. After several rewrites, it is hardly the same work. Still, it is safe to say that I could not have written the book I did without the support I received from UVa's political theory group—both during and after my time in Charlottesville. I thank my professors, Lawrie Balfour, Colin Bird, George Klosko, Melvin Rogers, Jennifer Rubenstein, Lynn Sanders, and Chad Wellmon, for their substantive feedback and general support in writing this book.

In particular, I would like to thank my dissertation adviser, mentor, and friend, Stephen White. Stephen has been a truly exceptional mentor. This project was much improved for his generous and incisive readings of multiple versions of each chapter. Stephen has a keen ability to engage with others' ideas on their own terms, and my work has benefited tremendously as a result.

Early work on this project was done during my predoctoral fellowship year at the Institute for Advanced Studies in Culture at the University of Virginia. I am grateful for the financial and intellectual support I received from the IASC. Thanks are also owed to Clarissa Hayward and Frank Lovett at Washington University for welcoming me into their political theory community during my time in St. Louis. The suggestions I received at Washington University were instrumental in the development of my critique of empathy. I am especially thankful to Ron Watson and Matt Chick for their feedback and friendship.

I wrote and revised this book as an assistant professor, first at Texas Christian University and then at Purdue University. I am grateful to my friends and colleagues at TCU, especially my fellow writing bootcampers: Sam Arnold, Stacie McCormick, Kathryn Sederberg, and our fearless leader, Charlotte Hogg. In 2016, I participated in the National Center for Faculty Development & Diversity's Faculty Success Program and had the good fortune of being matched with Lauren Cooper and Nora Williams, who provided immensely helpful professional advice and, dare I say, empathy. Their encouragement has had a profound effect on me.

At Purdue, my colleagues in the Political Science Department have provided a wonderfully supportive (and fun) environment in which to work. I look forward to coming in to the office. And there is no better group with which to celebrate—or commiserate—than the Wine Wednesday crew. A special thank-you is owed to Pat Boling, Nadia Brown, Ann Clark, Rosie Clawson, Tara Grillos, Manjana Milkoreit, Keith Shimko, Valeria Sinclair-Chapman, Swati Srivastava, and former colleagues Laurel Weldon and Aaron Hoffman, for their support and friendship throughout the process of writing this book. I wrote this book under Rosie's reign as department head, and I am so thankful for the support she showed me and this project from the very beginning.

I presented portions of this book at meetings of the American Political Science Association, the Midwest Political Science Association, the Western Political Science Association, and the Association of Political Theory, as well as workshops at the University of Notre Dame, the University of Virginia, and Washington University in St. Louis. I am grateful to those who organized and participated in these events. I received generous feedback from discussants and fellow panelists, including Emily Beausoleil, Susan Bickford, James Bohman, Quinlan Bowman, Mark Button, Kennan Ferguson, Ben Hertzberg, Nancy Hirschmann, Hélène Landemore, Michael Morrell, Michael Neblo, and Mark Warren. A portion of Chapter 2 is based on "The Ideal of Uptake in Democratic Deliberation," which was published in *Political Studies* 68, no. 2 (2020). I am thankful to have had the opportunity to develop these ideas further here. An earlier version of Chapter 3 was published as "Beyond Empathy: Strategies and Ideals of Democratic Deliberation," in *Polity* 48, no. 4 (2016). I am grateful for permission to reuse this material here.

I would also like to thank Steve Johnston, Sharon Krause, and Libby Anker, who commented on an early draft of the full manuscript as part of a book workshop hosted at the University of Virginia in 2016 with support from the College of Liberal Arts at Purdue University. The book benefited tremendously from Steve's, Sharon's, and Libby's sustained and critical engagement. I also want to acknowledge the tremendously constructive feedback I received from three anonymous reviewers and my editor at Oxford University Press, Angela Chnapko.

In writing this book, I also incurred a great number of personal debts. It is a delight to thank publicly the people whose help made this book possible. I have much appreciation for all of my teachers, especially Marie Bernard, Sister Frances Meyer, DC, David Pardini, and Michael Sanderl, who pushed me to reach my potential. Timothy J. Lukes of Santa Clara University first taught me to love political theory. My students will be fortunate if I am even half the teacher he is.

I am also grateful for the love and care that Bunchy Boldebuck provided my family and me during late revisions of the manuscript. And I am indebted to my friends from graduate school who supported me at the earliest stages of this project. My ideas and life would have been much poorer without Regev Ben Jacob, Emily Charnock, Anne Daniels, Ellie Kaknes, Nadim Khoury, Derek King, Kyle Lascurettes, Allison and Dave Novitsky, Emily Pears, Justin Peck, Hilde Restad, Kate Sanger, Greta Snyder, Emily Sydnor, Will Umphres, and Brandon Yoder. It was a great privilege to have landed in Charlottesville at the same time as these folks. Taking courses, studying for comprehensive exams, and writing a dissertation would have been a lot harder and no fun at all without the friendship and guidance of political theorists Evan Farr, Callum Ingram, Colin Kielty, and Claire Timperley.

I owe perhaps my largest debt to my parents and greatest teachers, John and Judy Scudder. As educators, they endowed my sister and me with a deep love of learning. I am forever grateful for their encouragement and unyielding confidence. I wrote and revised much of this work under their roof, while they fed and cared for me and my growing family. I could not have written this book without them. Big thanks are also owed to my Haynes family, especially to Bonnie and Tim for their love and support and help with moving, and to Amelia and Kepler for their FaceTime calls. I am also grateful to the rest of my Bauer and Scudder family, especially Paula and Bob Behmke for letting me take over their dining room table for weeks so that I could have a place to write, and Carol and Joe Zulich for putting up with me and my revisions during their vacation time in Sonoma. My Nana, Dolores Bauer, has provided a tremendous amount of support for my research. She always asks me how my work is going and has made an effort to understand what it is I do. And when she disagrees with one of my ideas, she lets me know.

I thank my sister, Annie Gabillet, who happily suffered my company from elementary school to college (and ultimately the same political science department). It was on Annie's recommendation that I took Lukes's advanced political theory course at Santa Clara University. I hesitated, having already satisfied that requirement, but ultimately heeded her advice. My life would never be the same after that. Annie has talked over many of these ideas with me, and they have been improved significantly thanks to her clear thinking. I will never be able to repay her for the time she has spent as my PR adviser! Let it be known that there is no better (or more ruthless) reader of abstracts or proposals. I am also grateful for the support from my brother-in-law Rémi Gabillet, who is quick to acknowledge and celebrate the successes of others. When I thought that writing and revising this book were hard, Annie and Rémi lovingly reminded me that it was the good kind of hard. Their daughters, Lucie and Iris, bring me so much joy and motivation to work hard and make them proud.

I dedicate this book to Kyle and Lola. Kyle Haynes will certainly be the most familiar with the arguments presented in these pages. I am grateful beyond words for the daily support and unconditional love he shows me, and for his editing. He read several drafts of every chapter and helped me clarify my arguments and language. I am thankful that he goes along with my summer writing bootcamps in Sonoma and is even willing to spend our short writing breaks helping me think through a challenging critique or idea while we walk around the block. His encouragement, love, and coffee sustain my work and my life. Lola Scudder-Haynes was born during the writing of this book. She, of course, will be the least familiar with the book's arguments, though her smiles and cuddles—and before that, her kicks—were no less integral to my writing process.

Mary F. (Molly) Scudder
West Lafayette, Indiana

1

The Challenge of Listening

The central claim of this book is that the more citizens listen to one another when forming their political opinions, the better.[1] Good listening is a virtue. All else equal, good listeners are thought to make better students, teachers, therapists, salespeople, managers, friends, and romantic partners. In this book, I show that listening has important political stakes as well. Without listening, there can be no democracy. Being heard by our fellow citizens is what ensures we have a say in the laws to which we are held. The act of listening has the power to change lived reality, infusing a decision-making process with democratic meaning. Conversely, a lack of listening necessarily leads to a democratic deficit.

To make processes of collective decision making more democratic, we need to find ways to promote greater listening. Listening is essential not only in the deliberation directly preceding a formal decision or vote but also in everyday and informal conversations during which citizens form their opinions on social and political issues. All else equal, a political system that facilitates and encourages sincere and careful listening among its citizens will produce more democratic decisions than one that does not.

This book not only defends listening as a central act of democratic citizenship, it also takes stock of the all-too-common tendency of people to shut down, ignore, or otherwise not listen to voices and perspectives they would rather not hear. Specifically, I show how democracy is threatened by people's unwillingness to seriously engage across difference and disagreement. As I show, in order to improve the democratic quality of a political system, we

---

[1] The word "citizen" raises complicated questions regarding what is owed *noncitizens* who live in a democratic nation. Importantly, by using the word "citizen," I do not mean to suggest that those without the legal status of "citizen" are not owed listening. Indeed, the arguments in this book would suggest that a political system that denied noncitizen residents a say in the laws should not be considered fully democratic. Deliberative democracies ought to include and consider the perspectives of "all the people potentially affected by a collective decision or regime." Michael A. Neblo, Kevin M. Esterling, and David Lazer, *Politics with the People: Building a Directly Representative Democracy* (Cambridge: Cambridge University Press, 2018), 4. André Bächtiger and John Parkinson, *Mapping and Measuring Deliberation: Towards a New Deliberative Quality* (Oxford: Oxford University Press, 2019), 9.

Beyond Empathy and Inclusion. Mary F. Scudder, Oxford University Press (2020). © Oxford University Press.
DOI: 10.1093/oso/9780197535455.001.0001.

must account for and address the obstacles that prevent people's voices from actually being heard.

Take, for example, the Occupy Wall Street (OWS) and Black Lives Matter movements, which have used their own collective "voice" to shed light on injustice and challenge the status quo. Despite substantial effort, these movements have struggled to get a fair hearing from dominant segments of society. A 2011 video, for example, showed Wharton MBA students chanting "get a job" at OWS protestors on the University of Pennsylvania's campus.[2] This quick and ungenerous reaction to the OWS movement demonstrates the limitations of democratic deliberation and political action when others refuse to listen. Similarly, the negative view of the Black Lives Matter movement that persists among a majority of Americans suggests that many citizens, especially those who enjoy economic or racial privilege, are unwilling or even unable to really hear voices that challenge their worldview or demand remediation of injustice.[3] What lasting influence can these movements have if most Americans refuse to fairly consider and deal with their messages?

These failures of listening would seem to reveal a major limitation of deliberative democratic theory, and importantly, one that cannot be overcome by procedural interventions aimed at making deliberation more inclusive. Even after people from marginalized groups succeed at breaking into the public sphere, there is no guarantee that their fellow citizens will actually listen to what they have to say. Without listening, hard-won battles for inclusion and empowerment will have no democratic impact.

Take, as another example, First Lady Michelle Obama's speech at the Democratic National Convention in 2016. There, she spoke of her experience living in the White House, tying her own story as the first black First Lady to the history of America:

> That is the story of this country, the story that has brought me to this stage tonight, the story of generations of people who felt the lash of bondage, the shame of servitude, the sting of segregation, but who kept on striving and hoping and doing what needed to be done so that today, I wake up every morning in a house that was built by slaves—and I watch my

[2] Zaid Jilani, "Video: Students at Elite Wharton Business School Mock 99 Percent Movement: 'Get a Job! Get a Job!,'" *Think Progress*, October 21, 2011, https://thinkprogress.org/video-students-at-elite-wharton-business-school-mock-99-percent-movement-get-a-job-get-a-job-1e0ed111fbd/.

[3] Jonathan Easley, "Poll: 57 Percent Have Negative View of Black Lives Matter Movement," *Thehill.com*, August 2, 2017, https://thehill.com/homenews/campaign/344985-poll-57-percent-have-negative-view-of-black-lives-matter-movement.

daughters—two beautiful, intelligent, black women—playing with their dogs on the White House lawn.[4]

Referring to the White House as a "house built by slaves," Obama reminds American citizens of the white supremacist legacy of their country. For an untold number of the estimated 26 million people who tuned in to Obama's speech, this was the first time they considered the extent to which the White House—and the country—was built on the backs of slaves. In the wake of the First Lady's speech, hundreds of articles were written and shared on social media examining the historical accuracy of her observation. The *New York Times* published a story with the headline, "Yes, Slaves Did Help Build the White House."

But some, especially conservative, critics of the Obamas tried to discount the First Lady's emphasis on the white supremacist legacy of the United States, revealing an unwillingness to consider, in other words, to deal with America's racist past and present. Then–Fox News host Bill O'Reilly, for example, stated that while Obama was "essentially correct in citing slaves as builders of the White House . . . there were others working as well." He also asserted, without citing any evidence, that the "slaves that worked there were well-fed and had decent lodgings provided by the government."[5] Conservative media "watchdog" *Newsbusters* challenged the significance of Obama's claim, noting that the White House "was actually gutted and renovated by [sic] multiple times post-slavery."[6] The implication was that since slaves were not responsible for the most recent renovations, their contribution could be ignored.

Of course, these reactions from political elites and the media are part of a well-choreographed and predictable strategy of partisan opposition. It would be naïve to expect opponents of the Democratic Party not to respond critically to a major convention speech. But these reactions to Obama's specific point regarding the use of slaves to build the White House also seem to reveal the resistance people often show toward considering others' input when it offends or indicts them. In an effort to avoid dealing with the implications of the White House being built by slaves, these commentators

---

[4] Michelle Obama, "Democratic National Convention Speech," July 25, 2016, https://www.youtube.com/watch?v=4ZNWYqDU948.

[5] Bill O'Reilly, *The O'Reilly Factor*, Fox News, July 26, 2016.

[6] Curtis Houck, "Networks Laud 'Artfully Painted,' 'Remarkable' Michelle Obama Speech; Touts People Crying," *NewsBusters*, July 2016, https://www.newsbusters.org/video/networks-laud-artfully-painted-remarkable-michelle-obama-speech-touts-people-crying.

sought to discount or diminish rather than fairly consider the actual content of Obama's claims. Interpreting these reactions to Obama's speech as more than just partisan politics, or even a conservative strategy of playing on middle-class Americans' racial resentment, offers another example of people dismissing inputs that trouble them. They reveal an all-too-common tendency people have to disregard perspectives that challenge their preferred view of the world.[7]

My aim is to better understand the prospects of democracy in a world where citizens are often uninterested or unwilling to engage across social divisions. As I show, however, failures to listen need not be willful or based in self-interest, as in the case of someone who refuses to listen to a claim of injustice because it challenges one's own position of privilege. People often struggle to hear the perspectives of those who are different from them, even when the relationship is not marked by unequal power or histories of oppression. Whatever the cause, citizens' failures to listen to what others have to say undermine the democratic nature and potential of large, complex, and diverse societies. Listening is what supplies deliberation with its democratic force. Unless citizens listen to one another when forming their opinions and until representatives or those with formal decision-making power really listen to their constituents so as to take into account their preferences, concerns, and perspectives, we will never achieve meaningfully democratic rule.

But while most lowercase-d democrats would agree that democracy suffers when the perspectives of the historically excluded and the marginalized are not fairly considered, it does not necessarily follow that listening is an absolute democratic good. Do citizens have to listen to the voices of people who wish them ill? How does democracy suffer, exactly, when its enemies are silenced, or if not silenced, then simply ignored?[8] Is it not a virtue of democratic citizenship to shut down and resist certain political movements, in particular, those that seek to destroy democracy?[9]

---

[7] In *The Racial Contract*, Charles Mills argues that white supremacy has its own "epistemology of ignorance." This would suggest that the inability of white Americans to understand or accept Obama's statement may go beyond the general difficulty people have seeing others' perspectives. According to Mills, this "particular pattern of localized and global cognitive dysfunctions" produces "the ironic outcomes that whites will in general be unable to understand the world they themselves have made." I think the case of Michelle Obama is illustrative of the difficulty we have hearing opposing views, even if symptomatic of something more than that. Charles W. Mills, *The Racial Contract* (Ithaca, NY: Cornell University Press, 1997), 18.

[8] John S. Dryzek, "The Forum, the System, and the Polity: Three Varieties of Democratic Theory," *Political Theory* 45, no. 5 (2017): 620.

[9] Steven Johnston, *American Dionysia: Violence, Tragedy, and Democratic Politics* (Cambridge: Cambridge University Press, 2015).

Consider, for example, the hundreds of white supremacists who descended on Charlottesville, Virginia, in August 2017 for a "Unite the Right" rally organized by Jason Kessler, a Charlottesville native. In addition to general intimidation, the proximate purpose of the rally was to protest the city's decision to remove a Robert E. Lee statue from the newly renamed Emancipation Park in the center of town. The city, which had reached that decision only after a long deliberative process, denied the protestors' request for a permit to hold a rally in Emancipation Park. The city stated that protestors should instead hold the rally in a larger park outside of the city center. The American Civil Liberties Union, however, successfully defended Kessler and his fellow protestors' right to hold their rally in Emancipation Park on the grounds of their First Amendment right to free speech.

This book is not about an expansive right to free speech. Instead, it is about the democratic expectation that citizens will listen even to those with whom they disagree. More specifically, this book is about the threat to democracy posed by citizens' refusal to listen to one another. But what do we lose, democratically speaking, by not hearing the hateful voices of white nationalists and other hate groups? Do democratic co-citizens have the right to shut out antidemocratic sentiments and forces that emerge from the democratic process itself? Or must committed democrats stand by and watch their enemies turn the democratic process of deliberation against itself?[10] Gains in support and visibility of white nationalist and neo-Nazi groups both in the United States and other Western democracies would seem to work against the absolute value of listening for democracy.[11]

A major goal of this book is to help us understand how to achieve democratic outcomes in real-world contexts where citizens not only disagree, but where some express dangerously undemocratic preferences and ideas. Reaffirming the democratic power of deliberation precisely in these contexts, I offer "uptake" or fair consideration as the relevant normative standard to assess the democratic quality of a deliberative system. I explain that deliberation helps achieve democracy to the extent that it allows citizens to have a say in the laws to which they are held. In order for a person's input to be brought to bear on a political decision, for it to have the opportunity to influence that

---

[10] Along these lines, Johnston, in *American Dionysia*, has identified what he calls the "tragedy of democracy." To save itself against its enemies, democracy cannot but violate its own commitments and so bring about its own death.

[11] Abigail Hauslohner, "Southern Poverty Law Center Says American Hate Groups Are on the Rise," *Washington Post*, February 15, 2017.

decision, others must hear and consider it. Importantly, the fair consideration required to recognize the moral equality of each citizen's voice does not demand equal influence, but equal *opportunity* to influence.

As I show, assessing deliberation according to the presence of fair consideration actually helps us resist the pernicious tendency to equate a committed democrat's considered rejection of a given proposal to someone's automatic dismissal of a claim because he believes it goes against his own interests.[12] According to this view, shutting down or shouting over Nazis in Charlottesville is democratic to the extent that citizens can say: we listened, we considered your input, but we reject it. By introducing the normative standard of fair consideration, I do not mean to suggest that committed democrats shouldn't feel empowered to reject Nazis on substantive grounds. They should! Moreover, doing so would be a sign of the proper—read, democratic—functioning of deliberative procedures. Still, in order for the substantive rejection (or acceptance) of a deliberative input to be democratically valid, it must come after that input was fairly considered. And for that, I argue, listening is essential.

Fair consideration, or what I call uptake, is ultimately predicated on careful listening. And in the chapters that follow, I offer an account of the specific interventions we ought to take to move citizens' deliberations in the direction of greater democracy. With recourse to the concept of uptake, I challenge proliferating appeals to empathy and inclusion, ultimately moving beyond these two supposedly unproblematic ideals of democracy. Furthermore I show that centering deliberation on the listening act not only makes room for difference in deliberation, but can even put difference to work toward productive ends.

1.1 Situating the Project

Aristotle famously wrote that it is our capacity for speech that sets humans apart as political animals.[13] Humans alone have the gift of speech, allowing us

---

[12] Mark Button has made a similar point in *Political Vices*, in which he draws a distinction between the vice of recalcitrance and the virtue of resilience. The committed democrat could be seen as resilient in opposing white supremacy, while the neo-Nazi who refuses to accept the city of Charlottesville's decision to remove the statue could be seen as recalcitrant. For Button, "in losing sight of these ethical distinctions we risk mistaking a virtue that can help sustain democratic commitments to equality and reciprocal freedom for a vice that imperils these same values." Mark Button, *Political Vices* (Oxford: Oxford University Press, 2016), 102.

[13] Aristotle, *The Politics* (New York: Penguin, 1981), 60.

to live together *politically*, coming to collective judgments about what is just and unjust. Starting from Aristotle's claim regarding the centrality of speech to politics, the importance of listening becomes clear. This book theorizes the democratic significance of listening, the necessary correlate of speech. Specifically, I consider how *in* listening citizens enact the deliberative ideal of fair consideration and thus realize the promise of democracy.

In many ways, my emphasis on listening can be seen as a natural outgrowth of deliberative democratic theory, which took root in the field of political theory over three decades ago. Since then, deliberation—understood as communication and debate among citizens—has replaced voting as the fundamental act of democratic citizenship in the eyes of political theorists. In his key articulation of deliberative politics, Habermas, citing John Dewey, explains that when it comes to democratic legitimacy, "the means by which a majority comes to be a majority is the more important thing."[14] Developed further over the last thirty years by Habermas, Iris Young, Jane Mansbridge, Simone Chambers, John Dryzek, and others, deliberative democratic theory maintains that the legitimacy of a decision is not simply a function of the number of votes received, but the quality of the deliberation that precedes voting.

Deliberative democratic theory represents a diverse research paradigm focused primarily on questions concerning the nature and value of political talk. As a theoretical approach, deliberative democracy can be "centered" on formal deliberative or decision-making institutions such as Congress and public deliberative forums open to citizens. But democratic deliberation can also be viewed as "de-centered," where "processes of discussion and decision making" occur "in multiple forums and sites connected to one another over broad spans of space and time."[15] In other words, deliberative democrats concern themselves with more than just the formal debates that occur in official decision-making bodies.

Those who take a decentered approach, including Habermas and Young, recognize the importance of formal deliberations, but simply view them as one chapter in a longer story. Indeed, according to the now dominant

---

[14] John Dewey, *The Public and Its Problems* (Chicago: Swallow Press, 1954), 207–8; Jürgen Habermas, *Between Facts and Norms: Contributions to a Discourse Theory of Law and Democracy* (Cambridge, MA: MIT Press, 1996), 304. In this famous statement, Dewey is actually quoting American politician Samuel Tilden.

[15] Iris Marion Young, "De-Centering Deliberative Democracy," in *Democratizing Deliberation: A Political Theory Anthology*, ed. Derek W. M. Barker, Noelle McAfee, and David W. McIvor (Dayton, OH: Kettering Foundation Press, 2012), 113; Jürgen Habermas, *Between Facts and Norms*.

systemic approach to deliberative democracy, the task of the democratic theorist is to evaluate the overall deliberativeness of a political system instead of focusing on a single site or instance of deliberation.[16]

Such systemic approaches are prefigured by the "two-track" model of democratic deliberation that Habermas presents in *Between Facts and Norms*. There, Habermas conceptualizes deliberation as operating along two tracks. The first track is made up of informal communication dispersed across public spheres. The second track includes the formal deliberation that occurs in official legislative bodies. According to Habermas, if the system is operating democratically, then the goings on in these two tracks will be connected. Specifically, the collective opinion formed in the informal deliberation of the first track will be transmitted to the formal representative institutions of the second track where a collective will is formed.

A key takeaway of the two-track model is that the decisions that are made (or not made) in a political system are the culmination of processes of opinion formation that begin long before particular options are weighed or a formal agenda is even set. These informal interactions (between neighbors, parishioners, coworkers, etc.) help determine what issues rise to the level of public consciousness and are taken up in formal debate in the first place. As André Bächtiger and John Parkinson explain, "While policy might *appear* to be made by the administration under direction from elected politicians, in a well-functioning democratic system it does so by explicit and implicit reference to the broad currents of public communication and not simply on its own initiative."[17]

According to systemic approaches to deliberation, important political work that will shape the democratic potential of a society's actions occurs in the everyday communication among citizens.[18] In other words, "The entire burden of decision making and legitimacy does not fall on one forum or institution but is distributed among different components in different cases."[19]

---

[16] Michael Neblo, "Thinking through Democracy: Between the Theory and Practice of Deliberative Politics," *Acta Politica* 40, no. 2 (2005): 169–81; John Parkinson, *Deliberating in the Real World: Problems of Legitimacy in Deliberative Democracy* (Oxford: Oxford University Press, 2006); Dennis F. Thompson, "Deliberative Democratic Theory and Empirical Political Science," *Annual Review of Political Science* 11 (2008): 497–520; Jane Mansbridge, James Bohman, Simone Chambers, Thomas Christiano, et al., "A Systemic Approach to Deliberative Democracy," in *Deliberative Systems: Deliberative Democracy at the Large Scale—Theories of Institutional Design*, ed. John Parkinson and Jane Mansbridge (Cambridge: Cambridge University Press, 2012), 1–26; Hayley Stevenson and John S. Dryzek, *Democratizing Global Climate Governance* (Cambridge: Cambridge University Press, 2014).

[17] Bächtiger and Parkinson, *Mapping and Measuring Deliberation*, 89.

[18] Young, "De-Centering Deliberative Democracy," 117.

[19] Mansbridge et al., "A Systemic Approach to Deliberative Democracy," 5.

Therefore, to determine whether a political system is functioning democratically, we have to pay as much attention to the diffuse and unstructured communication in public spheres as we do to the formal communication taking place in empowered spaces. Collective opinions discursively formed in the informal deliberation of the first track must ultimately be transmitted to the formal institutions of democratic decision making in the second track.

But the democratic functioning of a political system requires more than simply *that* formal decisions be made with reference to the broad currents of public communication. The currents of public communication must themselves be generated in a discursive fashion.[20] Systemic approaches to deliberation, however, have tended to overlook the fact that while the democratic impact of informal interactions in diffuse public spheres is real, it is not always positive.[21]

This informal deliberation involves a wide range of communicative practices, from protest to negotiation. And while it may not be directed at any actual decision, it still has important implications for the legitimacy of a political system and any decisions ultimately taken in that system. Nevertheless, it is important to recognize that this informal deliberation will vary in its democratic force.[22] In other words, to say that informal deliberation and everyday political talk help determine the democratic quality of a political system and the decisions it makes is not to say that they always enhance democratic possibilities. Indeed, democratic theorists must carefully attend to the informal deliberation in diffuse public spheres precisely because we cannot assume it will necessarily boost democracy.[23] Whether

[20] Habermas, *Between Facts and Norms*, 304.
[21] According to Mansbridge et al., "What might be considered low quality or undemocratic deliberation in an individual instance might from a systems perspective contribute to an overall healthy deliberation." As others have pointed out, however, in taking a systemic approach to deliberation, we run the risk of jumping "too soon to find positive deliberative consequences in intrinsically non-deliberative practices." David Owen and Graham Smith have offered a compelling account of this concern. But while this critique is fair as far as existing interpretations of deliberative systems go, we can begin to answer this critique by noting, as I do, that while the democratic impact of nondeliberative practices is real, it is not always positive. Mansbridge et al., "A Systemic Approach to Deliberative Democracy," 12; Stevenson and Dryzek, *Democratizing Global Climate Governance*, 33; David Owen and Graham Smith, "Deliberation, Democracy, and the Systemic Turn," *Journal of Political Philosophy* 23, no. 2 (2015): 213–34.
[22] Jane Mansbridge, "Everyday Talk in the Deliberative System," in *Deliberative Politics: Essays on Democracy and Disagreement*, ed. Stephen Macedo (Oxford: Oxford University Press, 1999), 211–40.
[23] Rather than being an absolute ideal at which to aim, I look at the deliberative model of democratic legitimacy as a critical tool that allows us to examine supposedly democratic values and procedures, assessing the extent to which they comply with or depart from our intentions and assumptions. The purpose of deliberative democratic theory, therefore, is not to sketch out a path to finding an ideal consensus or even the will of the people. Instead, the value of deliberative democracy

democratically constructive or not, these interactions are part of the means by which the majority comes to be the majority and so must be included in our assessment of the democratic quality of a deliberative system. I ask, what are the normative conditions required of informal deliberation in order for it to confer democratic legitimacy on our collective actions?

Answering this question, I argue that in order for our deliberation to fulfill its democratic function, indeed for speech to have any political effect whatsoever, speakers must have an attentive audience. A political system will capture the democratic force of deliberation only if citizens listen to one another. Until recently, however, little work has examined the ways in which our practices of listening affect the democratic potential of deliberation.[24] As deliberative democratic theory has matured over the last three decades, its proponents became absorbed with efforts to improve deliberative procedures and institutions so as to empower speakers and democratize the inputs to deliberation. In doing so, they largely overlooked the question of listening. This inattention to listening distances deliberative democratic theory from a political reality in which people often tune out alternative viewpoints and remain closed off to people who are different from them.[25]

Fortunately, this gap in the study of democracy has begun to close.[26] In their 2019 book, for example, Bächtiger and Parkinson identify reason-giving and listening as the "two core components of deliberation."[27] But

is its provision of a normative standard with which to judge existing practices and the outcomes they produce.

[24] Historically, there has been a dearth of literature on the topic of listening in political theory. The exception to this was Susan Bickford, *The Dissonance of Democracy* (Ithaca, NY: Cornell University Press, 1996).

[25] Failures to listen are not necessarily a sign of individual viciousness on the part of citizens. As I explain in Chapter 6, if we admit of the depth of the challenge to deliberation posed by the deep constitutive differences between citizens, we see that even admirably motivated and virtuous citizens can struggle with the expectation and practice of robust listening. See Button, *Political Vices*, 1.

[26] Tanja Dreher, "Listening across Difference: Media and Multiculturalism beyond the Politics of Voice," *Continuum* 23, no. 4 (2009): 445–58; Andrew Dobson, *Listening for Democracy: Recognition, Representation, Reconciliation* (Oxford: Oxford University Press, 2014); Mary F. Scudder, "Beyond Empathy: Strategies and Ideals of Democratic Deliberation," *Polity* 48, no. 4 (2016): 524–50; Emily Beausoleil, "Responsibility as Responsiveness: Enacting a Dispositional Ethics of Encounter," *Political Theory* 45, no. 3 (2017): 291–318; Jane Mansbridge and Audrey Latura, "The Polarization Crisis in the US and the Future of Listening," in *Strong Democracy in Crisis: Promise or Peril?*, ed. Trevor Norris (Lanham, MD: Lexington Books, 2017), 29–54; Tanja Dreher and Poppy de Souza, "Locating Listening," in *Ethical Responsiveness and the Politics of Difference*, ed. Tanja Dreher and Anshuman Mondal (Palgrave Macmillan, 2018), 21–39; Carolyn M. Hendriks, Selen A. Ercan, and Sonya Duus, "Listening in Polarised Controversies: A Study of Listening Practices in the Public Sphere," *Policy Sciences* 52, no. 1 (2019): 137–51; Mary F. Scudder, "The Ideal of Uptake in Democratic Deliberation," *Political Studies* 68, no. 2 (2020): 504–522.

[27] Downplaying the novelty of their emphasis on listening, Bächtiger and Parkinson trace it back to claims about the importance of mutual respect in deliberation. As they explain, "treating each other

though deliberativists have begun to recognize the importance of listening for deliberation, recent work has left us with an inadequate understanding of the *challenge* of listening. In what follows, I do more than explore listening as simply the next frontier of democratic theory. I also carefully consider the deep challenges that an expectation of listening creates for citizens deliberating across difference and disagreement.

There has been a rich discussion within democratic theory regarding the challenge that dissensus poses for democracy. The thinking of first-generation deliberative democrats, sometimes explicit and other times only implied, was that truly democratic decisions would come from communicatively derived *consensus,* representing the will of "the people," and not simply the will of the strongest (in numbers). But if the democratic power of deliberation comes from the resulting consensus, how can we reach meaningfully democratic decisions when "the people" do not agree? The democratic potential of deliberation would seem to dissipate in large pluralistic societies divided by space, interests, and ethical values.

Indeed, some agonistic critics identify dissensus as an insurmountable obstacle to deliberation and its perceived goal of reaching consensual democratic decisions. For them, agreement will inevitably come at too high of a price: namely, respect for difference. Thus, to respect difference, we must give up on deliberation. As Susan Bickford, the first political theorist to tackle the importance of listening for democracy, explains, "Those who take conflict seriously tend not to stress interaction, while those who value interaction tend to underestimate the presence and persistence of conflict."[28] This thinking has resulted in a perceived tradeoff between a commitment to democratic cooperation, on the one hand, and a respect for the difference that produces conflict on the other.[29]

In this book, I work *within* a deliberative framework to find answers to the important question of achieving democracy amid dissensus. Returning to the normative core of deliberative democratic theory, I find that deliberation's greatest democratic value comes precisely in contexts of difference,

with respect—a key deliberative good—requires listening to what they say." I argue, however, that listening is not just valuable as a means of showing respect. Instead, listening is central to the exercise of democratic power. Listening ensures citizens achieve democratic autonomy. My account of listening is, thus, part of a larger reimagining of the normative core of deliberation and democracy. Bächtiger and Parkinson, *Mapping and Measuring Deliberation,* 22–23.

[28] Bickford, *The Dissonance of Democracy,* 5.
[29] Ibid.

disagreement, and dissensus. Importantly, we turn to deliberation in the absence of agreement. The aim of deliberative democracy is to infuse decision-making processes with a deliberative quality so that citizens, as diverse as they are, can meaningfully participate in the authorship of the laws to which they are held. It is the decision-making process broadly understood, and not the outcome, whether unanimous or contested, that carries the democratic weight of a deliberative system. As I show, however, the challenges of deliberating across difference are not resolved simply by centering deliberation on listening instead of consensus. The kind of listening required for public communication to carry democratic force is difficult to achieve in contexts of deep difference.

In admitting the depth of the challenge that difference presents for deliberation, however, I do not conclude that the deliberative ideal is altogether out of reach. According to my account, listening is not just a more realistic aim of deliberation given the fact of difference and disagreement in large pluralistic societies, nor is it a stand-in for fair consideration. I remain hopeful in regards to citizens' ability to arrive at democratically legitimate decisions— through listening—so long as they remain aware and accepting of the many difficulties that will lie in their path.

In an effort to understand and meet these challenges, I go on to interpret the conditions of full and fair communication, filling in substantive details regarding what deliberation in diffuse and unstructured public spheres must look like in order to carry the normative weight that deliberative democrats hope it will. Specifically, I articulate the capacities and dispositions citizens must have in order for their deliberation to have democratic force. The listening approach that I propose, thus, pushes back on the procedural and institutional approaches that have dominated deliberative democratic theory since its inception.[30] This shift in focus toward the capacities of citizen-listeners also marks a departure from prior work in deliberative democratic theory that has put primary importance on empowering citizens to speak and reflect.

Significant theoretical payoffs come with understanding the listening act as an essential act of democratic citizenship. Indeed, by centering deliberation on the act of listening I am able to reconsider and clarify the nature of democracy itself. Introducing the concept of "performative democratic listening," I show that it is *in* the act of listening that we move our deliberation

---

[30] Owen and Smith, "Deliberation, Democracy, and the Systemic Turn," 221.

toward the ideal of fair consideration. Listening, I argue, helps constitute democratic autonomy insofar as it ensures that citizens are able participate in the authorship of the laws to which they are held.

Of course, no matter how much citizens listened to one another in diffuse and unstructured public spheres, if this informal political talk was all there was, we would not be talking about a *democratic* system at all. As Bächtiger and Parkinson show with their broadly sequential account of a deliberative system, people "listening to the narratives and claims of the informal public sphere" is only the first step.[31] This "wild debate" must eventually be given "some institutional focal points," to help "channel public debate into the agenda-setting process, and then provide focused deliberation on the issues at hand, providing recommendations for further action."[32] Finally, a formal decision must be made, either by "every member of that state in a referendum or by their duly authorized and accountable representatives in a legislature."[33]

Therefore, in assessing the democratic force of listening in the diffuse public communication of a deliberative system, I assume a system of popular sovereignty, where citizens wield decision-making power through elections and representation and have some input on the constitution or design of deliberative forums. Assuming these conditions, I show that citizens' practices of listening are essential to ensuring that the broad currents of communicative influence generated from public discourse will be democracy enhancing. By putting citizens at the center of my treatment of deliberative democracy, I do not mean to suggest that institutions and procedures are peripheral. My point is simply that while these institutional and procedural considerations are important, so too are the capacities and dispositions of citizens interacting within them and within the broader unstructured public spheres.

By adopting what I call a democratic listening approach to deliberation, I challenge previously settled assumptions regarding what it means to achieve meaningfully democratic decisions in large pluralistic societies. Specifically, I argue that without a robust commitment to listening, more inclusive deliberation among even the most empathetic citizens will not necessarily achieve the democratic outcomes deliberativists are after. By situating the listening act at the center of deliberative democratic theory, I am able to

[31] Bächtiger and Parkinson, *Mapping and Measuring Deliberation*, 92.
[32] Ibid.
[33] Ibid.

reveal the insufficiency of inclusion, the pathology of empathy, and the democratic power of difference in deliberation.

1.2 Outline of the Book

Fitting form to content, this book proceeds as a series of conversations. Each chapter engages with a different set of interlocutors to provide new answers to the question of how to improve the democratic quality of discourse among citizens in pluralistic polities.

Chapter 2 begins by reconstructing conversations between Jürgen Habermas, his critics, and his subsequent defenders, to show how deliberative democratic theory has stalled in recent years. I show that prior attempts to improve the democratic prospects of deliberation across difference have focused primarily on making deliberation more inclusive by incorporating marginalized voices and pluralizing the types of communication permitted in political debates. As a result, this literature has ignored the issue of fair consideration. I argue that even the most inclusive deliberative procedures will not guarantee democratic outcomes unless citizens really take up or consider what their fellow citizens say. When it comes to achieving democratic self-governance, the aim is not to *feel* included. Instead, the point is to have a say in the laws to which we are held. For that, inclusion is absolutely necessary, but insufficient.

Thus, to achieve meaningfully democratic outcomes through deliberation, uptake—or fair consideration—must follow inclusion. Fair consideration is what ensures people's inputs are actually put to work in deliberation. In order to understand and fight instances of political exclusion and domination, we must pursue the task of democratizing uptake, rather than just increasing input. For this, however, we must go beyond questions of procedure to consider the disposition and capacities of citizens. The book proceeds by evaluating particular practices and capacities that citizens might adopt and develop so as to achieve uptake.

For example, in recent years, democratic theorists looking to promote communication and consideration across differences have lauded the benefits of empathy, or imaginative perspective taking. Reviewing accounts of the democratic value of empathy—offered by Robert Goodin, Sharon Krause, Michael Morrell, and others—Chapter 3 shows the limits of empathy-based approaches to deliberation.

There, I focus on three qualities of the practice of empathy that ultimately make it ill-suited for democratizing deliberation. First, with empirical evidence from the field of psychology, I show that we are, in fact, not very good at accurately imagining the perspectives of others. The outcomes of the process of empathy are realized selectively and unevenly depending on the relationship of the observer to the target. Empathy's selective nature makes it an unlikely corrective for the problems of exclusion and selective uptake that undermine deliberation's democratic potential in diverse polities.[34] Second, I find that, although empathy is aimed at something like uptake, its reliance on imagination instead of communication is at odds with the normative core of deliberative democracy. Even when successful, empathy promises only a kind of spurious uptake rooted in imaginative rather than communicative engagement. Thus, even if we *could* accurately imagine others' perspectives, this would undermine deliberation by distracting us from the need to engage in the hard work of democratic listening. Consider, for example, that you do not have to engage in what can be difficult or uncomfortable conversations with others if you can simply imagine their perspectives.

Last in Chapter 3, I take issue with empathy's reliance on commonality. I show that empathy's emphasis on highlighting or uncovering commonalities among citizens puts it at odds with democratic deliberation, which is supposed to provide a model for meaningfully democratic decision making across difference and, indeed, when empathy is not readily available. I show that the assumption of commonality at the heart of calls for empathy make it potentially dangerous even when practiced *within* inclusive communication.

In Chapter 4, I begin to lay out an alternative to the empathic turn in deliberative democratic theory. To assess and improve the democratic quality of collective decisions, I argue that we must shift our attention to citizens' responsibility to listen to one another. Drawing on research in communications, this chapter introduces a theory of listening acts, which I then use to unpack and explicate the multiple and varied ways that listening contributes to democratic deliberation. Employing the categories of Austin's speech act theory, I show that listening amounts to more than simply hearing *what* is said. And it is not only valuable for its ability to *bring about* something like

---

[34] Significantly, social psychology research demonstrates the power of empathy to break down certain biases. I accept Morrell's evidence showing that successful attempts at empathic role taking can help overcome cognitive biases. My point about selective empathy, however, is that achieving empathy (with the hope of overcoming such biases) is itself limited by bias. Michael E. Morrell, *Empathy and Democracy: Feeling, Thinking, and Deliberation* (University Park: Pennsylvania State University Press, 2010).

consensus or mutual understanding. With the concept of performative democratic listening, I explain how *in* listening we constitute the deliberative act, ensuring that someone's message connects up with the relevant audience.

In Chapter 5, I further develop the category of performative democratic listening to show how *in* listening to our fellow citizens, we move our deliberation in the direction of greater democracy. *In* listening, we acknowledge that our fellow citizens have a rightful say in the decision at hand. I show that simple listening becomes *listening toward democracy* when we listen for the purpose of considering what others have to say. Thus, the democratic force of listening comes, in large part, from the affective-cognitive disposition of the citizen-listener. This chapter goes on to detail the cultural and institutional conditions needed to motivate citizens to listen toward democracy. Specifically, I explain the importance of a robust commitment to democratic self-rule, formalized expectations of listening, and a greater acceptance of conflict as a feature of the political life of a democratic citizen. I also discuss how we might assess the democratic quality of citizens' listening. To that end, I present empirical indicators of performative democratic listening.

I consider in Chapter 6 the challenges to achieving listening toward democracy in contexts of difference and disagreement. Listening to our political adversaries *so that* we can consider what they have to say is not always easy. Here, I take seriously the possible objection that practices of listening are just as limited as empathy when it comes to ensuring uptake across difference. I find, however, that in the context of a listening-centered approach to deliberation, differences can actually serve as a resource by showing citizens the limits of their ability to imagine and even understand each other, thus emphasizing the hard work and importance of continued engagement. The challenges to democratic discourse in a pluralistic world are significant, given that it occurs always already in the presence of disagreement. I show that calling attention to the hard work of deliberative uptake is a necessary first step in any effort to improve its practice.

In order to faithfully consider the opinions and perspectives of others, it is crucial to recognize that their experiences may be beyond your understanding. The realization of the limits of our ability to understand others in the presence of deep difference opens us more vividly to the ways in which we are inconspicuously limited in our opinions, our basic understanding of issues, and our relationship to the democratic community. This sort of engagement is less likely to occur if we imagine only our commonalities or assume that we can know or feel how another feels.

By identifying difference as a resource in listening-centered approaches to democratic deliberation, I recall my earlier critique of empathy-based approaches to democratic deliberation. Appeals to empathy, which collapse the distance and differences between citizens by assuming we are alike enough to imagine one another's feelings and perspectives, undermine the potential for discussion across differences. In contrast, highlighting differences between citizens helps keep our focus trained on the need to actually engage with others, while also alerting us to the challenges of that engagement. In the end, recognizing the limits of our ability to understand others can actually serve as a guarantor of meaningfully democratic deliberation.

Finally, in Chapter 7, I account for the risks and difficulties of pursuing the ideal of uptake in the real world. Here, I consider whether it is possible to develop a politics of listening that is sensitive to power differentials and historical injustice. In this chapter, I also explain how we ought to respond to failures of democratic listening and uptake. In sum, Chapter 7 examines the purpose of democratic ideals in a non-ideal world.

2

The Insufficiency of Inclusion and the Need for Uptake

Since the deliberative turn in democratic theory, deliberation—understood as fair communication and debate among citizens—has been considered as fundamental a dimension of democratic decision making as voting. While not offering its own decision rule, deliberative democracy contends that the legitimating force of a decision-making process depends as much on the quality of deliberation that precedes voting as it does on the outcome of the vote itself. According to the now dominant systemic approach to democratic deliberation, deliberation carries epistemic, ethical, and democratic value.[1] High-quality deliberation in a political system successfully performs these three functions, and so enhances the legitimacy of decisions made in that system.[2]

In what follows, I consider the conditions that allow deliberation to fulfill its democratizing function. According to the last twenty years of research in democratic deliberation, the democratic functioning of deliberation is determined by its level of inclusiveness.[3] As critics and defenders of deliberation have both pointed out, deliberation's democratizing potential will be greatly diminished if some citizens, perspectives, or voices are excluded from

---

[1] Jane Mansbridge, James Bohman, Simone Chambers, Thomas Christiano, et al., "A Systemic Approach to Deliberative Democracy," in *Deliberative Systems: Deliberative Democracy at the Large Scale. Theories of Institutional Design*, ed. John Parkinson and Jane Mansbridge (Cambridge: Cambridge University Press, 2012), 1–26.

[2] Outlining the idea of a systemic approach to deliberative democracy, Mansbridge et al. explain that the deliberative system includes not only the binding decisions of the state but also "societal decisions, many of which have only a very indirect impact on state legislation." These societal decisions include, for example, "the decision not to settle a particular matter through the state" Jane Mansbridge, James Bohman, Simone Chambers, Thomas Christiano, et al., "A Systemic Approach to Deliberative Democracy," in *Deliberative Systems: Deliberative Democracy at the Large Scale—Theories of Institutional Design*, ed. John Parkinson and Jane Mansbridge (Cambridge: Cambridge University Press, 2012) 10, 8.

[3] Iris Marion Young, *Inclusion and Democracy* (Oxford: Oxford University Press, 2000); Mansbridge et al., "A Systemic Approach to Deliberative Democracy"; Simone Chambers, "Balancing Epistemic Quality and Equal Participation in a System Approach to Deliberative Democracy," *Social Epistemology* 31, no. 3 (2017): 266–76.

Beyond Empathy and Inclusion. Mary F. Scudder, Oxford University Press (2020). © Oxford University Press.
DOI: 10.1093/oso/9780197535455.001.0001.

debate.[4] Consider, for example, that even a unanimous vote would lose its legitimacy if some citizens were disenfranchised. This emphasis on inclusion has remained even after deliberative democratic theory ushered in a "talk-centric" rather than a "voting-centric" model of democracy.[5]

But when it comes to making deliberative democratic processes democratic, inclusion only tells part of the story. In this chapter, I reinterpret the democratic force of deliberation, showing that it comes in large part from the uptake of citizens' inputs. By "uptake," I mean giving due consideration to the arguments, stories, and perspectives that particular citizens share in deliberation. After inclusion, uptake ensures that citizens have a say in the laws to which they are held.

The concept of uptake, however, has been undertheorized in deliberative democratic theory. Borrowing the term "securing uptake" from J. L. Austin's speech act theory, James Bohman introduced the term to deliberative democratic theory as a measure of "the success of dialogue."[6] Bohman's brief but valuable treatment is still the most significant analysis on the subject to date.[7] Iris Young also mentions the concept, defining it as "when someone speaks [and] others acknowledge the expression in ways that continue the engagement."[8] Although these two accounts have shed initial light on this aspect of the deliberative terrain, neither provides adequate elucidation of the distinctive significance that uptake has for democratic deliberation.[9]

Furthermore, while others have recognized the need for something like uptake in deliberation, for the most part they have stopped short of giving it pride of place in their accounts of the democratic force of deliberation. For example, deliberative democrats have long identified the importance

[4] Iris Marion Young, "Difference as a Resource for Democratic Communication," in *Deliberative Democracy: Essays on Reason and Politics*, ed. James Bohman and William Rehg (Cambridge, MA: MIT Press, 1997), 383–406.

[5] Simone Chambers, "Deliberative Democratic Theory," *Annual Review of Political Science* 6, no. 1 (2003): 307–26.

[6] See J. L. Austin, *How to Do Things with Words* (Cambridge, MA: Harvard University Press, 1962); James Bohman, *Public Deliberation: Pluralism, Complexity, and Democracy* (Cambridge, MA: MIT Press, 1996), 58.

[7] Bohman, *Public Deliberation*, 58–66, 116–118.

[8] Young, *Inclusion and Democracy*, 25.

[9] Bächtiger, Niemeyer, Neblo, Steenbergen, and Steiner identify the expectation that citizens will "consider the arguments and demands of others with respect" as a "key empirical blindspot" of deliberative democratic theory. I contend, however, that the limitations of our current understanding of uptake are not only empirical but normative as well. Uptake or fair consideration is not simply a precondition of effective deliberation, as Bächtiger and colleagues suggest, but an essential component of deliberation itself. André Bächtiger, Simon Niemeyer, Michael Neblo, Marco R. Steenbergen, and Jürg Steiner, "Disentangling Diversity in Deliberative Democracy: Competing Theories, Their Blind Spots and Complementarities," *Journal of Political Philosophy* 18, no. 1 (2010): 40, 56.

of mutual respect among participants as well as the need for citizens "to be flexible and open enough to undertake a genuine evaluation of [others'] opinions."[10] More often than not, however, these references to something like uptake or fair consideration (I use these terms interchangeably) are presented either as a background condition or as an ethical requirement. Uptake, however, is more than a background condition. And, similar to the claims others have made in regards to inclusion, uptake is "not simply an ethic added to democratic deliberation," but a "central element of what makes deliberative democratic processes democratic."[11] Uptake gets at the normative core of meaningfully democratic deliberation.

Further elucidation of uptake is warranted not only because of the significant normative weight it carries, but also because of the difficulty we have achieving it. The challenge we face really considering what others have to say, especially those with whom we disagree, fundamentally affects democratic possibilities in large, complex, and diverse societies. These issues surrounding what I call "limited uptake" are not typically captured in discussions about exclusion, nor are they adequately corrected by efforts to expand inclusion. To date, deliberativists desiring to enhance the democratic force of deliberation have sought "actively to promote and facilitate inclusion and the equal opportunities to participate in the system."[12] But as we succeed in broadening the diversity of voices included in the public sphere, we nevertheless must also confront the challenge of uptake: ensuring these voices are *actually heard and ultimately considered.*

Consider, once again, the Black Lives Matter movement, which has organized to protest racial injustice in the United States and resist an unequal status quo. Of particular concern to this movement is the impunity with which police officers use lethal force against black Americans.[13] As the movement gained attention in popular discourses, however, certain dominant segments of society, including many white middle-class American citizens and political

---

[10] Amy Gutmann and Dennis F. Thompson, *Democracy and Disagreement* (Cambridge, MA: Harvard University Press, 1996), 79; Simone Chambers, *Reasonable Democracy: Jürgen Habermas and the Politics of Discourse* (Ithaca, NY: Cornell University Press, 1996), 100.

[11] In this quote, Mansbridge et al. are referring only to inclusion ("A Systemic Approach to Deliberative Democracy," 12). See also Chambers, "Balancing Epistemic Quality and Equal Participation in a System Approach to Deliberative Democracy," 268.

[12] Mansbridge et al., "A Systemic Approach to Deliberative Democracy," 12.

[13] While much focus has been on these issues, Chris Lebron cautions against reducing the Black Lives Matter movement to claims about policing and laws. Lebron argues that the movement represents "a civic desire for equality and a human desire for respect, the intellectual roots of which lie deep in the history of black American thought." Christopher J. Lebron, *The Making of Black Lives Matter: A Brief History of an Idea* (Oxford: Oxford University Press, 2017), xiii.

elites, responded by insisting "all lives matter." This retort, essentially a non sequitur, reveals an ungenerous reading of the movement. Here, the actual arguments and grievances voiced by black Americans are ignored or else misunderstood, and as a result, their experiences are rendered invisible and their voices inaudible. Whether disingenuous or not, this response to the Black Lives Matter movement shows the limitations of democratic deliberation and political action when others do not conscientiously engage with a group's claims. If inclusive deliberation is to have a meaningfully democratic impact, we must search for ways to broaden the enactment of deliberative uptake.

Critics of deliberative democracy, often referred to as "difference democrats," have consistently contended that certain features of democratic deliberation make it ill-suited for achieving democracy in contexts of deep difference.[14] The difficulty we have securing uptake across difference would seem only to confirm these charges. As I show, however, a better understanding of the centrality of uptake can actually help deliberativists address concerns regarding deliberation's inability to accommodate the deep differences and disagreements in large pluralistic societies.

To develop a better understanding of the significance and character of uptake, especially in deliberation across difference, I proceed as follows. I begin by outlining the basic idea of deliberative democracy, paying special attention to the emphasis that defenders and critics of deliberation have both placed on inclusion as the element of deliberation that makes it democratic (2.1). I show that owing to the limitations of these overly procedural accounts, previous efforts to enhance the democratic force of deliberation have failed. Leaning too heavily on inclusion and aiming mainly at increasing access and pluralizing inputs, deliberativists have all but ignored the equally vital task of ensuring participants in deliberation understand the importance of adequately considering newly included perspectives and modes of communication (2.2). In order to respond more effectively to the many concerns gathered under the notion of exclusions, deliberative democratic theory must do a better job integrating the concept of uptake.

---

[14] I present the challenge to deliberative democracy leveled by difference democrats in greater detail later in this volume. For now, it's worth noting that the category of "difference democrat" transcends the typical categories of agonistic versus deliberative democrat. "Agonism" refers to a conception of politics that emphasizes the inevitability and legitimacy of conflict in democratic life. For agonists, difference and disagreement can only be tamed through exclusionary and homogenizing practices, many of which they associate with deliberative democracy's use of reason and dialogue. While all agonistic democrats are probably rightly understood as difference democrats, not all difference democrats are agonistic democrats. Though some difference democrats have abandoned deliberative democracy in favor of agonism, others have sought to rehabilitate deliberation in light of concerns of exclusion.

Correcting for this oversight, I present a theoretical account of what uptake entails and work through some of the challenges of improving the quality of uptake in a deliberative system characterized by deep difference (2.3). Finally, I offer a preliminary discussion—which I continue in Chapter 7—of the drawbacks of pursuing the ideal of uptake in a non-ideal world. For example, how should we deal with the inputs of democracy's enemies, for example, racists and authoritarians (2.4)?

2.1 Inclusion and the Democratic Force of Deliberation

Deliberativists tie their democratic aspirations to the procedures that produce outcomes instead of the outcomes themselves. Recall that for Habermas, when it comes to democratic legitimacy, "the means by which a majority comes to be a majority is the more important thing."[15] For him, decisions made within a political system will have the presumption of democratic legitimacy to the extent that they are reached through inclusive, even if informal and diffuse, communicative procedures. When it comes to assessing the democratic functioning of a deliberative system, deliberative democrats are looking for evidence that citizens participated in the lawmaking authority.

Like radical democrat Jean-Jacques Rousseau before him, Habermas is looking for ways to make our "chains" legitimate, to move the facticity of the law toward greater validity. Rather than trying to eliminate the chains—which would be impossible given the collective lives we live—Rousseau searches for a way to make those chains feel less like chains. Thus, to solve the puzzle of freedom and authority, Rousseau reinterprets what it means to be free. For him, freedom or autonomy is "obedience to the law one has prescribed to oneself."[16] Democratic autonomy means that in obeying the laws, citizens obey only themselves.

Following Rousseau, Habermas maintains that democracy makes us free by allowing us to see ourselves as both the addressees and authors of the law. But unlike Rousseau, whose radical communitarian brand of democracy relied on the maintenance of a thick ethical and cultural background consensus to help citizens recognize their own will in an objective general will,

[15] Jürgen Habermas, *Between Facts and Norms: Contributions to a Discourse Theory of Law and Democracy* (Cambridge, MA: MIT Press, 1996), 304.
[16] Jean-Jacques Rousseau, *The Social Contract and Other Later Political Writings*, ed. Victor Gourevitch (Cambridge: Cambridge University Press, 1997), 56.

Habermas relies on inclusive communicative practices to coordinate political action intersubjectively.[17] According to Habermas, democracy answers the puzzle of freedom and authority by allowing citizens to have a say in the laws to which they are held. Providing a simple yea or nay show of hands for a particular policy does not meet the bar of meaningful authorship.

All this is to say that for Habermas, the democratic quality of a collective decision is tied to the deliberation that precedes it and not the number of votes it receives, whether it serves the interests of a majority of citizens or accords with an objective general will. This move away from Rousseau's prepolitical ethical consensus is crucial for achieving democracy in a pluralistic and heterogeneous late-modern polity.[18]

According to Habermas, the normative weight of deliberation "is grounded ultimately in the interplay between institutionally structured political will-formation and spontaneous, unsubverted circuits of communication in a public sphere that is not programmed to reach decisions and thus is not organized."[19] Deliberation in diffuse public spheres generates what Habermas calls "communicative power." And if a political system is functioning democratically, then this communicative power is transformed into the administrative power that manifests in actual policies and laws.[20]

This link between democracy and communication can be traced back to Habermas's theory of communicative action in which he harnesses the potential of everyday communication to validate claims intersubjectively.[21] Through language we come to a mutual understanding with our interlocutors and thus are able to coordinate action legitimately, in the sense of being achieved intersubjectively through persuasion, rather than relying on force or manipulation.[22]

---

[17] Rousseau, *The Social Contract*; Jürgen Habermas, "Three Normative Models of Democracy," *Constellations* 1, no. 1 (1994): 1–10.

[18] Habermas, "Three Normative Models of Democracy" ; Seyla Benhabib, "The Democratic Moment and the Problem of Difference," in *Democracy and Difference: Contesting the Boundaries of the Political*, ed. Seyla Benhabib (Princeton, NJ: Princeton University Press, 1996), 3–18.

[19] Jürgen Habermas, "Popular Sovereignty as Procedure," in *Deliberative Democracy: Essays on Reason and Politics*, ed. James Bohman and William Rehg (Cambridge, MA: MIT Press, 1997), 57.

[20] Habermas, "Three Normative Models of Democracy," 8.

[21] As Simone Chambers explains, "Underpinning both [Habermas's] moral theory (discourse ethics) and his political theory (a discourse theory of law and democracy) today are, on the one hand, a sociological theory of communicative action and, on the other hand, a linguistic theory of argumentation." Simone Chambers, "The Philosophic Origins of Deliberative Ideals," in *The Oxford Handbook of Deliberative Democracy* (Oxford: Oxford University Press, 2018), 65.

[22] According to Habermas, "Reaching understanding is the inherent *telos* of human speech." But we do not have to accept Habermas's strong foundationalism in order to make the coordinating power of language into a key component of democratic life. Jürgen Habermas, *The Theory of Communicative*

Developing his research program further, Habermas applies his theory of communicative action to the realm of politics, where the question of interest becomes how we might democratically resolve ruptures in ongoing communicative action that occur when someone challenges the validity of a given law, practice, or claim.[23] Indeed, what makes Habermas's sociological theory of communicative action so distinct is that it seeks to explain not only the integration and reproduction of society but also the breakdown of this reproduction.[24] Specifically, Habermas thematizes the breakdown of ongoing communicative action that occurs when some norm or taken-for-granted assumption is challenged. For these disruptions of ongoing communicative action—the stuff of politics—to be resolved *democratically*, we need communicative procedures that recognize the "moral equality of voice" of all citizens.[25] Only then can all citizens see themselves as meaningful participants in the lawmaking authority.

Indeed, according to the last two decades of research in deliberative democracy, the democratizing force of deliberation comes from its level of inclusiveness. If citizens are to see themselves as the authors of the laws to which they are held, they must be included in processes of opinion formation and will formation. As Mansbridge and colleagues explain, "For those excluded, no deliberative democratic legitimacy is generated."[26] On the other hand, to enhance its democratic quality, a deliberative system ought "actively to promote

---

Action, Vol. 1 (Boston: Beacon Press, 1984), 287; Stephen K. White, *A Democratic Bearing: Admirable Citizens, Uneven Justice, and Critical Theory* (Cambridge: Cambridge University Press, 2017).

[23] As White and Farr's interpretation of Habermas's political theory shows, the whole framework of deliberative democracy begins within a scene of ongoing communicative action where norms of interaction are taken for granted, until they are not. Stephen K. White and Evan Robert Farr, "'No-Saying' in Habermas," *Political Theory* 40, no. 1 (2012): 32–57.

[24] It makes sense to understand Habermas's *Between Facts and Norms* as an extension of the larger research program he introduced in *The Theory of Communicative Action*. As White explains, "Ongoing communicative action is Habermas's account of unproblematic social interaction." Habermas's understanding of "discursive justification, both cognitive and normative," however, "is constitutively related to this intersubjective bond's becoming problematic in some way. In other words, communicative rationality has to be understood finally as a practice of *coping with* the emergence of *problems within a context of intersubjectivity*." Stephen K. White, "The Very Idea of a Critical Social Science: A Pragmatist Turn," in *The Cambridge Companion to Critical Theory*, ed. Fred Rush (Cambridge: Cambridge University Press, 2004), 319.

[25] I borrow the language of "moral equality of voice" from Stephen K. White. In his book *A Democratic Bearing*, White makes a convincing case, first, for recognizing autonomy and moral equality of voice as the two core commitments of Habermas's communicative action paradigm, and, second for understanding Habermas's political theory against the backdrop of that paradigm.

[26] Mansbridge et al., "A Systemic Approach to Deliberative Democracy," 12.

and facilitate inclusion and the equal opportunities to participate in the system."[27] Mansbridge and her estimable coauthors (James Bohman, Simone Chambers, Thomas Christiano, Archon Fung, John Parkinson, Dennis F. Thompson, and Mark E. Warren) assert that "the inclusion of multiple and plural voices, interests, concerns, and claims on the basis of feasible equality is not simply an ethic added to democratic deliberation; it is the central element of what makes deliberative democratic processes democratic."[28] In fact, they use the words "democratic" and "inclusive" interchangeably, referring at times to a deliberative system's "democratic function" as its "inclusive function."[29]

Given the importance of inclusion to the democratic power of deliberation, it is worrisome that critics have raised concerns regarding what they see as deliberation's inability to accommodate the deep differences and disagreements that exist in large pluralistic societies. Indeed, the normative link between democracy and deliberation has been challenged by prominent critics, often called "difference democrats," who argue that deliberation struggles to deliver on democracy's promise of inclusion.[30] According to these critics, the narrowly rational *means,* consensual *ends,* and unequal *conditions* of democratic deliberation make the process inhospitable to diversity, undermining the democratic nature of a deliberative system and reducing the legitimacy of decisions made in that system.

Those who take issue with the *means* of deliberation claim that rational argument can be "coercive and exclusive."[31] As James Bohman notes, even "standards of rationality are themselves subject to deeply conflicting interpretations."[32] By permitting only certain kinds of reasons and restricting the types of communication in public discourse, models of democratic deliberation run the risk of marginalizing some groups and individuals while privileging others. Restrictions on the means of deliberation undermine the

---

[27] Ibid.; Simone Chambers, "Making Referendums Safe for Democracy: A Call for More and Better Deliberation," *Swiss Political Science Review* 24, no. 3 (2018): 308.

[28] Mansbridge et al., "A Systemic Approach to Deliberative Democracy," 12. See also Chambers, "Balancing Epistemic Quality and Equal Participation in a System Approach to Deliberative Democracy," 268.

[29] Mansbridge et al., "A Systemic Approach to Deliberative Democracy," 13, 11.

[30] John S. Dryzek, *Deliberative Democracy and Beyond: Liberals, Critics, Contestations* (Oxford: Oxford University Press, 2000), 4.

[31] Ibid., 57. See also Young, *Inclusion and Democracy*; Lynn Sanders, "Against Deliberation," *Political Theory* 25, no. 3 (1997): 347–76; Cheryl Hall, "Recognizing the Passion in Deliberation: Toward a More Democratic Theory of Deliberative Democracy," *Hypatia* 22, no. 4 (2007): 81–95; Sharon R. Krause, *Civil Passions: Moral Sentiment and Democratic Deliberation* (Princeton, NJ: Princeton University Press, 2008).

[32] James Bohman, "Public Reason and Cultural Pluralism: Political Liberalism and the Problem of Moral Conflict," *Political Theory* 23, no. 2 (1995): 254.

moral equality of each citizens' voice and actually favor those in power, including white men, while discounting groups that use other means of communicating, such as emotional speech, testimony, and rhetoric.[33]

Similarly, those who take issue with the consensual *ends* of deliberation argue that the single-minded drive toward consensus and agreement creates "remainders" who are ultimately left out of the discussion. According to these critics, especially William Connolly and Chantal Mouffe, but Sanders and Young as well, the deliberative ideal of consensus, even when pursued through a variety of means, crowds out difference and disagreement.[34] As Michael Feola explains, the worry relates to the "depoliticizing force of consensus," or how an "emphasis on consensus ultimately defangs the unruly possibilities of democratic speech."[35] By definition, the political is that which is contested. Even a politics that is "neutral" to these differences can only be achieved through exclusionary and homogenizing practices.[36] Large pluralistic societies such as the United States cannot escape difference and disagreement, which permeate all aspects of political life. Difference, in fact, is tied up with and constitutive of personal identity.[37] Instead of futilely trying to overcome difference as models of deliberative democracy tend to do in their pursuit of consensus, we should work on overcoming the urge to exclude or discount differences that we perceive as posing a threat to our own identity.[38]

In the third category of difference democrats are those who take issue with the *conditions* of deliberation, or what critics identify as inherent power asymmetries present in society at the time of deliberation. Due to unequal social, political, and even economic conditions, deliberation cannot produce the legitimate outcomes many of its advocates believe it will.[39] The unequal and power-laden conditions of deliberation specifically and politics generally make fair deliberation a naïve, unattainable, and misguided goal.[40]

[33] Sanders, "Against Deliberation"; Young, *Inclusion and Democracy*.

[34] William Connolly, *The Ethos of Pluralization* (Minneapolis: University of Minnesota Press, 1995); Chantal Mouffe, *The Democratic Paradox* (New York: Verso, 2000); Sanders, "Against Deliberation"; Young, *Inclusion and Democracy*, 44.

[35] Michael Feola, "Speaking Subjects and Democratic Space: Rancière and the Politics of Speech," *Polity* 46, no. 4 (2014): 500.

[36] As I explain in Chapter 3, agonistic democrats like Mouffe would reject empathy precisely because it fits with deliberative democratic theory's exclusionary drive toward consensus, though I contest this reading of deliberation as such.

[37] William E. Connolly, *Identity\Difference: Democratic Negotiations of Political Paradox* (Minneapolis: University of Minnesota Press, 2002).

[38] Ibid.

[39] Jeff Jackson, "Dividing Deliberative and Participatory Democracy through John Dewey," *Democratic Theory* 2, no. 1 (2015): 63–84.

[40] Sanders, "Against Deliberation."

Highlighting the inextricability of power and politics, these critics contend that our energies should be directed toward designing institutions that redistribute power (specifically decision-making power) rather than guarantee access to communicative venues.[41] Only such a distribution of power is thought to ensure that all relevant parties' interests and concerns will be represented.

If true in either theory or practice, the concerns raised by difference democrats would undermine the democratic force of deliberation. Unless deliberation can be made to accommodate persistent disagreement and difference, deliberative systems will have no greater claim to democratic legitimacy than alternative models of democracy. But while these now well-known suspicions of exclusion have led agonistically minded critics to dispense with the deliberative ideal, others have tried to correct it. Among those seeking to rehabilitate deliberative democracy, a marked focus has been on designing procedures that pluralize the voices included in deliberation and amplify the dissenting voices that remain after a decision has been made.[42] Seen in this way, the exclusion of difference is not a problem *of* deliberation, so much as a problem *for* deliberation. The first step is to identify and then (dis)solve the specific feature of the deliberative system that thwarts the incorporation of minority perspectives or dissenting voices.

For example, worried about the exclusionary tendencies of supposedly neutral procedures or *means* of deliberation, Cheryl Hall, Sharon Krause, and Iris Young all advocate for a broader conception of what is considered acceptable input.[43] Specifically, they reject Habermas's preference for rational argumentation, narrowly defined. Indeed, these more sympathetic critics argue that deliberative models of democracy always already rely on the very passions that are formally excluded from their procedures.

Other would-be defenders of Habermas have reinterpreted the *ends* of deliberation, arguing that his perceived problem of consensus may not be as dire

---

[41] Ian Shapiro, *The State of Democratic Theory* (Princeton, NJ: Princeton University Press, 2003).

[42] Young, *Inclusion and Democracy*; Sanders, "Against Deliberation"; Patchen Markell, "Contesting Consensus: Rereading Habermas on the Public Sphere," *Constellations* 3, no. 3 (1997): 377–400; Lincoln Dahlberg, "The Habermasian Public Sphere: Taking Difference Seriously?," *Theory and Society* 34, no. 2 (2005): 111–36; White and Farr, " 'No-Saying' in Habermas."

[43] For Young, "demonstration and protest, the use of emotionally charged language and symbols, publicly ridiculing or mocking exclusive or dismissive behavior of others, are sometimes appropriate and effective ways of getting attention for issues of legitimate public concern." Hall writes that "the best strategy for making deliberative theory more democratic is to demonstrate the ways in which deliberation already involves passion." Young, *Inclusion and Democracy*, 66; Hall, "Recognizing the Passion in Deliberation," 92.

as it first appears.[44] Patchen Markell, for example, recasts the Habermasian public sphere as inherently contestatory and therefore able to accommodate the difference and disagreement found in large pluralistic democracies. For Markell, Habermas's public sphere not only allows for dissent, it very much depends on it. Accordingly, Habermas sees democratic politics as a "never-ending process of contestation."[45] Agreements on Monday can be challenged on Tuesday. Lincoln Dahlberg comes to a similar conclusion by highlighting the two-track nature of Habermas's deliberative system. Unlike the formal decision-making processes, the process of public opinion formation that takes place in diffuse public spheres never ends and therefore need not crowd out dissent or difference for the sake of coming to a decision.[46]

Cautiously, White and Farr aim to alleviate some of the concerns of difference democrats, with whom they sympathize, by reinterpreting Habermas's paradigm of communicative action—which they argue should be seen as the basis of his theory of deliberative democracy.[47] According to White and Farr, Habermas's brand of deliberative democracy is more hospitable to deep difference and disagreement than many critics realize.[48] Specifically, they argue that the initial moment of disagreement (or no-saying) that interrupts communicative action cannot be reduced to merely a "discursively framed normative argument" intended to bring about renewed consensus.[49] Importantly, they identify the moment of no-saying in Habermas as also representing a diffuse "existential taking-of-a-stand against the normative force of a dominant form of life."[50] Through their reinterpretation of "no-saying" in Habermas, White and Farr show that Habermas's model of deliberation has the potential to accommodate deep, inarticulate, and existential differences that exist between people, produce disagreement, and inform our communicative interactions.[51]

[44] Robert W. T. Martin, "Between Consensus and Conflict: Habermas, Post-Modern Agonism and the Early American Public Sphere," *Polity* 37, no. 3 (2005): 365–88.

[45] Markell, "Contesting Consensus," 378–79.

[46] Dahlberg, "The Habermasian Public Sphere."

[47] White and Farr, "'No-Saying' in Habermas," 52.

[48] Ibid., 33. White develops this line of thinking further in his 2017 book, wherein he searches for ways to attend to the dynamic of identity/difference thematized by Connolly from within Habermas's paradigm of communicative action. White, *A Democratic Bearing*.

[49] White and Farr, "'No-Saying' in Habermas," 40.

[50] Ibid., 38.

[51] Furthermore, White and Farr emphasize that they "are not speaking of the rational-moral, 'yes/ no position . . . in deliberation' (Thomassen, 210) but rather the existential, aesthetic-expressive no-saying." So in addition to reinterpreting the *ends* of deliberation to include contestation, White and Farr also show how the *means* of contestation can be more than just carefully articulated normative arguments (White and Farr, "'No-Saying' in Habermas," 55 n.36). White and Farr are citing Lasse

Lastly, responding to the unequal and power-laden *conditions* of deliberation, defenders have begun searching for ways that democratic deliberation can exist within and resist (rather than completely overcome or transcend) the inevitably unequal and non-ideal conditions of contemporary politics.[52] According to this line of thinking, designing decision-making procedures so that they protect the influence of otherwise marginalized groups can mitigate the problems of an exclusionary public sphere. As James Bohman explains, "If power over decisions is widely dispersed in institutions . . . excluding groups from deliberation is more difficult to accomplish."[53] Giving historically underrepresented groups veto power over issue domains that directly affect them, for example, not only mitigates the effects of inevitably unequal deliberative conditions but can also improve these conditions by ensuring marginalized groups are not ignored out of hand. Deliberativists have also highlighted the potential for using discourse itself to help resist unequal conditions by helping "expose uncomfortable valences of privilege, highlight moments of collective shame, or disrupt cherished communal narratives."[54]

The approach taken by these defenders of the democratic force of deliberation is telling. Each of these lines of defense acknowledges that suspicions of exclusion in deliberative democracy are of urgent importance. Indeed, Habermas's model of democracy is specifically intended to work across difference and disagreement.[55] Charges of exclusion, therefore, should worry even the most committed deliberative democrat as they threaten deliberation's normative core and undermine its democratizing potential. Still, these more sympathetic critics maintain that exclusion is not an essential feature of deliberative democracy. As such, they have made efforts to redesign or reinterpret deliberative procedures such that they can accommodate difference and disagreement, making room for contestation and even agonism within deliberative practices.[56]

Though necessary for addressing the concerns thematized by difference democrats, the remedies just discussed are not enough. Concerns regarding the democratic potential of deliberation, especially in large

---

Thomassen, "Within the Limits of Deliberative Reason Alone: Habermas, Civil Disobedience, and Constitutional Democracy," *European Journal of Political Theory* 6, no. 2 (2007): 200–218.

[52] Shapiro, *The State of Democratic Theory*.
[53] Bohman, *Public Deliberation*, 148.
[54] Feola, "Speaking Subjects and Democratic Space," 514.
[55] Habermas, "Three Normative Models of Democracy."
[56] White, *A Democratic Bearing*, 17.

pluralistic societies, persist even after greater levels of inclusion are achieved. Furthermore, these concerns originate from within deliberative democratic theory itself.

Mark Warren, himself an architect of the deliberative turn, has recently conceded that deliberation "functions weakly as a means of empowering inclusion."[57] Warren goes on to argue, however, that "we should not expect deliberation to address problems of empowered inclusion," which are better addressed by practices of voting, especially the universal franchise.[58] While deliberation is superior to voting when it comes to "collective agenda and will formation," a political system will always rely on voting to ensure that it is sufficiently inclusive and thus democratic.[59]

Pace Warren, even the most inclusive voting procedures would not let deliberation off the inclusive hook, so to speak. If the means by which the majority comes to be the majority is the most important thing for democratic legitimacy, then a political system's deliberation, and not just its voting procedures, must be sufficiently inclusive. It's a problem for democracy, in other words, if deliberation functions weakly as a means of empowering inclusion. I argue, however, that practices of deliberation are not necessarily at a disadvantage, compared to voting, when it comes to empowering inclusion. A more accurate conclusion, reached only once we update our thinking on inclusion, is that deliberation requires *more* than inclusion, namely uptake, to function democratically.

Importantly, however, the need for uptake is not unique to deliberative models of democracy; it is just as important, though normally automatic, in aggregative models that rely on voting. When it comes to voting, procedures are usually designed to ensure that inclusion implies uptake. It is assumed, for example, that a vote cast is necessarily a vote counted. And in aggregating the votes, we have immediate feedback or evidence regarding whether someone's vote was, indeed, counted equally and taken up. In the case of voting in elections, achieving uptake does not guarantee one's candidate will win, but simply that one's vote will be counted the same as everyone else's. Similarly, as I explain shortly, in the case of deliberative models of democracy, uptake does not guarantee your fellow citizens will share your perspective or find your argument persuasive. Instead, it guarantees that your preferences and

[57] Mark E. Warren, "A Problem-Based Approach to Democratic Theory," *American Political Science Review* 111, no. 1 (2017): 39.
[58] Ibid., 48.
[59] Ibid., 47.

perspectives will be considered and so brought to bear on any eventual decision. Your input will be integrated into the deliberative process, even if not ultimately reflected in the output. This integration is what allows you to participate in the lawmaking authority.

A deliberative system's democratic function cannot be achieved without uptake. According to its own normative commitments, deliberative democratic theory is incomplete without an account of the extent to which included perspectives, passions, dissent, and so on are *received and ultimately considered*.[60] This is the issue to which my discussion of uptake is addressed.

2.2 The Insufficiency of Inclusion

In what follows, I lay out the theoretical stakes of deliberative uptake by showing the insufficiency of inclusion for ensuring the democratic functioning of a deliberative system. Efforts to address problems of exclusion in deliberation will be incomplete until we attend to the question of ensuring uptake. Problematically, neither the importance nor the challenge of achieving uptake (especially in contexts of deep difference and contestation) is captured by existing efforts to make deliberation more democratic.

In order for all citizens to meaningfully participate in the lawmaking authority, a deliberative system must somehow more effectively affirm the moral equality of each. Citizens' inputs, therefore, need to be both included *and* duly considered. Young, who literally wrote the book on inclusion and democracy, makes a similar point when she highlights the need for citizens not only to be included in the decision-making process but to also have the opportunity to actually influence decisions.[61] Importantly, Young recognizes that having the opportunity to influence outcomes requires more than just equal access to deliberative forums and public spheres. Namely, it requires what she calls "internal inclusion."[62] As she explains, when citizens' inputs

---

[60] John Boswell, Carolyn M. Hendriks, and Selen A. Ercan have identified a related gap in deliberative systems literature, what they refer to as the issue of "transmission." Specifically, Boswell and colleagues aim to identify whether and how political messages and discourses are transmitted between deliberative settings. Transmission ensures that individual sites of deliberation are linked so that messages are disseminated throughout a deliberative system. Boswell et al.'s transmission and my uptake, both of which are interested in ensuring that messages are received, are undoubtedly allied in spirit. I address their relationship more when I discuss empirical indicators of uptake in Chapter 5. John Boswell, Carolyn M. Hendriks, and Selen A. Ercan, "Message Received? Examining Transmission in Deliberative Systems," *Critical Policy Studies* 10, no. 3 (2016): 264.

[61] Young, *Inclusion and Democracy*, 5–6.

[62] Ibid., 55.

are ignored and dismissed because "the dominant mood may find their ideas or modes of expression silly or simple, and not worthy of consideration," they are denied any real opportunity to influence outcomes and are, thus, internally excluded.[63]

The concept of inclusion, typically understood, does not adequately capture the kind of harm that is done when one is allowed to speak, but is then ignored or not taken seriously. These instances of what I call "failed uptake" can have a chilling effect on political talk and even reduce a person's sense of political efficacy.[64] Why should I spend time and energy sharing my perspective if I know, from past experience, that others are not going to seriously consider it? But more than these *indirect* negative effects on discourse, failed uptake also leads *directly* to a democratic deficit insofar as citizens are denied a say in the laws to which they are held.

Helpfully, Young's discussion of internal inclusion and exclusion actually begins to move the conversation beyond inclusion. Still, she diminishes the impact of her insight insofar as she describes the opportunity to influence outcomes as simply another side of the same coin of inclusion. Folding the opportunity to influence into the concept of inclusion has the effect of overburdening inclusion with the responsibility of guaranteeing not only equal access but fair consideration. And as I show, this overburdening of inclusion is both theoretically and practically untenable.

Wrapping the issue of serious consideration into the concept of inclusion poses practical challenges insofar as the usual strategies we use for improving inclusion are ill-suited for ensuring uptake, something that defies procedural guarantees. Young even concedes that "no rules or formalities can ensure that people will treat others in the political public with respect, and really listen to their claims."[65] Indeed, Young is right about this, but instead of tackling this crucial challenge head on, Young turns back to that which rules and formalities *can* ensure: namely, inclusion or access to deliberative forums and public

---

[63] Ibid.

[64] For example, Tara Grillos, studying women's participation in environmental decision-making fora in Kenya, found that efforts to include women in community decision making made women "more likely to attend community decision-making meetings . . . ," but that these women were "not likely to speak at those meetings." This might be because, as Grillos found, these included women were actually less likely than women in the control group "to feel that local leaders pay attention to what they think." These findings speak to the ways in which nominally including, but then ignoring people might damage their confidence, sense of self-worth, or political efficacy. Tara Grillos, "Women's Participation in Environmental Decision-Making: Quasi-Experimental Evidence from Northern Kenya," *World Development* 108 (2018): 115–30.

[65] Young, *Inclusion and Democracy*, 57.

spheres. And so, in a very unsatisfying move, Young proposes combating the problem of "internal exclusion" by loosening the restrictions typically placed on the types of reasons and the forms of communication permitted in deliberation.[66] Specifically, Young recommends broadening our conception of political communication to include greeting, rhetoric, and narrative, as well as explicitly disruptive modes of communication.[67] This innovation certainly makes deliberation more accommodating, inclusive, and accessible. But it remains unclear whether these procedural changes can effectively promote fair consideration. No matter how inclusive a decision-making procedure or deliberative forum, we know that individual closed-mindedness or unequal social conditions can affect which people, groups, ideas, or kinds of communication are seen as worthy of our consideration and thus given a real opportunity to influence outcomes.[68]

Young does not explain why (or even if) citizens would be better able or more likely to listen to these disorderly, disruptive, or annoying forms of communication than the rational and orderly argumentation endorsed by Habermas.[69] Even the most engaging storytelling will not necessarily make a perspective more amenable to uptake. What I take to be a compelling story, another person may dismiss as mere rhetoric. Of course, Young's goal is to change what is considered acceptable input in the first place so that storytelling is not dismissed as an inappropriate way of conveying perspectives in politics. Still, missing from her treatment of these issues is an account of the conditions of receptivity that will help or hinder citizens' fair consideration of what is shared.

In focusing on pluralizing the inputs to deliberation, Young would allow more inclusive procedures to stand in for greater receptivity on the part of citizens. But simply amplifying the voices of relevant parties, or making processes of deliberation more formally inclusive or accommodating, cannot ensure that citizens' voices will be heard and their ideas considered. We should simply admit the *insufficiency* of inclusion for ensuring that citizens have equal opportunity to influence democratic decisions.[70] Instead of stretching

---

[66] See Section 2.1 in this chapter.

[67] Young, *Inclusion and Democracy*, 57.

[68] Miranda Fricker, *Epistemic Injustice: Power and the Ethics of Knowing* (Oxford: Oxford University Press, 2007).

[69] Habermas, *The Theory of Communicative Action*, 1:10.

[70] I would argue that Dryzek makes a related point when he argues that deliberative inclusion should not be seen as "additive." While systems theorists acknowledge that the inclusivity of a deliberative system could be greater than the sum of its parts, Dryzek pushes us to recognize that it could also be *less* than the sum of its parts. Using the example of internet trolls, Dryzek argues that we must be "alive to the possibility that particular inclusions could have consequences that turn out to be

the concept of inclusion to cover all necessary conditions of democratic deliberation, I contend that we get more critical purchase on democratic deliberation if we distinguish between inclusion and fair consideration.

Even after the conceptual overhaul that Young offers, inclusion fits within democratic theory like pieces of old plumbing overburdened after a large-scale renovation. Just as deliberative democracy replaced more "minimalist" understandings of aggregative democracy by supplementing voting with deliberation, so too must a conception of inclusion be supported by something more. Inclusion will not guarantee fair consideration in deliberation across deep difference when encounters with others are more likely to be experienced as existential threats or affronts to one's own identity.[71] If we are to begin to address seriously the issues raised by difference democrats that undermine the democratic functioning of a deliberative system, we must go beyond inclusion to examine the related, though distinct, issue of fair consideration. The inclusion of all citizens in a deliberative system, including those with dissenting opinions, must be followed by the fair consideration of their input.[72]

2.3 Unpacking Uptake

Without the connection of inclusion to uptake, hard-won battles over political access will not make much of a democratic impact. A rich diversity of voices and types of speech can flow through an inclusive deliberative system, but without uptake, they will flow right back out or otherwise dissolve to no effect. A deficit of uptake (at either the collective opinion- or will-formation stage) runs the risk of derailing even the most inclusive deliberative procedures.[73]

exclusive." I argue that we can protect against the exclusionary outcomes of inclusion by pursuing a critical politics of uptake. John S. Dryzek, "The Forum, the System, and the Polity: Three Varieties of Democratic Theory," *Political Theory* 45, no. 5 (2017): 620.

[71] Connolly, *Identity\Difference*.

[72] I use the language of fair consideration rather than equal consideration to acknowledge that while all inputs deserve to be heard, not all inputs are necessarily deserving of equal time on the floor. If someone's proposal or grievance is not given equal time and attention in deliberation, he would have a justifiable complaint of exclusion only if the relative inattention to his input was caused by insufficient or unfair consideration and not the collective and considered (if prompt) rejection of the proposal, grievance, etc.

[73] As I explained in Chapter 1, according to Habermas, deliberative democracy operates along two tracks: the informal communication dispersed across public spheres in which a collective opinion is formed, and the formal deliberation that occurs in official decision-making bodies like Parliament

Subsequent chapters examine how to motivate citizens to enact the deliberative ideal of uptake as well as how we might know when they have succeeded in doing so. In what follows, I define "deliberative uptake" and explain its democratic significance. Again, by uptake, I mean giving due consideration to the arguments, stories, and perspectives that particular citizens share in inclusive deliberation. As I argue, it is only by having our inputs taken up in the sense of being fairly considered that we achieve moral equality of voice and thus can see ourselves as meaningful participants in the means by which the majority comes to be the majority.

2.3.1 Defining Uptake

Bohman, who first introduced the concept of uptake to deliberative democratic theory, argues that in order for an individual engaging in the collective decision-making process to accept the outcome, he must "recognize his own intentions as part of the deliberative activity, even if it is not directly a part of its specific outcome."[74] Being sensitive to the "dilemmas of difference," Bohman knows that deliberation will not always resolve disagreements or reveal common ground.[75] As he explains, the success of dialogue is measured instead "in the uptake of other points of view and reasons into speakers' own interpretations of the ongoing course of discussion."[76]

For Bohman, uptake is the key to understanding how deliberation can repair a "problematic situation" caused by a breakdown in coordination.[77] As he explains, uptake allows actors divided by disagreement to cooperate once again not by "restoring equilibrium" or "balancing reasons," but by helping them "revis[e] the common understandings that are operative in ongoing cooperative activity."[78] While taking up a particular input does not mean it will necessarily determine the output in a direct way, uptake allows us to, at the

and Congress, from which emerges a collective will. The collective opinion of citizens must be reflected in the collective will. Uptake is needed both *along* and *between* these two tracks of deliberation. See Habermas, "Popular Sovereignty as Procedure," 57. In what follows, I focus primarily on uptake in deliberation between citizens in their informal deliberations in diffuse public spheres.

[74] Bohman, *Public Deliberation*, 56.
[75] Ibid., 59.
[76] Ibid., 58.
[77] Ibid., 55.
[78] Ibid., 59.

very least, incorporate others' intentions and perspectives in a "dynamic process of reflection and revision."[79]

As will be clear from the following, my treatment of uptake is not at odds with Bohman's. In fact, some of my discussion here elaborates on the theoretical insights uncovered in his examination of the topic. Still, compared to Bohman's focus on uptake as a means to an end, namely a means to restoring coordination that has broken down, I take uptake to be an end in itself. While uptake is certainly essential to achieving desirable deliberative outcomes, I also contend that achieving uptake is itself a normatively significant outcome, one that infuses deliberative encounters with democratic force. In taking up what others say, we recognize their moral equality of voice. As such, uptake is constitutive of the democratic force of deliberation. Put differently, citizens have not meaningfully participated in the lawmaking authority unless they secure uptake from their fellow citizens. Borrowing the language that Mansbridge and colleagues use to describe the democratic force of inclusion, I argue that uptake "is not simply an ethic added to democratic deliberation; it is [a] central element of what makes deliberative democratic processes democratic."[80]

To help explain the constitutive power of uptake in deliberation, let me return to the concept of uptake in speech acts developed by Austin. According to Austin, one must secure uptake in order to act in speaking.[81] But while uptake is required for someone to act in speaking, Austin distinguishes it from the effects or consequences of that speech act. As he explains, "I cannot be said to have warned an audience unless it hears what I say and takes what I say in a certain sense."[82] Still, the uptake that is required for me to effectively act in, say, warning people is distinct from and prior to any consequences that my warning may produce, including their judging my warning to be valid. For example, I have not acted in warning people unless they hear me yell, "Fire!," and understand that utterance to be an assessment of our current surroundings. But so long as they hear and understand me, even if they do not heed my warning or otherwise respond, I can be said to have successfully acted in warning them.[83]

[79] Ibid.
[80] Mansbridge et al., "A Systemic Approach to Deliberative Democracy," 12.
[81] Austin, *How to Do Things with Words* .
[82] Ibid., 116.
[83] Since Austin, speech act theorists have debated whether uptake is necessary for all illocutionary acts. Alexander Bird, for example, argues it is not, using the example of "a soldier being tried for the war-crime of shooting someone who had surrendered. . . . It would be no defense that the soldier had not taken him to surrender—and therefore he had not in fact surrendered." In such a case, we

When it comes to deliberative uptake, hearing and understanding are essential. For example, you cannot consider a person's input if she does not speak audibly or if, in the absence of an interpreter, she speaks or signs a language you do not understand. In the context of deliberation, however, uptake involves not only receiving and understanding the utterance, but actually considering it as well, in the sense of entertaining it as a serious normative claim.

Still, deliberative uptake is distinct from the result of that consideration. Thus, just as we should keep inclusion separate from the responsibility of uptake, we must also be mindful not to burden uptake with the responsibility for a system's outcome or output. While uptake ensures that deliberative inputs are duly evaluated in the deliberative *process*, it does not guarantee they will be reflected in the particular direction of the decision itself. Importantly, we can consider a fellow citizen's point of view without integrating it into the character of what we see as legitimate in that specific case. Indeed, successful uptake will not always involve reshaping a common understanding among citizens as Bohman suggests it will. Still, if we include and consider, but ultimately reject, a particular citizen's point of view, that person does not necessarily have a valid claim of exclusion to make against the deliberative system. While uptake ensures each citizen has a real opportunity to influence the collective thinking on a particular subject of public concern, not all ideas and proposals will be equally persuasive and therefore equally influential in the social and political decisions made in a particular system.[84] The deliberative system will still have a greater presumption of generating democratic legitimacy to the extent that all arguments, even those ultimately rejected, are considered as a matter of course.

To illustrate the relationship of uptake to output in processes of deliberation, consider the example of a town meeting held to select a new recycling program. Imagine one citizen proposes a single-stream recycling program

could admit of a person having acted in surrendering despite being denied uptake. These debates, however, do not weaken the explanatory value of Austin's uptake for deliberative democratic theory. I am not arguing that Austin's uptake is literally what is owed to citizens in deliberation, but rather that it serves as a useful comparison. Alexander Bird, "Illocutionary Silencing," *Pacific Philosophical Quarterly* 83, no. 1 (2002): 8.

[84] In their discussion of uptake between mini-publics and macro-political institutions, Goodin and Dryzek equate uptake with impact or influence. Here, I argue that, especially within informal deliberations between citizens, it would be wrong to equate uptake with actual influence. Robert E. Goodin and John S. Dryzek, "Deliberative Impacts: The Macro-Political Uptake of Mini-Publics," *Politics & Society* 34, no. 2 (2006): 219–44.

in which recyclables are separated in a plant after they are collected. Another citizen proposes a three-bin recycling system in which citizens separate their recyclables from their waste and compostable items. This system depends on the cooperation of citizens, but helps prevent unnecessary loss that occurs when recyclable items are contaminated by waste. Now, let's imagine that a third citizen proposes eliminating all municipal recycling efforts based on his unsubstantiated claim that they are part of a grand conspiracy to raise taxes and weaken the local economy.

In order for the citizens' deliberation to function democratically with the hope of generating legitimacy for an eventual decision, all three of these citizens must be allowed to share their perspectives and offer proposals. Furthermore, citizens participating in the meeting would have to listen to and consider all proposals before reaching a decision. The demands of inclusion and uptake, however, do not require that each of these proposals have equal influence on resulting decisions, or even be given equal time on the floor. Dismissing the unfounded claims of conspiracy and affirming their commitment to a city recycling program, the other citizens might spend most of their time debating the relative advantages of a single-stream versus a multi-bin recycling program. They would be justified in promptly rejecting the third citizen's proposal, so long as they considered it first, listening to the proposal and attempting to understand the speaker's meaning.

As the preceding discussion suggests, the realization of uptake will not necessarily generate any immediately observable change in the world.[85] Consider, for example, that my deliberation with a white supremacist will not necessarily shape my preferences or alter my thinking regarding the best course of collective action. Our deliberation is also unlikely to produce a "meta-consensus" whereby I accept the legitimacy of my interlocutor's values.[86] Indeed, contra Bohman, my taking up this individual's input may very well lead to further breakdown in coordination. Even if I walk away

[85] Though there may not be an observable change in the world, a change will still have occurred. With uptake, the claim of my interlocutor as well as the implications of that claim would be included, if not in the decision we reach, then at the very least in the story we might tell about our discussion and decision-making process. In taking up a perspective that I ultimately reject as invalid, my view or understanding of the world might widen to incorporate my understanding of the other's perspective, even if my assessment or judgment of the world does not. Here, I follow Bohman's assessment, but contend that this change will not always repair a breakdown in coordination. Bohman, *Public Deliberation*, 58.

[86] Dryzek and Niemeyer acknowledge that "any meta-consensus is characterized by exclusions as well as inclusions" and that it need not "strive to cover (say) Nazi values." Still, we need uptake to know which values ought to be excluded. John S. Dryzek and Simon Niemeyer, "Reconciling Pluralism and Consensus as Political Ideals," *American Journal of Political Science* 50, no. 3 (2006): 638.

from or shout over the person, I do not weaken the normative power of deliberation, so long as I have first considered the sense and meaning of the claims. Assuming uptake was secured, my racist interlocutors would have no persuasive claim of democratic illegitimacy if resulting decisions were not shaped by their input.

When it comes to making decisions under conditions of deep difference and disagreement, even the most inclusive and considerate deliberation will not result in agreement. Therefore, when decisions are made, either through discourse or discursively grounded bargaining, some citizens may not see their own wills reflected in the collective will. Now, according to Rousseau's republican conception of autonomy, dissent from the general will is unacceptable, and so must be overcome—by force if necessary. The presence of dissent, however, does not necessarily speak against the democratic functioning of a deliberative system, thanks to the proceduralist conception of democratic autonomy it offers.

Reinterpreting popular sovereignty intersubjectively, Habermas shows how citizens' participation in communicative processes of opinion and will formation allows them to see themselves as the authors of even those laws they do not personally support. For Habermas, the "self," of the autonomous sovereign self, is located in neither the individual subject nor in the "macrosubject of a people or nation."[87] Instead, the " 'self' of the self-organizing legal community disappears in the subjectless forms of communication that regulate the flow of discursive opinion- and will-formation in such a way that their fallible results enjoy the presumption of being reasonable."[88] Reasonable or fair results are presumed to follow from discursive processes of opinion and will formation so long "as the flow of relevant information and its proper handling have not been obstructed."[89] Uptake, which amounts to letting someone's input enter into your consideration, is essential to the unobstructed flow of relevant information within a deliberative system.

Uptake, then, is a kind of processing. Sometimes the inputs are processed out and rejected before they can directly shape a decision, and sometimes they are put to use in assessing the full range of legitimate alternatives. By focusing on uptake as a condition for achieving the democratic functioning of a deliberative system, we keep our focus on the processing and not the

[87] Habermas, *Between Facts and Norms*, 103.
[88] Ibid., 301.
[89] Ibid., 296.

output of deliberation, whether agreement, consensus, compromise, reinterpretation, and so on.[90] Through uptake, citizens are able to see themselves as having meaningfully participated in the lawmaking authority even when their input is rejected.

Uptake, then, appears to be a potentially attainable democratic ideal in a world of difference and disagreement, insofar as we do not have to agree or find common ground with our interlocutors in order to consider what they have to say. Still, as I explain below, uptake is not always straightforward. Distinct from inclusion, uptake faces its own obstacles, especially in large pluralistic societies in which people have to make decisions with real and disparate consequences for themselves and others.

2.3.2   Securing Uptake

Fair consideration is not automatic and should not be assumed to follow inclusion, especially given the dynamics of identity/difference that characterize the relationships of citizens within large pluralistic societies. In deliberation, citizens have to negotiate different experiences and perspectives, as well as competing interests and clashing values. When confronted with ideas or life experiences that contradict our own, our initial impulse is often to dismiss, reject, and even delegitimize them.[91] Due to the limits of our ability to understand those who are different from us, uptake can fail even when admirably motivated citizens take the time to engage with one another.

Ultimately, in this discussion of uptake, I have two goals. Not only do I want to show that uptake is essential for achieving the democratic functioning of a deliberative system. I also want to illustrate the challenges to achieving uptake in a political context of deep difference. Inputs in deliberation are not the communicative equivalent of presliced bread waiting to be jammed into our mind-toaster. We often struggle to fully understand, let alone clearly articulate, our *own* feelings, grievances, or political positions. These challenges of articulation are only heightened when we try to express certain ideas to segments of society we expect will be unmoved by our input. Moreover,

---

[90] In the case of formal decision-making bodies considering the input of constituents, policy output may be a potentially relevant, though indirect, empirical indicator of whether uptake occurred.
[91] Connolly, *Identity\Difference*.

meaning is often partially constituted in deliberation itself: speakers do not always start out with a clear message in mind.

With these issues on our radar, we can begin to consider an example more complicated than the earlier one of deliberation regarding which recycling program to adopt. Imagine we are discussing workplace gender discrimination in the 1970s. And now, the person being dismissed as paranoid is a woman who raises the issue of sexual harassment. Maybe her colleagues understood *what* she was saying, but they could not understand *why* she would feel that way and thus concluded that her concerns were unfounded. Such a conclusion would lead them to prematurely dismiss her input. Maybe she explained that she took offense to someone's words, but the others failed to understand how that "joke" would make her feel uncomfortable. And so, while they understand *that* she had been made to feel uncomfortable, they did not deem that feeling worthy of careful consideration. Maybe they believed she was too sensitive and had herself failed to take up the joker's true meaning. In such a case, it would be hard to conclude that the woman's input was fairly considered.

If others cannot understand what this woman is trying to say, how can her perspective be incorporated into any plan of collective action? Butting up against the walls of intelligibility, women had to literally invent language to explain and even make sense of the particular injustice of sexual harassment they were experiencing.[92] Still, even with more sophisticated language and clear legal categories to use when making claims of sexual harassment, uptake on the part of federal agencies and the general public did not automatically follow.

As we see with this example, uptake is not easily achieved and it is not always straightforward. Like more agonistic difference democrats, I too accept an ontology of identity/difference as a background condition of democratic engagement. As such, I recognize the ways in which citizens are not only divided but constituted by their differences. And I acknowledge that this ontological reality affects both our ability and willingness to fairly consider others' ideas. These relations of identity/difference are only compounded when deliberative procedures become more inclusive.[93] Moreover, the

---

[92] Young, *Inclusion and Democracy*, 72.

[93] In introducing the concept of "communicative plenty," Ercan and colleagues identify another potential obstacle to achieving deliberative uptake: the sheer quantity of voices and perspectives included in a deliberative system. While distinct from the issues of identity/difference raised here, the challenges of reflection in an era of communicative plenty support my call to differentiate between inclusion and uptake. Indeed, Ercan et al. show how these two deliberative ideals can even be directly at odds with each other. Importantly, however, remedies to the pathologies of communicative plenty

challenges of securing uptake that exist even across horizontal relations of social distance—when people have little in common or little opportunity to interact—are exacerbated by power differentials.

The difficulty we have securing uptake under the political conditions we currently confront would seem to present a new challenge to difference-minded democrats attempting to rehabilitate deliberation instead of abandoning it in favor of agonism. Despite the challenges to securing uptake, I argue that pursuing it as an ideal still offers our best chance of achieving meaningfully democratic deliberation across difference and disagreement. Importantly, however, we must pursue uptake while remaining sensitive to an ontology of identity/difference. To this end, efforts to secure uptake should be aimed at fostering the *conditions* for uptake, rather than fruitlessly trying to guarantee uptake itself. Crucially, however, the conditions for uptake require more than having certain procedures in place. To promote uptake, especially in unstructured public communication, we must go beyond questions of procedure to consider the capacities and dispositions of citizens acting within an otherwise inclusive deliberative system.

As I show, however, even well-intentioned and open-minded citizens can struggle to fairly consider another person's input due to limitations in their ability to understand others' experiences and perspectives. But while it's important to recognize these failures of uptake and their impact on our democratic prospects, we should differentiate them from failures of uptake that result from ideological rigidity, willful misinterpretations, and prejudice. In other words, not all failures of uptake are created equal. Uptake can be purposefully denied, for example, if someone willfully misinterprets an input that she takes to challenge her political dominance. Alternatively, uptake can fail as a result of limits to understanding that are caused by epistemologies of ignorance rather than horizontal relations of social distance.[94] Conditions of inequality and oppression make it harder for some not only to share their stories, but for their stories to be validated and even understood. By studying the concept of uptake, we can gain a better understanding of these barriers to democracy in large, complex societies.

will not necessarily address challenges of consideration that emanate from relations of identity/difference. Selen A. Ercan, Carolyn M. Hendriks, and John S. Dryzek, "Public Deliberation in an Era of Communicative Plenty," *Policy & Politics* 47, no. 1 (2019): 19–36.

[94] Charles W. Mills, "White Ignorance," in *Race and Epistemologies of Ignorance*, ed. Shannon Sullivan and Nancy Tuana (Albany, NY: SUNY Press, 2007), 13–38.

Failures of uptake that result from our best efforts to understand and consider another's perspective may be an inevitable part of deliberating across difference. And the democratic functioning of a polity will not necessarily be improved if we were to somehow remove these kinks, say, by avoiding certain topics in debate, or as I discuss in the next chapter, by downplaying differences between citizens through appeals to empathy. Even when elusive, the ideal of uptake can contribute to the democratic functioning of a political system by helping to identify and diagnose issues of unequal standing and epistemic injustice caused by structural inequalities or prejudice, which, unlike the simple presence of difference and disagreement, *do* represent flaws in a supposedly democratic system.[95]

Absent appeals to uptake, claims made against a democratic system can only be evaluated according to the norm of inclusion or the expectation of influence. As such, claims of domination that cannot be easily validated by pointing to formal exclusion are often assessed according to whether one agrees with the substance of the input that was rejected. Uptake, which offers a middle ground between mere inclusion and actual influence, is valuable precisely because it encourages us to continually strive to differentiate between times when a person's voice is ignored and prematurely dismissed, on the one hand, and instances when a group of citizens was included and had their arguments considered, but simply did not see their will reflected in the law, on the other.

2.4 Uptake as a Universal Ideal?

From the preceding, fair consideration emerges as an essential standard for evaluating claims of exclusion or domination made in a supposedly democratic polity marked by dissensus. In the remaining chapters, I consider how to achieve uptake in practice. But first I want to briefly address what may be some initial skepticism toward my claim that the democratic quality of deliberation is always improved by more uptake. I return to these questions in Chapter 7.

So far, I have presented uptake as a universal deliberative ideal. But we know that, in practice, deliberation will include the input and perspectives

---

[95] For an account of how prejudice can undermine uptake, see Okim Kang and Donald L. Rubin, "Reverse Linguistic Stereotyping: Measuring the Effect of Listener Expectations on Speech Evaluation," *Journal of Language and Social Psychology* 28, no. 4 (2009): 441–56.

of not only the marginalized and powerless, but democracy's enemies as well—for example, white nationalists, misogynists, and authoritarians. Is democracy improved when we take up these messages? Should citizens really be expected to expose themselves to this kind of hate and enmity? Or might there be a democratic equivalent of poison that, as a rule, ought to be expelled immediately without being meaningfully taken up?

These questions must figure into any discussion of deliberative uptake, and are particularly relevant in light of recent political events in the United States. Here, I am thinking about the rise of white nationalist violence and rhetoric since the 2016 US presidential campaign and election of Donald Trump.[96] In what follows, I consider how these issues bear on uptake's status as a universal ideal.

The challenges of securing uptake, which exist even across horizontal social lines, are exacerbated in contexts of social and political inequality. The relatively powerful "middle segments" of society are often unaccustomed, if not unwilling, to fairly consider the inputs of minority groups, including those who are disadvantaged and oppressed.[97] Such instances of failed uptake seem to present an obvious democratic deficit for a deliberative system. But the democratic advantage of encouraging members of less powerful or marginalized groups to take up dominant discourses is not as clear. Perhaps our aim should be to encourage dominant segments of society to listen, while empowering others to tune out certain voices, particularly the voices of those who seek to oppress.[98]

Indeed, others have argued that holding all citizens to the same deliberative standards, standards that are not sensitive to power differentials and historic injustice, is bad for democracy.[99] For example, Pedrini, Bächtiger, and Steenbergen contend that the "burden of reciprocity" should not be imposed on majority and minority groups alike.[100] While majorities and privileged

---

[96] Henry A. Giroux, "White Nationalism, Armed Culture and State Violence in the Age of Donald Trump," *Philosophy & Social Criticism* 43, no. 9 (2017): 887–910.

[97] White, *A Democratic Bearing*.

[98] Suzanne Dovi, "In Praise of Exclusion," *Journal of Politics* 71, no. 3 (2009): 1182. Seraina Pedrini, André Bächtiger, and Marco R. Steenbergen, "Deliberative Inclusion of Minorities: Patterns of Reciprocity among Linguistic Groups in Switzerland," *European Political Science Review* 5, no. 3 (2013): 483–512.

[99] André Bächtiger and John Parkinson, *Mapping and Measuring Deliberation: Towards a New Deliberative Quality* (Oxford: Oxford University Press, 2019), 134; Tanja Dreher and Poppy de Souza, "Locating Listening," in *Ethical Responsiveness and the Politics of Difference*, ed. Tanja Dreher and Anshuman Mondal (New York: Palgrave Macmillan, 2018), 21–39; Pedrini, Bächtiger, and Steenbergen, "Deliberative Inclusion of Minorities," 508.

[100] Pedrini, Bächtiger, and Steenbergen, "Deliberative Inclusion of Minorities."

groups should always "approach the claims of structural minorities and disadvantaged groups with serious listening and respect," minorities should not be "held fully accountable to these standards."[101]

Going still further, Suzanne Dovi has written "In Praise of Exclusion," arguing that "democratic institutions can sometimes function better when certain groups are excluded from the political arena."[102] Though Dovi is writing about democratic representation and not deliberation, her concept of democratic exclusion is relevant here. According to Dovi, to counter undue influence and domination we need democratic exclusion. Specifically, she argues that we must consider how to effectively "marginalize" certain voices so as to "curtail the influence of powerful groups, such as the wealthy, whites, or males."[103] While Dovi opposes "formal prohibitions that bar certain citizens from being full participants in representative institutions based on their group memberships," she argues that democratic institutions can actually function more democratically when they informally silence certain voices, specifically the voices of those who oppress and those who benefit from oppression.[104]

As such, Dovi recommends using informal norms and practices to prevent "certain groups from having an effective political voice."[105] According to this view, in order to deny a group undue influence, Dovi would have us deny them uptake, or what she calls "informal inclusion." Specifically, Dovi argues that democratic citizens ought not to consider the voices of those groups and ideologies that seek to oppress others.[106]

But while sympathetic to Dovi's aims and aware of the fact that in pursuing the ideal of uptake we run the risk of normalizing and legitimizing dangerous and undemocratic inputs, I would argue that it is precisely by pursuing uptake as a universal democratic ideal that we can begin to correct for the undue influence of dominant groups and discourses. Only through fair consideration can citizens determine which ideas and perspectives ought to be "marginalized" in the first place—in other words, processed out—and therefore denied *influence* in democratic institutions.[107] And in the case of

---

[101] Ibid., 489.
[102] Dovi, "In Praise of Exclusion," 1172.
[103] Ibid., 1173.
[104] Dovi introduces this "Oppression Principle" as the standard to use when deciding whose voices we should marginalize. Ibid., 1182.
[105] Ibid., 1174.
[106] Ibid., 1182.
[107] Ibid., 1173.

dangerously antidemocratic inputs, if functioning properly, uptake can effectively sound an alarm, helping citizens identify and defend against threats to democracy. In other words, uptake can be used defensively by democratic citizens.

Importantly, the expectation of fair consideration is not just about being receptive to what others have to say, but being critical as well. According to the ideal of uptake, democracy suffers as much when the voices of the oppressed are included without consideration as when the voices of dominant groups achieve influence without being critically assessed.[108] Pursuing the ideal of uptake, our goal is to prevent citizens from summarily rejecting or accepting what others say. This critical, discursive processing at the heart of uptake is crucial precisely because inclusive deliberation introduces the inputs of the marginalized and powerless, alongside the inputs of the dominant and powerful.

In the end, only by attending to the question of uptake do we come to understand both the promise and perils of inclusive deliberation. Relying solely on the ideal of inclusion, however, we lose sight of the critical engagement that must occur in meaningfully democratic deliberation. Without recourse to uptake and the critical engagement it ensures, we have no choice but to exclude voices and perspectives that we think could damage our democracy. The crucial point, however, is that we cannot, prior to the act of uptake itself, determine who is and is not owed fair consideration. In presuming we can, we risk reproducing "simplistic and essentializing binaries of privileged and marginalized, silenced and silencer" and losing "sight of the complexities of the workings of privilege and power. . . ."[109] A democratic theory with uptake at its center, on the other hand, emphasizes the need to be critical and vigilant in our processing of inputs, while still aligning with our strong intuitions about the importance of inclusion for democracy.

2.5 Conclusion

On the basis of what I have argued in this chapter, it should now be clear that the fair consideration that occurs after inclusion is what ensures people

---

[108] Mark E. Button and Jacob Garrett, "Impartiality in Political Judgment: Deliberative Not Philosophical," *Political Studies* 64, no. 15 (2016): 48.

[109] Tanja Dreher, "Listening across Difference: Media and Multiculturalism beyond the Politics of Voice," *Continuum* 23, no. 4 (2009): 451–52.

have the opportunity to participate as full democratic citizens in a deliberative system. Indeed, we value deliberative inclusion in the first place because we want our ideas to be taken up by our fellow citizens and representatives. Only then can we see ourselves as having helped shape the laws to which we are held. Recognizing the insufficiency of inclusion and the need for uptake is essential if deliberative democratic theory is to respond to persistent concerns of exclusion.

Beyond showing that deliberative uptake is essential for achieving the democratic force of deliberation, I also illustrated the challenges to achieving uptake in political contexts of deep difference. Importantly, my defense of uptake as a deliberative ideal is not based on it being readily available or a more realistic goal for deliberation than, say, consensus. Instead, I turn to uptake because it is the relevant standard by which to assess the democratic nature of collective decisions. Far from suggesting that the question of how to democratize deliberative uptake has a straightforward answer, I have shown that it is a question in urgent need of attention. Acknowledging uptake as a deliberative ideal helpfully reveals when full and fair deliberation, and so the promise of democracy, is being enhanced and, just as importantly, when it is not. Without recourse to the concept of uptake, however, we cannot fully understand, let alone address the challenges to the normative core of democratic deliberation raised by difference democrats.

What it means to consider someone's point of view is not immediately obvious. And it is inevitably less straightforward than counting a person's vote or even granting a person access to deliberative forums. Despite the difficulty we have observing uptake, it still warrants further investigation given the role it plays in ensuring the democratic functioning of a deliberative system. It is the promise of having one's interests, preferences, or perspective meaningfully considered (and not just tallied) by one's fellow citizens that makes deliberation, at once, admittedly more burdensome than aggregation or "mere majority rule," but also more meaningfully democratic.[110] Deliberative uptake, then, gets at the heart of both the advantages and the challenges of a deliberative model of democracy, capturing the hard work that must occur between the inclusion of deliberative inputs and the production of meaningfully democratic outputs.

---

[110] And according to some research, though potentially more burdensome, deliberative democracy may ultimately be more attractive to citizens. Michael A. Neblo, Kevin M. Esterling, Ryan P. Kennedy, David M. J. Lazer, Anand E. Sokhey, "Who Wants to Deliberate—And Why?," *American Political Science Review* 104, no. 03 (2010): 566–83.

One important set of questions remains: How do we improve and assess the deliberative uptake that ensures the democratic functioning of a deliberative system? A project, such as mine, aimed at democratizing deliberative uptake is not without its challenges. For one, while we can design procedures ensuring equal access and inclusion, it is less obvious how to ensure the corresponding consideration that makes the inclusion democratically meaningful. Uptake, it seems, defies procedural guarantees. Furthermore, there are no unambiguous arguments or empirical indicators to which we can appeal in either redeeming or challenging claims of failed uptake. As I explain in Chapter 5, the only way to know whether uptake has been secured is through further engagement.[111] Failures of uptake "can be *revealed*" over time through a citizen's treatment of and interactions with those whose inputs they are supposed to be taking up.[112]

Though perhaps difficult to achieve and operationalize, accounting for how (or whether) included voices are actually considered by their fellow citizens is an essential part of democratizing "the means by which a majority comes to be a majority." In Chapter 3, I consider one possible resource for securing the conditions of uptake in democratic deliberation across difference: empathy. Arguments for improving and expanding our practices of empathy have exploded in popularity over the last ten years in both political and scholarly debate. As I show, however, empathy, relying as it does on imaginative perspective taking and seeking to uncover underlying or preexisting commonalities among citizens, may ultimately exacerbate problems of uptake in large pluralistic societies. Providing some critical purchase with which to assess proliferating appeals to empathy as an unproblematic democratic ideal, I argue that we must move beyond empathy in order to achieve the uptake on which full and fair deliberation depends.

---

[111] Susan Bickford, *The Dissonance of Democracy* (Ithaca, NY: Cornell University Press, 1996), 157.
[112] Habermas, *The Theory of Communicative Action*, 1: 41.

3

Empathy as a Strategy and Ideal
of Deliberation

The Promise and Perils

Democracy is enacted when citizens participate in the authorship of the laws
to which they are held. Thus, to carry democratic force, political communication must be inclusive and considerate of all voices. People need not only a
chance to speak, but also a guarantee that their contributions will be taken up
by their fellow citizens. But while much thought has been given to making a
deliberative system more inclusive and democratizing inputs to deliberation,
we still lack an understanding of how to ensure those inputs are taken up and
actually considered.

One exception to the dearth in attention paid to something like uptake in
deliberative democratic theory is the recent turn toward empathy as both a
strategy and ideal of democratic discourse. Defenses of empathy in democratic deliberation, typified by the work of Sharon Krause, Michael Morrell,
and Robert Goodin—but also that of Michael Frazer, Martha Nussbaum, and
others—claim that enhancing practices of empathy among citizens would
improve the democratic functioning of a deliberative system by promoting
greater inclusiveness and consideration in political communication among
citizens.[1] In this chapter, I consider both the promise and perils of relying on
empathy as a means of improving democratic deliberation.

Specifically, in what follows, I examine the role that empathy might play in
deliberative democratic theory and practice. To begin, I elucidate the ways in
which empathy can be used to support both inclusion and uptake (**3.1**). Then,
problematizing and complicating recent accounts of empathy, I go on to reveal potential pathologies of the practice (**3.2**). Because of the variation in our

---

[1] Sharon R. Krause, *Civil Passions: Moral Sentiment and Democratic Deliberation* (Princeton,
NJ: Princeton University Press, 2008); Michael E. Morrell, *Empathy and Democracy: Feeling,
Thinking, and Deliberation* (University Park: Pennsylvania State University Press, 2010); Robert E.
Goodin, *Reflective Democracy* (Oxford: Oxford University Press, 2003).

Beyond Empathy and Inclusion. Mary F. Scudder, Oxford University Press (2020). © Oxford University Press.
DOI: 10.1093/oso/9780197535455.001.0001.

ability to empathize and our tendency to project our own views onto others, we should not rely on empathy to play as central a role in deliberation as its supporters propose. Furthermore, I show why even improving our practices of empathy is an unlikely answer to these pathologies of empathy. Contrary to our intuitions, and perhaps paradoxically, empathy will not always support deliberative inclusion and uptake in the way its promoters think.

3.1 The Empathic Turn in Democratic Deliberation

The recent appeals to empathy by political theorists reflect a new emphasis on the value of affect, emotion, and passion in democratic discourse.[2] As James Bohman explains, theories of democratic deliberation "share the common demand that democracy is the rule by citizens of their common affairs *through the public use of reason*."[3] The recent turn to empathy developed as a reaction to what was considered a narrow or singular understanding of reason in theories of deliberation, especially those of John Rawls and Jürgen Habermas.[4]

While disputes over reason and affect in democratic deliberation persist (including debates over whether that distinction is even tenable), empathy is often seen as an unproblematic addition to deliberative democratic theory. Empathy has been described as one of a few " 'good' emotions"—compatible with rational discourse and reasoned argumentation.[5] Describing empathy as a good *emotion*, however, confuses more than it clarifies. We do not feel empathy; empathy is not, itself, an emotion.[6] Instead, if we empathize with someone, it means that we may share or at least understand her feelings (sadness, happiness, fear, anger, etc.).

---

[2] Krause, *Civil Passions*; Morrell, *Empathy and Democracy*; Michael Frazer, *The Enlightenment of Sympathy: Justice and the Moral Sentiments in the Eighteenth Century and Today* (New York: Oxford University Press, 2010); Goodin, *Reflective Democracy*; Martha Nussbaum, *Poetic Justice: The Literary Imagination and Public Life* (Boston: Beacon Press, 1995).

[3] James Bohman, "Realizing Deliberative Democracy as a Mode of Inquiry: Pragmatism, Social Facts, and Normative Theory," *Journal of Speculative Philosophy* 18, no. 1 (2004): 23–24 (emphasis added).

[4] George Marcus, "Reason, Passion, and Democratic Politics," in *Passions and Emotions: Nomos LIII*, ed. James E. Fleming (New York: NYU Press, 2012).

[5] Ibid., 131. The literature on the value of emotion in politics extends well beyond the specific focus of deliberative democratic theory. For a helpful review see Eric Groenendyk, "Current Emotion Research in Political Science: How Emotions Help Democracy Overcome Its Collective Action Problem," *Emotion Review* 3, no. 4 (2011): 455–63.

[6] Morrell, *Empathy and Democracy*, 62.

Though empathy is not itself an emotion, deliberative democrats turn to empathy as a way to acknowledge and formalize the role of emotions, affect, and passions in democratic politics. Through the practice of empathy, of putting ourselves in another's shoes, citizens can encounter and therefore consider the sentiments of others.[7]

We can better understand empathy as a practice (rather than a discrete emotion) by tracing its relatively recent etymological roots. The English word "empathy," coined in the early twentieth century, comes from the German *Einfühlung*, which means "feeling-into." According to Michael Frazer, Johann Gottfried von Herder used this term to describe a practice of reading historical texts, where historians could only understand ancient peoples through a "process of self-projection."[8] Herder's study of history involved imagining ourselves in the place of others, " 'feeling our way into' their experience of the world."[9] The practice of empathy or feeling one's self into another person's situation was supposed to foster better understanding of peoples who were distant and different from the historian.

Interestingly, the English word "empathy" did not exist when David Hume and Adam Smith wrote about imaginative perspective taking and shared feelings, which they included under the concept of "sympathy." In her own work on affect and democratic deliberation, Sharon Krause, following Hume, refers exclusively to "sympathy." But as she and Michael Morrell acknowledge, their preferred terms of sympathy and empathy, respectively, have a common meaning.[10] For them, empathy is the "affective-cognitive communication of sentiments between persons that transpires through perspective-taking."[11]

Whether called sympathy, empathy, or Goodin's preferred "deliberation within," political theorists argue that this process of imaginative perspective taking—which allows us to understand the sentiments of others—contributes

---

[7] Students of politics, philosophy, law, and psychology have all offered their own definitions of empathy. Across all of these disciplines, however, empathy is understood as both a process and an outcome. Empathy-as-process, which involves imagining another's perspective, is supposed to bring about empathy-as-outcome, of which there are two types: cognitive and affective. Cognitive empathy is the "awareness of another's feelings," whereas affective empathy is "feeling what another feels." Cognitive empathy, which emerges from the process of imagined perspective taking, allows us to understand another's perspective or feelings, even if we do not ultimately come to share them. Martin L. Hoffman, "Empathy, Justice, and the Law," in *Empathy: Philosophical and Psychological Perspectives*, ed. Amy Coplan and Peter Goldie (Oxford: Oxford University Press, 2011), 230.

[8] Frazer, *The Enlightenment of Sympathy*, 155.

[9] Ibid., 154.

[10] Sharon R. Krause, "Empathy, Democratic Politics, and the Impartial Juror," *Law, Culture and the Humanities* 7, no. 1 (2011): 83; Morrell, *Empathy and Democracy*, 194.

[11] Krause, "Empathy, Democratic Politics, and the Impartial Juror," 83.

to democratic deliberation by improving both inclusion and uptake.[12] Taken together, I argue, these interventions constitute an "empathic turn" in regard to how we should enhance the democratic quality of deliberation.[13]

For Krause, the democratic potential of empathy is rooted in its contribution to the inclusiveness of our deliberation. Krause explains that to be democratically legitimate, decisions must be made impartially. While an impartial perspective is often assumed to be one free of passion or emotion, Krause shows that impartiality comes, instead, from the inclusion and consideration of others' feelings and passions alongside our own.[14] Judgments cannot be made without reference to passions. Therefore, trying to exclude passion and sentiment is impossible and counterproductive. According to Krause's crucial reinterpretation of the concept, impartiality, in fact, requires the inclusion of all relevant people's passions and sentiments.[15] And sympathy is the mechanism through which we encounter the sentiments and situated perspectives of others.

In *Civil Passions*, Krause identifies two distinct, though related, meanings of sympathy in the work of Hume: one cognitive, the other affective. The primary meaning of sympathy for Hume is what Krause calls "S1." S1 "is not itself a passion, hence not itself an affective state, but it communicates passions to us and stimulates similar passions in us."[16] As a cognitive faculty of the mind "with an informational function," S1 provides affective inputs for our consideration in deliberation.[17] S1 serves an important informational function, allowing us to know how another is feeling. According to Krause, the feelings of others do not need to be explicitly communicated to us, and instead are often imagined.[18] Although our cognitive faculty of sympathy (S1) is "automatic" and "a natural feature of our moral psychology," it "is not naturally as extensive or as free from self-love as impartial judgment requires."[19]

---

[12] Krause, Morrell, and Goodin do not refer to the concept of "uptake," as such, but discuss the ways in which empathy brings about the consideration of and concern for the ideas of others.

[13] In order to keep the discussion here manageable, and since Krause, Morrell, and Goodin provide the most in-depth and detailed accounts of empathy's contribution to democratic deliberation, I engage primarily with their work, taking it to be a proxy for proponents of empathy in general. For more on empathy and politics see James E. Fleming, ed., *Passions and Emotions: Nomos LIII* (New York: NYU Press, 2012); Amy Coplan and Peter Goldie, ed. *Empathy: Philosophical and Psychological Perspectives* (Oxford: Oxford University Press, 2011).

[14] Krause, *Civil Passions*, 5.

[15] Ibid., 73.

[16] Ibid., 80.

[17] Ibid., 79.

[18] Ibid., 85.

[19] Ibid., 84.

For Krause, sympathy is an important, though limited, first step in knowing the sentiments of others so as to include them in deliberation. And again, this inclusion is what allows citizens to make impartial decisions, or decisions that are not based solely on self-interest.

Though primarily serving a cognitive and informational function, sympathy in this sense "enables us to resonate with the affective experiences of others, to be moved by the sentiments that others express."[20] Krause refers to Hume's second sense of sympathy as "S2." S2 "*is* itself an affective state, or a form of passion."[21] Sympathy in this sense involves caring for another person. Krause explains that S2 is the benevolence or pity that, quoting Hume, "makes me concern'd for the present sorrows of a stranger."[22]

Though Hume does not differentiate between S1 and S2, Krause shows how the two senses of sympathy are different, though related. Deploying the cognitive faculty of sympathy (S1) can often lead to affective concern for others (S2).[23] Even if exercising the cognitive faculty of sympathy, or engaging in the practice of empathy, does not produce feelings of sympathy for others, it is still an important contribution to the impartiality of moral judgment insofar as it introduces the sentiments of others as relevant inputs for deliberation.[24] According to Krause, the value of empathy, or imaginative perspective taking, comes in large part from the resulting empathic (cognitive) understanding of others' feelings.

Echoing Krause's endorsement of both the cognitive and affective sides of sympathy, Morrell argues that the process of empathy helps deliver on the democratic promise of both inclusion and equal consideration.[25] In fact, Morrell goes so far as to base the legitimacy of deliberative decisions on the extent to which citizens empathized with one another. For Morrell, empathy is a process that includes, but is not limited to, imaginatively taking the perspective of another person. This process can then lead to both affective and cognitive outcomes.[26] For example, imaginatively putting yourself

---

[20] Ibid., 80.
[21] Ibid.
[22] Ibid.
[23] Ibid., 81.
[24] Ibid.
[25] Morrell uses the term "equal consideration." But as I explain in Chapter 2, "fair consideration" may be more apt. Morrell, *Empathy and Democracy*, 193.
[26] Morrell details the various elements of the process of empathy, beginning with the "antecedents" to the process, which include a person's biological capacity to empathize (which may be inherited) as well as the similarity between the "target" of empathy and the "observer" or would-be empathizer. These "personal and situational characteristics" interact with the "mechanisms of empathy," especially perspective taking, or imaginatively putting yourself in another's shoes. Together, the antecedents and mechanism of perspective taking lead to both affective and cognitive outcomes.

in another's shoes may lead to *feelings* of empathic concern for others. But even if this exercise does not result in greater feelings of empathic concern, the mechanism of perspective taking still produces the cognitive outcome of empathic understanding. Morrell's discussion of empathic understanding mirrors Krause's claim that S1 is valuable in its informational capacity even when it does not lead to S2 or feelings of concern for others.

Morrell's central claim is that without the practice of empathy, "deliberation cannot provide a basis for legitimate, justified democratic decision-making that truly takes all into consideration."[27] By formalizing the role of affect in democratic deliberation, empathy is supposed to help maximize inclusion while also promoting uptake and therefore bolstering the legitimating force of the decision-making process. According to Morrell, empathy contributes to uptake by providing us knowledge of others' emotions and by helping us see that our fellow citizens are not so dissimilar from ourselves.[28] Through empathy we recognize the fundamental desires, fears, and needs that we share with others. Empirically, Morrell finds that simply encouraging individuals to practice empathy can reduce certain biases that work against fair consideration in deliberation.

Morrell shows, for example, that empathy can reduce attribution bias.[29] Attribution bias describes the errors people make when evaluating the reasons for their own behavior compared to the reasons for others' behavior. Individuals often attribute their own successes to their personal qualities or dispositional factors, while attributing their failures to situational circumstances. In contrast, we are more likely to attribute the behavior of others solely to dispositional factors. So while I see my reliance on unemployment benefits as the result of bad luck or rough economic conditions, I am more likely to blame my neighbor's economic misfortune on laziness or incompetence. This kind of bias undermines the democratic potential of deliberation insofar as citizens' reasoning is inadvertently self-interested. Importantly, however, Morrell finds that when citizens are invited to practice empathy or to put themselves in another's shoes, they are less likely to demonstrate attribution bias. With this, Morrell seems to show that fair

---

Ibid., 56; Mark H. Davis, *Empathy: A Social Psychological Approach* (Madison, WI: Brown & Benchmark, 1994), 62–70.

[27] Morrell, *Empathy and Democracy*, 194.
[28] Ibid., 2.
[29] Ibid., 103.

consideration is not an exclusively cognitive process; our ability (and willing-ness) to take up the perspectives of others is, in part, driven by affect.

Taking an even stronger position than either Morrell or Krause, Goodin argues that empathy does more than improve communication among citi-zens; it can actually replace it. In *Reflective Democracy*, Goodin argues that "democratic deliberation within," or the act of "imagining ourselves in the place of others," "offers the best way" and in some cases the only way to ad-dress the problem of "social exclusion."[30] Goodin explains that "empathetic imagining" can solve the practical challenges of external deliberation. For him, empathy—again, the practice of imagining ourselves into the place of others—ensures that inputs in deliberation are broad and inclusive when face-to-face encounters are infeasible because of the "problem of scale," or, even in the absence of a problem of scale, in the case of excluded or mute interests.[31] Goodin talks about the power of film or fiction to fire our imagi-nation, such that we "imagine vividly what it would be like to be they, or to be in that situation."[32] Ideally, all people would speak for themselves, but when social or political inequalities or exclusions prevent equal voice, Goodin thinks that imagining others' perspectives is the best alternative.

But for Goodin, our empathic imaginings not only make deliberation more inclusive, they are also essential for ensuring that citizens' perspectives are actually taken up and meaningfully considered. Like me, Goodin points to the insufficiency of conceptions of inclusion currently on offer in delib-erative democratic theory when he writes, "Once upon a time, 'democratic inclusion' was regarded as mainly a matter of expanding the franchise."[33] Due to persistent problems of "social exclusion," however, "our faith in that sim-plistic model of democratic inclusion has waned."[34] Goodin explains that inclusion understood according to the "mechanistic model of aggregative democracy" is problematic because in deliberation "some affected interests will always be left out through those sorts of processes."[35] Here, Goodin acknowledges the need for more than inclusion.

He addresses this need by introducing the concept of "democratic delib-eration within," by which he means internal reflection rather than public

---

[30] Goodin, *Reflective Democracy*, 209, 194.
[31] Ibid., 194.
[32] Robert E. Goodin, "Democratic Deliberation Within," *Philosophy and Public Affairs* 29, no. 1 (2000): 95.
[33] Goodin, *Reflective Democracy*, 194.
[34] Ibid.
[35] Ibid.

discussion. In other words, for Goodin, the answer to facilitating uptake is turning deliberation inward. In deliberation "without," inclusion may not guarantee fair consideration, but with the use of our imaginations and deliberation within, all interests and perspectives can be both included and duly considered.

For Krause, Morrell, and Goodin, empathy is a fundamental democratic practice that is in vital need of expansion and development. Besides these, other theorists have argued that practices similar to Krause's sympathy, Morrell's empathy, and Goodin's deliberation within make important contributions to democracy. For example, Richard Rorty offers "imaginative identification" as the basis of solidarity.[36] Even more common are references or appeals to the assumed benefit of empathy. Diana Boros and Martha Nussbaum, for example, both write on the value of art in democracy for its ability to generate empathic concern for one's fellow citizens.[37] And in popular discourse as well, empathy is cited as the solution to disparate challenges of the twenty-first century, from bullying to racism.[38] In fact, during the 2016 election, some pointed to a failure on the part of liberal elites to empathize with white working-class voters as an explanation for Donald Trump's rise in popularity.[39] And in the wake of the election, low levels of empathy were blamed for the discursive echo chambers that may have prevented pollsters and party leaders from anticipating Trump's victory.[40] On the other hand, empathy is often credited for those instances when discourse succeeds in transcending ideological divides. For example, conservative pundit Glenn Beck explained that his change of heart toward the progressive Black Lives Matter movement was achieved through empathy.[41]

---

[36] Richard Rorty, *Contingency, Irony, and Solidarity* (Cambridge: Cambridge University Press, 1989).

[37] Diana Boros, *Creative Rebellion for the Twenty-First Century: The Importance of Public and Interactive Art to Political Life in America* (New York: Palgrave Macmillan, 2012); Nussbaum, *Poetic Justice.*

[38] See Roman Krznaric, "The One Thing That Could Save the World: Why We Need Empathy Now More Than Ever," *Salon*, November 9, 2014, https://www.salon.com/2014/11/08/the_one_thing_that_could_save_the_world_why_we_need_empathy_now_more_than_ever/.

[39] Colby Itkowitz, "What Is This Election Missing? Empathy for Trump Voters," *Washington Post*, November 2, 2016.

[40] Akash Wasil, "On Trump, Empathy, and Discourse," *Harvard Political Review*, November 11, 2016, https://harvardpolitics.com/united-states/trump-empathy-discourse/; Asma Khalid, "Tech Creates our Political Echo Chambers. It Might Also be a Solution," *All Things Considered*. NPR, April 12, 2017, https://www.npr.org/sections/alltechconsidered/2017/04/12/522760479/tech-creates-our-political-echo-chambers-it-might-also-be-a-solution.

[41] Glenn Beck, "Empathy for Black Lives Matter," *New York Times*, September 7, 2016.

I challenge the conventional wisdom, operating in both popular and scholarly debate, according to which empathy is seen as a straightforward way to boost democratic prospects.[42] My goal is to provide the critical purchase needed to assess proliferating appeals to empathy as a supposedly unproblematic ideal of democracy. Despite its wide acceptance, the practice of empathy suffers from pathologies that should worry deliberative democrats. My concerns relate primarily to the practice of putting one's self in another's shoes and the presumed value of such imaginative perspective taking for deliberative democratic theory and practice.

3.2 Pathologies of Empathy

Proponents of an empathy approach to deliberation argue that the expansion and development of our practices of empathy would contribute to the democratic prospects of deliberation. While Krause points to empathy as a way to make deliberation more inclusive of the sentiments and passions of all citizens, Morrell argues that empathy provides the affective component needed to sustain fair consideration of all perspectives included in deliberation. Meanwhile, Goodin argues that empathy, which he sees as largely a cognitive process, ensures the consideration of others' perspectives and feelings even when deliberative encounters are less than ideally wide and inclusive. According to these views, the democratic functioning of a deliberative system would be enhanced through the promotion of practices of empathy among citizens.

In this section, I take a critical look at these claims and raise questions regarding empathy's ability to improve the democratic quality of our deliberation. First, I present reasons for doubting the power of empathy to make deliberation more inclusive (3.2.1). While proponents of empathy are right to want to include affective inputs in our deliberation, I show that given practical limitations in our ability to put ourselves in others' shoes, empathy is not an effective way of achieving this kind of inclusion. In other words, while the

---

[42] Critiques of empathy exist in the broader moral philosophy and psychology literature. See Jesse Prinz, "Against Empathy," *Southern Journal of Philosophy* 49 (September 1, 2011): 214–33; and Paul Bloom, *Against Empathy: The Case for Rational Compassion* (New York: HarperCollins, 2016). These critics of empathy, however, focus on the limits of emotional empathy rather than cognitive empathy. Bloom sees cognitive empathy or empathic understanding as a more modest and less problematic outcome of the process of empathy, or putting yourself in another's shoes. In this chapter, I show why even this more modest goal does not sustain democratic deliberation.

goal of including citizens' affective inputs in deliberation is desirable, I have deep suspicions regarding empathy's ability to achieve it.

Second, I argue that even if our practices of empathy could be designed and perfected such that they effectively gave us access to and facilitated fair consideration of our fellow citizens' affective inputs, empathy would still fit uneasily as a deliberative ideal (3.2.2). Leaving behind concerns of infeasibility and practicality, here I argue that calls for more imaginative perspective taking run the risk of diverting citizens' attention from the need to actually engage with one another in the first place.

Lastly, I consider the role that empathy might play in democratizing deliberative uptake *within* inclusive and real—not imagined—communication across social divisions (3.2.3). Of course, no effort to improve uptake can succeed if inclusion has not been secured. And so, in this section, I evaluate empathy in a context where deliberation is sufficiently inclusive. Still, I present reasons for being skeptical of empathy's ability to promote uptake across difference and disagreement. But now, the problem with empathy is not its focus on imagination but its reliance on commonality. Supporters of empathy value imaginative perspective taking, in part, for its ability to reduce the distance between citizens, thus implying that such distance can and should be overcome in order to achieve productive deliberation. A more deliberative ideal, I contend, would show citizens the importance of reorienting themselves toward their fellow citizens in a way that allows them to communicate precisely with those people with whom they struggle to empathize effectively.

3.2.1 Practical Limits to Empathy

To begin my critical assessment of the empathy approach to democratic deliberation, I show that the practice of putting one's self in another's shoes is not always effective at achieving either affective or cognitive empathy. And so, while I agree that meaningfully democratic deliberation must be inclusive of citizens' feelings and sentiments and that affective inputs should be both included and considered, I show that the practice of empathy is not an effective or reliable way of accessing those inputs. Empathy functions weakly as a way to boost inclusion.

Empirical research regarding perspective taking points to the difficulty we have accurately imagining the perspectives of others or even our future selves. Not only does perspective taking rarely lead to affective empathy, but our ability to even understand the feelings of others through empathy is also limited. That is to say, the practice of empathy—in which we try to imaginatively encounter the feelings of others—does not give us access to the actual feelings and sentiments of our fellow citizens. Thus, even the more modest outcome of empathic understanding is difficult to attain from the practice of imaginative perspective taking.

Social psychologists Leaf Von Boven and George Loewenstein identify what they call the "empathy gap," which divides imagined perspectives from actual perspectives.[43] The source of this empathy gap is an egocentric bias in perspective taking that leads individuals to judge others in light of their own thoughts, feelings, or social context. When imagining the perspectives of others, people show significant bias in favor of their own feelings at that particular moment: "Judgments of others are made in comparison to the self, in service of the self, and in the direction of the self."[44] Indeed, people base their judgments and predictions about others on themselves "even when they have evidence that their own reactions are anomalous and even when they should recognize that their own experiences are of limited relevance—for example when others' experience is blatantly different from their own."[45] The authors contend that this projection may well be unavoidable—our own judgments are often our best source of information regarding how others would judge or think in a particular context.[46] In other words, projection of our own thoughts onto others may be the best way for us to engage in imaginative role taking, and yet it does not adequately inform us about the actual perspectives of others.

Iris Young vividly demonstrates the dangers of such a projection bias with the example of the Oregon Health Plan in the 1990s.[47] The Oregon Health Plan was designed in such a way that it disqualified disabled patients from certain treatments because their lives were considered less valuable than those of nondisabled patients. Oregon public policy makers devised their

---

[43] Leaf Von Boven and George Loewenstein, "Empathy Gaps in Emotional Perspective Taking," in *Other Minds: How Humans Bridge the Divide between Self and Others*, ed. Bertram Malle and Sara Hodges (New York: Guilford Press, 2005), 284–97.

[44] Ibid., 293.

[45] Ibid., 288.

[46] Ibid., 297.

[47] Young draws the example of the Oregon Health Plan from Anita Silver's essay "'Defective' Agents: Equality, Difference and the Tyranny of the Normal," *Journal of Social Philosophy* 25, no. 1 (1994): 154–75; Iris Marion Young, "Asymmetrical Reciprocity: On Moral Respect, Wonder, and Enlarged Thought," *Constellations* 3, no. 3 (1997): 340–63.

plan with the aid of a telephone survey, asking able-bodied respondents to imagine having a disability. These respondents frequently claimed "they would rather be dead than confined to a wheelchair."[48] Horrifically, "This claim was the grounds for a political judgment that health services for people with disabilities would not be subsidized in the same way as those for able-bodied people."[49] Ultimately these regulations were found to violate the Americans with Disabilities Act, though the example is still instructive.

Just as supporters of empathy would recommend, the participants in the survey "empathized" in the sense of imaginatively taking the perspective of disabled Oregonians. But contra the dictates of Morrell's process model of empathy, the participants or would-be empathizers failed to "maintain a healthy distinction between themselves and others."[50] This distinction is needed to guard against the dangerous assumption that the observers' imagined perspectives map on to the actual perspectives of the targets of empathy. But as Von Boven and Loewenstein's findings regarding the empathy gap show, maintaining the distinction between ourselves and others may be impossible when it comes to perspective taking. Though they drew incorrect conclusions about others' perspectives, the survey participants likely empathized to the best of their ability. And the process led to outcomes that Morrell and other proponents of the empathic turn do not discuss—namely, a failure of empathic understanding and misguided or unsolicited empathic concern. This example of the empathic process demonstrates the potential for perspective taking to lead to incorrect judgments and misunderstandings of how others feel. Furthermore, in so actively exercising their empathic imaginations, the people involved probably thought they had done something admirable and therefore, as I discuss below, may not take kindly to challenges or criticism.

Related to the pathologies of self-projection is a second challenge to empathy that occurs precisely when the observer and the target of empathy have little in common. In practice, people empathize selectively—and most often with others who are similar to them. Empathy is hardest to achieve for "outgroups" and those who are most different from ourselves.[51] The limits to

---

[48] Silvers, " 'Defective' Agents," 159.

[49] Young, "Asymmetrical Reciprocity," 344.

[50] Morrell, Empathy and Democracy, 167.

[51] See Davis, Empathy: A Social Psychological Approach; Diana C. Mutz, "Cross-Cutting Social Networks: Testing Democratic Theory in Practice," American Political Science Review 96, no. 1 (2002): 111–26; Elizabeth N. Simas, Scott Clifford, and Justin H. Kirkland, "How Empathic Concern Fuels Political Polarization," American Political Science Review, 114, no. 1 (2020): 258–269.

and errors in our attempts to empathically understand others are exaggerated when we try to imagine the perspectives of people most different from ourselves.

In response to the practical problems of empathy across difference, including the problem of projection, Krause and Morrell might remind us that exercises in perspective taking should never stand in for actual deliberation.[52] Morrell explicitly cites actual deliberation as the appropriate corrective to the problem of projection.[53] In the case of the Oregon Health Plan, this argument would go as follows: if lawmakers compared the imagined perspectives of able-bodied respondents to the actual beliefs and opinions of disabled citizens in deliberation, the thought experiment would have been quickly debunked. Accordingly, the outcomes of perspective taking should *inform* deliberation, not *replace* it. Similarly, deliberation itself should *inform* perspective taking. As Krause points out, "We can imagine the sentiments of others much better if they are able to tell us about them, after all."[54] Insofar as all citizens have a chance to present their own view and speak for themselves, we minimize the risk of incorrectly projecting our own view onto another.

Not only does deliberation keep the dangers of empathy in check, Krause explains that it can actually help us *overcome* the limits of our faculty of empathy. Sympathy and deliberation, it would seem, are bound together in a mutually beneficial loop, whereby deliberative encounters expand the faculty of sympathy (S1). Meanwhile, S1 feeds back into deliberation, making citizens open to more people in discourse. For example, Krause admits that "sympathy can extend only as far as does our awareness of others' sentiments."[55] As such, "the sentiments of marginalized persons—those whose identity or status sets them outside the majority's frame of reference—may tend not to register within the generalized standpoint of average citizens."[56] In other words, the sympathetic imagination on which we are relying to bring some concerns and issues to the attention of the polity does not necessarily extend to the most marginalized. Fortunately, however, deliberation—wherein citizens encounter perspectives they could not previously imagine—can correct for initial deficiencies in sympathy. "The access to public deliberation

---

[52] As I discuss shortly, Krause and Morrell's insistence on this point distinguishes their position from Goodin's take on deliberation within as a potential substitute for deliberation without. Morrell, *Empathy and Democracy*, 166.

[53] Ibid., 167.

[54] Krause, *Civil Passions*, 113.

[55] Ibid.

[56] Ibid.

that individual rights protect for members of minority groups facilitates such communication and supports regular contestation and debate, which extend the reach of the imagination and influence the contents of our judgments accordingly."[57] In other words, the sympathetic imagination itself can be expanded to reach excluded minorities through the process of deliberation. Empathy improves deliberation, while deliberation improves our capacity to empathize with those who are different from us.

But deliberation will not always correct for distortions and misperceptions brought about by limits in our ability to empathize. In the case of the Oregon Health Plan, for example, the same differences in perspective and experience that make it hard for able-bodied people to empathize with disabled individuals will also limit able-bodied people's ability to take up and hear what disabled people are really saying. In other words, deliberation will likely be most difficult in precisely those situations wherein Krause is counting on it to correct and expand empathy.

Moreover, the projection bias in perspective taking can lead to distortions and misperceptions of others' points of view for which discussion will not always correct. As Krause would certainly recognize, deliberation cannot correct the errors or limits of empathy when it comes to groups that are formally excluded from deliberation in the first place. People who have immigrated to the United States without documentation, for example, are denied both sympathy and inclusion in formal and informal deliberation. The denial of sympathy for these individuals often originates in the belief (whether true or not) that they freely chose to come to the United States without documentation, knowing that they would be denied certain rights and protections. Sympathetic exclusion, in this case, however, is never corrected as these immigrants are also excluded from deliberative forums and debate in the public sphere. Immigrants living in the United States who lack the necessary documents are not only prohibited from voting, holding office, and other formal political forums but are also discouraged from speaking up in informal deliberative settings due to the threat of detection and deportation.

The virtuous circle of wider empathy and more inclusive deliberation that Krause identifies turns into a vicious cycle for groups that are excluded from both empathy and deliberation. This can be the case not only for people who have immigrated to the United States without documentation, but also closeted gay men and women, victims of rape, disenfranchised felons, and

---

[57] Ibid.

numerous other groups of people who are empathically and politically marginalized. For members of these marginalized groups, the empathy approach offers little support for achieving either inclusion or uptake in deliberation.

Despite the challenges of accurately imagining how others feel and think, Goodin recommends empathy precisely in cases when people are already excluded from deliberation. Goodin explains:

> It is undeniably hard to imagine ourselves into the place of a homeless person or a Kurdish peasant, much less into the place of an orangutan or of people a thousand years from now. Still, imperfect though our imagination might be, we will almost certainly be more successful in our imaginings than such agents would be in speaking for themselves in the councils of state.[58]

Pace Goodin, imagining the interests of the politically excluded or voiceless is not a suitable stand-in for actual deliberation, even if only temporarily. Given the difficulty we face in empathizing with those most different from us, we should never assume that our imaginings map on to the real perspectives of particular others.[59] Doing so may actually obscure and exclude claims of injustice that do not fit easily within the majority's empathic imagination.

Furthermore, trying to empathize with such excluded individuals can distract us from the need to continually search for ways that they can speak for themselves. In the case of undocumented immigrants, a recent analysis of community-police forums found that when they feel secure "speaking for themselves," undocumented immigrants are quite effective in doing so.[60] While achieving empathic understanding through the process of imaginative perspective taking is supposed to sustain deliberation, in what follows I argue that it is just as likely to distract us from the need to listen to one another. In other words, gaining a better (and even an accurate) understanding

---

[58] Goodin, *Reflective Democracy*, 114.

[59] Frazer explains the value Herder placed on empathy or *Einfühlung* when studying ancient peoples. Herder, as a historian, was imagining the perspectives of people who were no longer able to speak for themselves. But we must be careful not to conflate subjects incapable of speaking (e.g., animals, the dead, and unborn future generations) and present, but silent or ignored, subjects. Empathy may be appropriate in trying to represent the interests of past or future generations or in the case of animals. These cases are beyond the scope of this project and must be distinguished from the case of present but ignored people. Frazer, *The Enlightenment of Sympathy*, 155.

[60] Rachel Wahl and Stephen K. White, "Deliberation, Accountability, and Legitimacy: A Case Study of Police-Community Forums," *Polity* 49, no. 4 (2017): 489–517.

of others through empathy runs the risk of short-circuiting uptake or the consideration of actual voices.

3.2.2 Imaginative Uptake and Communicative Uptake

Through their appeals to empathy, Krause, Morrell, and Goodin highlight the importance of attending to the affective dimension of deliberation. Here, I concede the importance of formalizing the role of affect in democratic deliberation and moral judgment. And leaving behind the practical concerns of projection bias discussed earlier, I argue that even if our practices of empathy could be designed and perfected such that they brought about appropriate empathic concern and accurate empathic understanding, the practices would still be ill-suited to sustain the kind of engagement needed for deliberative democracy. In other words, there are reasons to doubt that such empathically achieved inclusion and uptake would necessarily bolster democratic deliberation. Drawing on the relationship of inclusion and uptake presented in Chapter 2, I show that empathy may actually undermine rather than contribute to the very deliberation the democratic force of which we are trying to enhance.

For Goodin, when we access the perspectives of others through our imagination, they are always already taken up. A message imaginatively encountered is necessarily a message received. Accordingly, it seems that deliberation-within would be a strong ally of uptake. But in attempting to achieve consideration through empathic imagination, we alter our conception of deliberation such that the communicative component almost completely falls out. As such, instead of strengthening what Goodin calls "mere inclusion," empathy waters down the concept further. Imaginative or virtual inclusion replaces the real thing. What are considered are not so much the actual voices of our fellow citizens but their perspectives as we imagine them.

In Chapter 2, I showed that inclusion alone cannot ensure the democratic functioning of a deliberative system. Though real inclusion in actual (not just virtual) deliberative encounters is insufficient, it is still necessary for achieving meaningfully democratic deliberation. And so, it's a problem if, by helping individuals become more internally reflective and *deliberate*, empathy diverts their attention from the need to actually engage with one another in the first place. Indeed, in what follows I argue that the architects of the empathic turn propose a mechanism of inclusion and uptake that, even

when successful, is at least partially at odds with the basic tenets of the deliberative model of democracy. Efforts to improve the democratic functioning
of a deliberative system are counterproductive if they come at the expense of
that system's very deliberativeness.

To make good on this claim, I want to call our attention once again to
the distinctiveness of the deliberative model of democracy. Despite its wide
usage, "deliberation" remains an essentially contested concept.[61] *To deliberate* comes from the Latin word *librare*, which means to balance or weigh.
In English, the verb has two related, though different, meanings. These two
meanings are often conflated, as they are in the *Merriam-Webster Dictionary*,
which gives the following definition: *to deliberate*, "to think about *or* discuss
something very carefully in order to make a decision."[62] According to this
everyday understanding of the word, people can deliberate through thought
or speech. Deliberation can occur both within and without, independently
and collectively.

The *Oxford English Dictionary* parses out these two meanings in its definition of *to deliberate*. Definition 1A in the *Oxford English Dictionary* does not
mention communication. Instead *to deliberate* is defined as 'to weigh in the
mind; to consider carefully with a view to decision; to think over.' Definition
2B, on the other hand, offers a definition in relation to "a body of persons"
as "to take counsel together, considering and examining the reasons for and
against a proposal or course of action."[63] Only with this second definition is
there any mention of deliberation without, understood as communication
for the purpose of coming to a collective decision.

In separating out these two meanings of deliberation, I aim to demonstrate
two distinct claims that are often conflated in deliberative democratic theory.
While some students of democratic deliberation emphasize the value of
thoughtful consideration and reflection on the part of citizens, others point
to actual speech and communication between citizens as the vital contribution of deliberative theories of democracy. The latter model I call "deliberative democracy," while the former may be more accurately called "deliberate
democracy."[64] The two meanings of deliberation—deliberation-as-thought

[61] André Bächtiger, Simon Niemeyer, Michael Neblo, Marco R. Steenbergen, and Jürg Steiner,
"Disentangling Diversity in Deliberative Democracy: Competing Theories, Their Blind Spots and
Complementarities," *Journal of Political Philosophy* 18, no. 1 (2010): 32–63.

[62] *Merriam-Webster.com Dictionary*, s.v. "deliberate" (emphasis added).

[63] *Oxford English Dictionary Online* (Oxford: Oxford University Press), s.v. "deliberate."

[64] Other typologies of deliberation do not capture this distinction (see Bächtiger et al.,
"Disentangling Diversity in Deliberative Democracy"; Goodin, *Reflective Democracy*; and Morrell,
Empathy and Democracy). Bächtiger et al. distinguish between Type I and Type II deliberation, both

and deliberation-as-speech—have vastly different implications for democratic theory.

To make a political system more *deliberate* is not the same as making it more *deliberative*. Can these values come into conflict? If they do, which value should we prioritize? Consider that if the *deliberate*-ness of a political system is the priority, and if this *deliberate*-ness can be heightened by encouraging citizens to be more internally reflective, then we could improve democracy even in the absence of public discussion. If we find other, noncommunicative ways to induce reflection, such as empathy, should we adopt these practices and procedures instead of focusing on improving communicative practices? Whether you are a *deliberate* or a *deliberative* democrat determines how you answer these questions.

Goodin, a quintessential *deliberate* democrat, goes so far as to call his model "reflective democracy." He notes that deliberative democracy alerts us to the need to be "more sensitive to what precedes and underlies" voting, namely deliberation.[65] But as we saw above, for Goodin, that deliberation need not be external: "Internal-reflective and external-collective deliberative processes, I submit, stand in a similar relation to one another" in regard to rendering a decision "*democratically deliberative.*"[66] Goodin explains, however, that neither internal nor external deliberation is sufficient for rendering a decision *legitimate*. For that, voting needs to occur. To achieve democratically deliberative decisions that can then be legitimated through voting, Goodin advocates for "seeing democratic deliberation as being inevitably a largely internal mental process."[67]

Deliberative democrats would agree with Goodin that we need to be more sensitive to the deliberation that precedes voting. Further, they would acknowledge the desirable effects that communication among citizens can

---

of which focus on deliberation-as-speech. Like me, Goodin distinguishes between deliberation-within and deliberation-without, but not between deliberateness and deliberativeness. Contra Goodin, I maintain that deliberation-within and deliberation-without aim at different kinds of deliberation. Finally, Morrell distinguishes between two different deliberative turns, wherein the first emphasizes deliberation as a way to bring about more *informed* and *reflective* decisions and the second values deliberation for its ability to generate *reasonable* or *rational* decisions. According to Morrell, both of these schools of deliberative democratic theory ignore the importance of empathy at their own peril. I would argue that in missing the inherently *communicative* aspect of Habermas's deliberative democratic theory, Morrell overlooks the potential of empathy to distract from the need to communicate.

[65] Goodin, *Reflective Democracy*, 2.
[66] Ibid., 192.
[67] Ibid., 8.

have, such as transferring information and therefore improving the epistemic value of collective decisions. Indeed, according to the now-dominant systemic approach to democratic deliberation, deliberation is supposed to carry not only democratic benefits but epistemic and ethical ones too.[68] Quality deliberation encourages careful reflection or deliberation-as-thought, as individual citizens are called to provide reasons for their positions. But more importantly, or more fundamentally, for deliberative democrats in the tradition of Jürgen Habermas, communicative practices that recognize the moral equality of each citizens' voice improve the democratic quality of decisions taken by ensuring that individuals participate in the authorship of the laws to which they are held. For them, it is only through deliberation-as-speech that we can achieve democratic self-government.[69]

As Habermas explains, democracy, or "The idea of self-legislation *by citizens* . . . requires that those subject to law as its addressees can at the same time understand themselves as authors of law."[70] In order to meet this requirement, administrative power must be responsive to and reflective of the "communicative power" generated by informal and diffuse deliberations in the public sphere. According to Habermas, communication among citizens creates "influence," and through elections and other media this influence becomes "communicative power."[71] Communicative power is transformed into "administrative power" through legislation.[72] "The flow of communication between public opinion-formation, institutionalized elections, and legislative decisions is meant to guarantee that influence and communicative power are transformed through legislation into administrative power."[73]

---

[68] As Chambers points out, these functions need to be balanced and can sometimes come into conflict with one another. Simone Chambers, "Balancing Epistemic Quality and Equal Participation in a System Approach to Deliberative Democracy," *Social Epistemology* 31, no. 3 (2017): 266–76.

[69] Goodin's concern regarding external collective deliberation centers on the problem of scale. Dispensing with face-to-face interactions because they are plagued by the problem of scale, Goodin focuses on helping us reflect better. But Habermas's model, like other "systemic approaches" to deliberation, does not rest on the fact that all citizens participate in it. For Habermas, deliberation is seen to the extent that "communicative power" is generated through deliberations occurring at several sites, including diffuse and informal public spheres. The aim is to diligently increase the deliberativeness of the decision-making process, at both the opinion- and will-formation stages. Jane Mansbridge, James Bohman, Simone Chambers, Thomas Christiano, et al., "A Systemic Approach to Deliberative Democracy," in *Deliberative Systems: Deliberative Democracy at the Large Scale—Theories of Institutional Design*, ed. John Parkinson and Jane Mansbridge (Cambridge: Cambridge University Press, 2012), 1–26.

[70] Jürgen Habermas, *Between Facts and Norms: Contributions to a Discourse Theory of Law and Democracy* (Cambridge, MA: MIT Press, 1996), 120.

[71] Jürgen Habermas, "Three Normative Models of Democracy," *Constellations* 1, no. 1 (1994), 8.

[72] Ibid.

[73] Habermas, *Between Facts and Norms*, 299.

With this transformation, collective opinion is reflected in the collective will, which is then executed through the law. It is the realization of this process, which I showed in the previous chapter to be dependent on the inclusion and uptake of all relevant perspectives in communication, that ensures that the people themselves shape the laws. The facticity of the law meets with validity as citizens recognize themselves as the authors of the laws to which they are held.

The distinctiveness of *deliberative* democracy, therefore, is that popular sovereignty must be interpreted intersubjectively.[74] The "self" of democratic self-rule is not a collection of subjects who are internally reflective and *deliberate*, imagining what others feel or think, but rather the "subjectless" will formed only out of the intersubjective communication between citizens. Full and fair communication between citizens who share decision-making power is not just a means to encourage greater reflection, but the realization of democracy itself.

Nonetheless, as we see from my discussion of uptake in the previous chapter, it would be meaningless to value communication that was not, itself, reflective. Uptake requires that citizens reflect on what they hear in deliberative encounters. Thus, for a deliberative system to function democratically, it must encourage both deliberation-as-speech and deliberation-as-thought. I contend, however, that deliberation (as in actual communication between citizens) is lexically prior to internal reflection or deliberation within. As such, if deliberation-within ever conflicts with deliberation-without, our democratic commitment urges us to prioritize deliberation-without. Deliberation-as-speech cannot be sacrificed for greater levels of internal reflection.

In privileging internal reflection over external communication, then, Goodin along with other *deliberate* democrats seems to miss one of the founding assumptions of *deliberative* democratic theory: namely, the normative value of communication among citizens. For *deliberative* democracy to be achieved, the process of opinion-formation that precedes formal will-formation must be deliberative or communicative, not simply reflective. While Goodin is right to note that reflection is essential to meaningfully democratic decisions, he misses the fact that the reflection must occur within actual communication.

[74] Ibid.

Therefore, with Habermas, I contend that we cannot dispense with communication among citizens, no matter how effectively we can induce *deliberate*-ness and reflection through other means. A commitment to *deliberative* democracy prohibits us from substituting internal reflection for democratic communication, as the former can only make a political system and the decisions it takes more *deliberate*.

With this distinction in mind, we can better assess the claim that empathy or imaginative perspective taking sustains deliberative democracy. Defenders of the empathy approach to deliberation depart from the *deliberative* ideal to the extent that they prioritize the internal reflection of citizens over actual communication between citizens. While the substitution of deliberation-as-speech in favor of deliberation-as-thought is explicit in Goodin's model, I argue that it haunts both Krause's and Morrell's models as well. Specifically, calls for improving our practices of empathy can distract us from the need to engage and listen to those with whom we cannot empathize. My worry, thus, is that efforts to promote imaginative perspective taking may come at the expense of the *deliberative*-ness of a political system.

While empathy may result in further reflection, this reflection is not the same as true uptake insofar as what are taken up are not necessarily the perspectives and voices of actual citizens included in deliberation, but their perspectives as we imagine them. Rooted in imaginative rather than communicative engagement, even successful attempts at empathy, where citizens gain an understanding of their fellow citizens' perspectives, represent a premature (read noncommunicative) uptake that undermines the very possibility of achieving the uptake of actual voices included in political discourse. Empathy's reliance on imagination does not necessarily support and foster the communicative procedures, especially the hard listening that is required for uptake—that is, listening precisely in situations where one might prefer to tune out. As such, empathy fails as an ideal of deliberative democracy.

In the end, Goodin's reflective deliberation exacerbates the threat of (internal and external) exclusion by making citizens responsible not only for considering others' perspectives but imaginatively representing them as well. Though real inclusion in actual (not just imagined) deliberative forums is insufficient, it is still necessary for achieving democratic deliberation. We should be suspicious, then, of calls for increased reliance on empathy in democratic deliberation insofar as the understanding it facilitates is based on imagined perspectives, and not the inclusive communicative procedures that provide the normative core of deliberative democratic theory.

Still, Goodin is on the right track insofar as he tries to move beyond "mere inclusion" in order to ensure that people give careful thought to the perspectives, experiences, and opinions of others. In turning deliberation inward, however, Goodin would maximize consideration at the expense of inclusion. Recalling the arguments from the previous chapter, in turning to uptake, I mean to emphasize not only that a perspective must be considered in order to have democratic meaning (hence the insufficiency of inclusion), but also that a perspective must be actually shared or communicated before it can be considered (hence the insufficiency of internal reflection or deliberation within). The challenge, then, is to encourage reflection and promote fair consideration without weakening the inclusiveness of actual communication.

3.2.3 Empathy and Difference

In the foregoing, I have highlighted the limitations of relying on empathy to promote meaningfully democratic deliberation. Given the difficulty we have putting ourselves in others' shoes, we should not expect empathy to give us access to the actual feelings and perspectives of particular others. Furthermore, even if empathy could give us access to deliberative inputs, its reliance on imagination rather than communication put it at odds with *deliberative* models of democracy. Despite these limitations, empathy might still be defensible as a deliberative ideal that, if practiced *within* actual deliberation, might help promote the fair consideration at the normative core of deliberative democracy. Recall, that unlike Goodin, both Krause and Morrell argue that empathy must never replace actual deliberation.

Defenders of empathy might argue, for example, that it certainly could not hurt to encourage citizens to pursue empathy while they listened to others. Perhaps we could foster engagement and consideration if we asked people, again, *while* they are listening to others, to try and imagine being in their position.[75] If workable, this "empathetic listening" strategy would mark an improvement over Goodin's empathy approach discussed earlier, insofar as

---

[75] Michael Morrell, "Listening and Deliberation," *The Oxford Handbook of Deliberative Democracy* (Oxford: Oxford University Press, 2018), 236–50; Jane Mansbridge and Audrey Latura, "The Polarization Crisis in the US and the Future of Listening," in *Strong Democracy in Crisis: Promise or Peril?*, ed. Trevor Norris (Lanham, MD: Lexington Books, 2017), 29–54; Benjamin Barber, *Strong Democracy: Participatory Politics for a New Age* (Berkeley: University of California Press, 1984), 175.

imaginative uptake would not be the end goal. Rather, common ground and solidarity would be pursued *within* deliberation in order to facilitate the hard work of fair consideration.

In what follows, I caution against even such a modified empathy approach. Leaving behind the practical concerns regarding the difficulty we have empathizing with others, I elucidate the problem with pursuing the ideal of empathy even within our practices of democratic deliberation. My fear is that by taking empathy as either the starting point or goal of deliberation, we may actually weaken the power of discourse to function in contexts marked by deep difference. I argue that the very goal of bridging differences among citizens is misguided. Thus, it's not just that we are generally bad at empathy. The problem I discuss here is that what it would take to be *better* at empathy is bad for democracy.

As I explained in Chapter 2, deliberative democratic theory has been challenged on the basis of its perceived privileging of consensus at the expense of respecting difference. For difference democrats and more radical agonistic critics, empathy is problematic precisely because it fits with deliberative democratic theory's objectionable drive for consensus and disregard for differences among citizens. In contrast to this line of critique, I argue that the empathy approach suffers from a disregard for difference that actually contradicts deliberative democratic theory's commitment to fair (and actual) argumentation in pluralistic societies.

In creating a democratic model that does not assume shared interests, experiences, and conceptions of the good, Habermas makes room for difference in deliberation.[76] Even if the conditions of full inclusion and fair consideration are not always achieved in practice, deliberative democracy in theory should be able to accommodate deep differences among citizens.[77] Successful appeals to empathy, on the other hand, often depend on either the assumption or realization of commonality between the target and the observer.[78] Empathy trades in similarities. These appeals to shared sentiments, interests, or conceptions of the good fit uneasily within deliberative democratic theory where deliberation is seen as a way to achieve cooperation and democratic decisions across difference.

---

[76] Habermas, "Three Normative Models of Democracy."

[77] See Section 2.1 in this volume.

[78] Adam Gerace, Andrew Day, Sharon Casey, and Philip Mohr, "Perspective Taking and Empathy: Does Having Similar Past Experience to Another Person Make It Easier to Take Their Perspective?," *Journal of Relationships Research* 6, e10 (2015), 1–14; Mansbridge and Latura, "The Polarization Crisis in the US and the Future of Listening," 31.

Moreover, relying too much on empathy to sustain deliberation may lead us to systematically exclude or devalue concerns and perspectives that do not map onto the interests or ethical priorities of the majority. Not only does the majority remain unaware of these others' concerns, but that cluelessness may be accompanied by a comforting sense of self-satisfaction.

For an example of empathy's reliance on a culturally established and dominant background consensus, consider President Barack Obama's endorsement of same-sex marriage in 2012. In May of that year, President Obama came out in support of legalizing same-sex marriage in the United States. At the time, he suggested that empathy (both imaginative perspective taking and empathic concern for gay couples) was the driving force behind the evolution of his position.[79] Many people celebrated Obama's position as well as the empathic justification he provided for his shift in opinion.[80] I believe that closer inspection shows that, rather than expanding and opening our deliberative practices, empathy can function to constrict deliberation by burdening it with appeals to or assumptions of a preexisting consensus.

Obama's appeal, insofar as it is effective, implicitly relies on a preexisting consensus among the dominant cultural group about the good life, specifically the role that marriage between life partners plays in the good life. After bringing the American public through his empathic thought process, helping us imagine how gay people "feel constrained" because they are unable to "commit themselves in a marriage," Obama explained,

> At a certain point, I've just concluded that—for me personally, it is important for me to go ahead and affirm that—I think same-sex couples should be able to get married. And what you're seeing is, I think, states working through this issue—in fits and starts, all across the country. Different communities are arriving at different conclusions, at different times. And I think that's a healthy process and a healthy debate.[81]

---

[79] Obama explains that his position on gay marriage evolved as he "[thought] about members of [his] own staff who are incredibly committed, in monogamous relationships, same-sex relationships, who are raising kids together" as well as members of the military who are not able to "commit themselves in a marriage." Barack Obama, interview by Robin Roberts, "Transcript: Robin Roberts ABC News Interview with President Obama—ABC News," *Good Morning America*, ABC, May 9, 2012.

[80] Dahlia Lithwick, "It's about the Empathy, Stupid," *Slate*, May 10, 2012, https://slate.com/news-and-politics/2012/05/barack-obamas-decision-to-support-gay-marriage-was-a-rare-act-of-empathy-in-this-presidential-election.html; Charles Krauthammer, "Same-Sex Marriage Empathy or Right?," *Washington Post*, May 17, 2012.

[81] Obama, interview by Roberts.

This example illustrates how empathic approaches to democracy have the potential to limit the power of deliberation to contexts where commonality and agreement, at least among a majority of citizens, already exists. Obama's empathic endorsement amounts to a call to legalize same-sex marriage in communities where the norms and moral sensibilities allow the majority to empathically understand the minority of gay couples. But in those communities where the norms make it hard for the majority of straight citizens to put themselves in the shoes of same-sex couples, banning same-sex marriage, or even putting off conversations about its legality, would be legitimate. The deliberative model of democracy, however, is supposed to mark an improvement over the republican model of democracy, and thereby function to coordinate action across difference, by decentering appeals to common or shared conceptions of the good.[82] And insofar as empathy operates along tracks of preexisting commonalities, it will not correct for failures of uptake in contexts of deep difference. In other words, there appears to be a redundancy to empathy as a deliberative practice. Empathy is available to us precisely when it is not needed—when we can accurately imagine someone else's feelings and perspectives, often due to preexisting background similarities or shared priorities and commitments. Conversely, empathy is out of our reach precisely when the threat of dialogical closure is most acute, when citizens encounter those most different from themselves and conversation (as well as imagination) is most likely to break down.[83]

Since Obama gave this interview, there has been much development regarding the question of same-sex marriage. In 2015, the Supreme Court ruled state bans on same-sex marriage unconstitutional, a decision supported by nearly six out of ten Americans.[84] What's more, the growing support for

[82] As I explained in the previous chapter, while Rousseau happily relies on a thick communitarian ethical consensus to form a collective will and guide collective action, Habermas relies instead on fair and inclusive communicative procedures. This move away from an objective general will based on preexisting ethical consensus toward an intersubjectively and communicatively derived collective opinion and will is crucial for achieving democracy in a pluralistic and heterogeneous late-modern polity. Habermas, "Three Normative Models of Democracy," 5.

[83] There appear to be real limits to how far empathy can be extended even under ideal circumstances. In fact, as Jesse Prinz explains, empathy's reliance on commonality means that "We can no more overcome [empathy's] limits than we can ride a bicycle across the ocean; it is designed for local travel." Empathy trades in similarities and therefore is an unlikely corrective for issues of exclusion in deliberation across difference. Hidetsugu Komeda. Kohei Tsunemi, Keisuke, Inohara, Takashi, Kusumi, David Rapp, "Beyond Disposition: The Processing Consequences of Explicit and Implicit Invocations of Empathy," *Acta Psychologica* 142, no. 3 (2013): 349–55; Prinz, "Against Empathy," 229.

[84] *Obergefell v. Hodges*, 576 U.S. ___ (2015); Justin McCarthy, "U.S. Support for Gay Marriage Stable after High Court Ruling," *Gallup*, July 17, 2015, http://www.gallup.com/poll/184217/support-gay-marriage-stable-high-court-ruling.aspx.

same-sex marriage among the American public seems to have been driven, in part, by the ever-expanding ability of straight Americans to put themselves in the shoes of their gay neighbors, friends, or family members.[85] But my worry is that *when* empathy is successful in sparking debate and highlighting claims of injustice, an underlying and preexisting commonality seems to be doing much of the work. In these cases, deliberation is circumscribed by our empathic imaginings and yet we assume in these moments of successful perspective taking that empathy is expanding our deliberations and making them more inclusive and more broadly considerate. While appeals to empathy may succeed in that effort to some degree, they may also simultaneously and inconspicuously restrict fair consideration by not decentering common conceptions of the good. By allowing preexisting (though perhaps not previously recognized or salient) commonalities to drive deliberation, empathy is just as likely to restrict discourse as it is to expand it.

Furthermore, when we try to empathize and fail, we might be set back further from full and fair deliberation than before we started. Recalling my discussion in the previous section, there is a risk that a person, having engaged in perspective taking and presuming to have learned the other's perspective, will be less likely to engage in deliberation, especially if she is accused of having understood that perspective wrongly.[86] As Young explains, "If you think you can look at things from their point of view, then you may avoid the sometimes arduous and painful process in which they confront you with your prejudices, fantasies, and misunderstandings about them, which you have because of your point of view."[87] The problems with relying on perspective taking persist even when it is incorporated alongside discussion:

> If you enter into a dialogue with all the best intentions of taking the other people's perspectives and then in the course of the discussion they express anger and frustration at you for misunderstanding their position, you are likely to become defensive and shut down the dialogue.[88]

---

[85] Lymari Morales, "Knowing Someone Gay/Lesbian Affects Views of Gay Issues," *Gallup*, May 29, 2009, http://www.gallup.com/poll/118931/knowing-someone-gay-lesbian-affects-views-gay-issues.aspx; Edward Schiappa, Peter B. Gregg, and Dean E. Hewes, "Can One TV Show Make a Difference?," *Journal of Homosexuality* 51, no. 4 (2006): 15–37.

[86] Young, "Asymmetrical Reciprocity," 350.

[87] Ibid.

[88] Ibid.

Not only are our attempts at perspective taking often biased, resulting in misguided empathic concern or empathic misunderstanding, but in practice, these attempts have the potential to truncate deliberation itself.[89] And as I explained earlier, this is problematic given communication's centrality to deliberative democracy.

What, then, should we make of Habermas's seeming endorsement of imaginative perspective taking at various points in *Between Facts and Norms*? He writes, for example, that "under discursive conditions that encourage each to adopt the perspectives of the other members or even of all other persons, rationally motivated changes in one's initial views are possible."[90] With this reference to perspective taking, Habermas is distancing himself from a transcendent conception of rationality for which he had previously been criticized.[91] In other words, he is acknowledging the situatedness of our practices of reason. As Young points out, however, calls to put one's self in the place of others go too far in the other direction. Part of what it means to recognize the situatedness of our practices of reason is accepting that we cannot simply imagine being otherwise situated.

In assuming that "moral respect entails being able to adopt the standpoint of others," we risk collapsing the distance between ourselves and others in deliberation.[92] Helpfully, Young distinguishes "between taking the perspectives of other people into account, on the one hand, and imaginatively taking their positions, on the other."[93] She endorses the former and rejects the latter. No matter how much I can imagine your perspective, it remains your perspective. This mediation is less obvious when we encourage citizens to try and put themselves in the shoes of those with whom they are deliberating. By focusing on our ability to imagine how others feel, the empathy approach tends to underestimate the distance between citizens, minimizing the challenges to uptake and rendering the need to engage less urgent.

As I develop further in Chapter 6, without recognizing the distance between citizens, the need to actually deliberate with others is muted. You do

---

[89] In fact, investigating how empathy relates to political polarization, Simas and colleagues find that highly empathic individuals express a greater desire to censor speakers from outgroups, specifically speakers from an opposing political party. Simas, Clifford, and Kirkland, "How Empathic Concern Fuels Political Polarization," 264.

[90] Habermas, *Between Facts and Norms*, 274.

[91] Seyla Benhabib, *Situating the Self: Gender, Community, and Postmodernism in Contemporary Ethics* (New York: Routledge, 1992).

[92] Young, "Asymmetrical Reciprocity," 343.

[93] Ibid., 341.

not have to listen to someone you already understand. In pursuing empathy as a deliberative ideal even within real communicative encounters, we risk distracting citizens from the need to actually engage with one another and, thus, undermining the normative core of deliberative democracy.

3.3 Conclusion

Through their appeals to empathy, Krause, Morrell, and Goodin highlight the importance of internalizing the inputs of others when engaging in democratic deliberation. In this way, the empathy approach to deliberation is allied in spirit with my claim regarding the centrality of uptake to meaningfully democratic deliberation. Still, empathy's emphasis on both imagination and commonality make it ill-suited for promoting uptake across difference. Empathy is not itself communication, nor does it necessarily lead to more communication, and so violates the normative core of democratic deliberation. I do not need to have a conversation with someone whose perspective I can simply imagine. Furthermore, empathy trades in similarities and so is out of our reach precisely when we need it most, when differences make it most difficult both to imagine and consider another's perspective. Ultimately, investing too much energy in improving our practices of empathy can distract us from the difficult yet necessary task of actually engaging with our fellow citizens, especially those with whom we disagree or whom we do not immediately understand.

Given these practical and theoretical limits to empathy, we should be cautious about relying too heavily on it for the sake of improving deliberation. Ultimately, empathic approaches exacerbate rather than alleviate the risks of exclusion and domination in democratic deliberation. It seems, therefore, that to sustain democratic deliberation in contexts of difference, we need an alternative to empathy. Specifically, we need to consider how to promote inclusion and uptake when empathy is not readily available and how to decenter it when it is available but deceptive in its effects. How can we foster full and fair deliberation when underlying similarities that sustain empathy are not available to us?

In the next three chapters, I sketch an alternative to the empathy approach to improving deliberative practices. In the place of efforts to improve our practices of empathy, I turn our attention to the need to improve listening.

Listening, however, has been an understudied and undervalued act of democratic citizenship.[94] For example, when Young pluralizes modes of communication, she privileges a conception of citizens as speakers. Similarly, when Goodin introduces deliberation-within, he focuses on an individual's reflection, which need not occur communicatively or even intersubjectively. Only in turning our attention to citizens in their role as listeners, however, can we begin to understand the extent to which what has been included has been taken up and put to use in the deliberative system.

In what follows, I argue that deliberative uptake is dependent on listening. It's essential, therefore, that we move beyond an exclusive focus on citizens' responsibility to speak and reflect and toward the importance of listening. Good listening practices, especially listening-with-humility, are vital to achieving the uptake that democratic deliberation requires.

Moreover, focusing on listening allows us to better sustain deliberation in contexts of difference. Importantly, then, I do not turn to listening as a means of expanding empathic understanding, though this may be an unintended consequence. Rather, as I explain, by focusing on the need to enhance our practices of listening we are better able to reconcile an attention to difference with the deliberative project itself. Agonistic critics of deliberative democracy have considered such a goal misguided, preferring instead to abandon the deliberative project altogether.[95] Supporters of empathy, on the other hand, value imaginative perspective taking precisely because of its ability to reduce the distance between citizens, thus implying that such distance can and should be decreased in order to achieve productive deliberation.[96] Both of these approaches, it seems, would resolve the tension between deliberation and difference by abandoning one or the other. As

---

[94] The exceptions that prove the rule are Susan Bickford's *Dissonance of Democracy* and more recently Dobson's own *Listening for Democracy*. Neither of these accounts, however, point to the ways in which listening facilitates uptake in deliberation. According to my understanding of the normative core of deliberative democratic theory, however, it is having one's inputs considered, and not just included or even heard, that ensures the enactment of democracy. Susan Bickford, *The Dissonance of Democracy* (Ithaca, NY: Cornell University Press, 1996); Andrew Dobson, *Listening for Democracy: Recognition, Representation, Reconciliation* (Oxford: Oxford University Press, 2014). See also Emily Beausoleil, "Responsibility as Responsiveness: Enacting a Dispositional Ethics of Encounter," *Political Theory* 45, no. 3 (2017): 291–318; Tanja Dreher and Poppy De Souza, "Locating Listening," in *Ethical Responsiveness and the Politics of Difference*, ed. Tanja Dreher and Anshuman Mondal (New York: Palgrave Macmillan, 2018), 21–39.

[95] Chantal Mouffe, *The Democratic Paradox* (New York: Verso, 2000), 104–5.

[96] Mansbridge and Latura, "The Polarization Crisis in the US and the Future of Listening."

I explain in Chapters 5 and 6, however, the listening approach offers an alternative path forward, finding a way to actually put difference to work in democratic deliberation.[97] Helpfully, the listening approach that I present offers a set of strategies to sustain uptake in inclusive deliberation when empathy fails us or is beyond our reach.

[97] As I show in Chapter 6, greater attention to citizens in their role as listeners reveals a new way of thinking of difference as a resource in deliberation, one that Iris Young, for example, did not develop in her work. See Iris Marion Young, "Difference as a Resource for Democratic Communication," in Deliberative Democracy: Essays on Reason and Politics, ed. James Bohman and William Rehg (Cambridge, MA: MIT Press, 1997), 383–406.

4

A Listening-Centered Approach
to Democratic Deliberation

The challenges to democratic discourse in pluralistic societies are significant. In order to deliver on deliberation's promise of democracy we must attend not only to the question of inclusion but also uptake. Recent accounts of how to ensure full and fair communication have focused on practices of empathy, or the value of encouraging people to try to imagine the feelings and perspectives of their fellow citizens. Robert Goodin, for example, turns to empathy for its ability to bring about uptake even in the absence of deliberation. Michael Morrell and Sharon Krause, on the other hand, see empathy more as a way to boost uptake *within* deliberation.[1] Whether empathy is seen as a shortcut (Goodin) or a training regimen (Morrell and Krause) for achieving meaningfully democratic deliberation, it is often assumed that the path to meaningful engagement between citizens goes through imaginative perspective taking. As I showed in the previous chapter, however, not only is the road to empathy itself a steep one, but it does not necessarily lead us toward deliberative uptake. If uptake is our objective, we are better off taking a different route. In this chapter and the next, I make the case for a democratic listening approach to deliberation.

Here I articulate the centrality of listening to deliberation. Specifically, I show that deliberative uptake is predicated on listening. Only with an account of listening, then, can we determine the democratic quality of a deliberative system. Turning our attention to citizens in their role as listeners, I aim to bring the deliberative acts of speech and reflection together in a meaningful way. Listening enacts the communicative act of deliberation, connecting speakers with their relevant audience. With this discussion, I am able to show why empathy's ability to undermine listening poses such

---

[1] Robert E. Goodin, *Reflective Democracy* (Oxford: Oxford University Press, 2003); Michael E. Morrell, *Empathy and Democracy: Feeling, Thinking, and Deliberation* (University Park: Pennsylvania State University Press, 2010); Sharon R. Krause, *Civil Passions: Moral Sentiment and Democratic Deliberation* (Princeton, NJ: Princeton University Press, 2008).

Beyond Empathy and Inclusion. Mary F. Scudder, Oxford University Press (2020). © Oxford University Press.
DOI: 10.1093/oso/9780197535455.001.0001.

a problem for deliberative democracy. We cannot dispense with listening in deliberation, no matter how reflective citizens are.

Compared to speaking and reflecting, however, listening has been an understudied and undervalued act of democratic citizenship. Little work to date has thoroughly examined the ways in which our practices of listening affect the quality and, therefore, the democratic potential of deliberation. Andrew Dobson refers to the dearth of political science research on the topic of listening as "the new democratic deficit."[2]

From all accounts, Susan Bickford was the first to fully appreciate the importance of listening for democracy.[3] In her 1996 *Dissonance of Democracy*, Bickford argues that we should assess our supposedly democratic procedures based on the "presence of listening" rather than the possibility of consensus.[4] Though presented as a critique of deliberative models of democracy, I understand Bickford's rejection of consensus and her turn to listening to be consistent with and even required by the normative core of deliberative democratic theory. The democratic force of a deliberative system comes from the communicative exchange among citizens. Listening is crucial to that exchange. As Jürgen Habermas explained in the same year that Bickford's book was published, the democratic nature of collective decisions depends on the means by which the majority comes to be the majority.[5] The decision-making process confers legitimacy on the outcome, not the other way around. Even a decision enjoying total consensus would lack the democratic quality that Habermas is after if not reached through full and fair deliberation.[6] Bickford is right, and Habermas would agree, that consensus cannot, on its own, legitimize a decision and thus carries little normative weight in deliberation.

[2] Andrew Dobson, "Listening: The New Democratic Deficit," *Political Studies* 60, no. 4 (2012): 843–59.

[3] And before Bickford, Benjamin Barber acknowledged that democratic talk involved listening as much as speaking. But Bickford is still the first to offer a dedicated account of the significance of listening for democracy. Susan Bickford, *The Dissonance of Democracy* (Ithaca, NY: Cornell University Press, 1996); Benjamin Barber, *Strong Democracy: Participatory Politics for a New Age* (Berkeley: University of California Press, 1984), 173–74.

[4] Bickford, *The Dissonance of Democracy*, 18.

[5] Jürgen Habermas, *Between Facts and Norms: Contributions to a Discourse Theory of Law and Democracy* (Cambridge, MA: MIT Press, 1996). *Between Facts and Norms* was published in the original German four years earlier.

[6] Hélène Landemore and Scott E. Page have discussed the epistemic value of consensus in deliberation. They argue that the normative appeal of consensus varies depending on the nature of the deliberative task at hand, whether it's a problem-solving task or an evaluative task. Here, I am not addressing the epistemic value of consensus, or whether aiming at it would help us reach better or "truer" decisions. Rather, I am evaluating the moral value of consensus. Hélène Landemore and Scott E. Page, "Deliberation and Disagreement: Problem Solving, Prediction, and Positive Dissensus," *Politics, Philosophy & Economics* 14, no. 3 (2015): 229–54.

A deliberative system generates democratic legitimacy only insofar as citizens actually consider the arguments and perspectives shared by their fellow citizens. Securing fair consideration from our fellow citizens allows us to meaningfully participate in the lawmaking authority. It is what gives us a say in the laws to which we are held. Listening, in the sense of hearing what another person says, is crucial for that fair consideration. In what follows, I explore the various ways that listening affects the democratic quality of deliberation. My analysis of the democratic power of listening builds on previous work, including Bickford's and Dobson's, incorporating insights from this literature into the account of uptake offered in Chapter 2. At its most basic, listening would refer to the reception of messages put in to deliberation. As I argue, however, listening does much more than allow for the reception of discrete messages.

My treatment of a listening-approach to democratic deliberation begins with an evaluation of how listening is used in everyday language (4.1). Next, I introduce a theory of listening acts in an effort to better explain the democratic force of listening (4.2). With its origins in communications scholarship, listening act theory breaks down the listening act into categories borrowed from Austin's speech act theory.[7] I go on to apply these categories of the listening act to the political context of democratic deliberation. Specifically, I describe the democratic relevance of the *auditory* (4.2.1), *perauditory* (4.2.2), and finally the *ilauditory* (4.2.3) force of listening. Using these categories, I am able to synthesize existing literature on listening in deliberative democratic theory, while revealing gaps in our understanding of the democratic significance of listening acts. As I show, the quality of listening has a varied and dynamic impact on the democratic nature of deliberation. Indeed, my analysis even reveals potentially undemocratic outcomes of the listening act. The chapter concludes by introducing the concept of "listening toward democracy," which I develop further in Chapter 5 (4.3). There I explain the central role that listening plays in achieving the deliberative ideal of fair consideration.

---

[7] In his own discussion of how we act in speaking, Austin refers to the listening act only in passing and in regards to "securing uptake." Austin argues that to act in speaking, one must secure uptake. To him, uptake refers to people hearing and understanding a particular utterance. In developing the categories of the "listening act" I mean to build out our understanding of "uptake" and show how it contributes to the democratic quality of our political decisions by allowing us to enact the deliberative ideal. J. L. Austin, *How to Do Things with Words* (Cambridge, MA: Harvard University Press, 1962).

4.1 The Politics of Listening

A useful way to begin my discussion of the politics of listening is by analyzing how "listening" is both employed in ordinary language and deployed in contemporary American politics. The goal of this section is to canvass the various assumptions and implications embedded in our everyday understanding of what it means to listen.

To begin, consider the various references to listening that were made in the lead-up to the 2016 presidential election. Hillary Clinton kicked off her 2016 US presidential bid with a "listening tour." Usually political campaigning involves "going on the stump," meaning a candidate travels city to city giving speeches. With this listening tour, borrowed from her 2000 Senate campaign and dismissed by some as a gimmick, Clinton tried to distinguish herself as a different kind of candidate.

It would be a mistake, I think, to ignore the gender dynamics at play in this listening tour. Leaving aside questions regarding the sincerity of Clinton's listening, it's safe to assume that she perceived strategic advantages to this move.[8] For example, the listening tour offered Clinton a way to break into the historically male role of presidential candidate while conforming to the traditional role of women who are expected to be more attentive, caring, and receptive than their male counterparts.[9] As with most traditionally feminine virtues, good listening is often underappreciated or even devalued. While listening may be a virtue, it is not always seen as a virtue of strength. Indeed, listening is just as often seen as a conciliatory act.

Here again, the 2016 US presidential election offers an instructive example. When asked to whom he speaks about foreign policy matters, Donald Trump answered: himself. He explained, "I'm speaking with myself, number one, because I have a very good brain and I've said a lot of things."[10] In his response, Trump implies that the need to listen to others is a sign of weakness. For him, listening implies inadequacy, ignorance, dependency.

---

[8] When listening is wielded by the powerful, it often has strategic undertones, as seen when chief executive officers go on listening tours of their own companies, trying to understand the worker's experience. Facebook founder, Mark Zuckerberg fueled rumors of his own presidential bid by going on a listening tour throughout the United States in 2017.

[9] Hillary Rodham Clinton, *What Happened* (New York: Simon & Schuster, 2017), 135.

[10] Eliza Collins, "Trump: I Consult Myself on Foreign Policy," *Politico*, March 16, 2016, https://www.politico.com/blogs/2016-gop-primary-live-updates-and-results/2016/03/trump-foreign-policy-adviser-220853.

The point I want to make with these examples is not a political or even a normative one, but a conceptual one. Listening is typically something that can be demanded by those in power. And the need to listen to someone can imply a lack of autonomy, while refusing to listen can be interpreted as an act of strength and even independence. For example, compare the image of a politician listening (or not listening) to constituents and experts with the image of a public crier calling, "Hear Ye, Hear Ye, Hear Ye." The public crier demands the attention of the people in order to make an official proclamation. In this case, the people are compelled to listen. Moreover, their listening carries the implication of heeding another's words, changing their thinking or behavior to bring it in line with what they hear. Whether *in* a position of authority or listening *to* authority, the listeners in these examples listen so that they can know what others expect of them.

In the following discussion, which is by no means comprehensive, I untangle the various ways we use "to listen" and articulate what each of these uses really means. Then, in the next section, I build out a more systematic theory of listening acts that can be applied to politics.

At times, to listen means to simply let someone have a chance to speak, but without any expectation that the listeners will do anything with what they hear. In interpersonal relationships, for example, there are times when we want someone to "*just* listen." The instructive example is the friend who is always ready with a piece of advice when all we want is for her to lend an ear and pay witness to our experience or perspective. Here, "listening" refers to that initial auditory act. In the case of a classroom, we want students to be quiet while another is talking so that they can literally hear what the speaker is saying.

Consider, in contrast to the classroom example, the expectation, among most parents, that their young children will listen to them. The expectation for children to listen implies much more than simply hearing what their parents say. Indeed, the expectation implies that the children will actually *do* what their parents tell them to, in the sense of taking their advice, or even following their orders. In this example, "to listen" implies deference on the part of the listener. Thus, if your child "doesn't listen," he is not respecting your wishes. Perhaps he listened, in the sense of literally hearing what you said, but is now refusing to comply with your wishes. Here, listening refers more to what a person *does* in response to the message they auditorily receive from another. In other words, sometimes by "listening," we mean more than the simple auditory act of receiving what is said, and instead are referring to what is brought about as a result of listening—in this case, obedience.

Compare the parent-child example with the case of a child being mocked or bullied by her classmates. "*Don't listen* to them. What do they know?" is a common refrain in just such an instance. With this reply, the speaker dismisses the authority of the bully, insisting that the child should "be herself," and not care about what other people think. The hope is that the child is able to ignore or brush off the insult and not let it enter into her consciousness. While we certainly might encourage a person to walk away from a conversation aimed at mocking or demeaning him, when we tell a hearing person, "Don't listen to them," we usually do not mean that he should physically cover his ears. Rather, we are saying, don't take it to heart. In other words, pay no attention to what they are saying. Ignore it.

With these examples, we see that the language of listening can, at times, carry the connotation of agreeing or aligning oneself with what is heard. Consider, for example, the sayings "I hear you," or "Hear, hear," both of which imply approbation for what the speaker says. Conversely, when someone says, "I won't hear of it," what they really mean is, "I reject what I have just heard!" Crucially, they likely *have* heard it, in an auditory sense, but have rejected it.

Once again, the insights that I want to draw from the foregoing discussion are descriptive, not normative. With these examples, we begin to see the general outlines of the listening act theory that I develop later. On the one hand, we have simple auditory listening, what I described in the preceding as "*just* listening." And on the other hand, we have the perauditory outcomes of listening, or what is brought about *through* listening.

But while the categories of listening revealed in the everyday interpersonal contexts described above are instructive, they must be developed further before they can be applied to the realm of politics. While "*just* listening" might, on its own, contribute to the proper functioning of an interpersonal or therapeutic relationship, it does not carry much democratic weight. Democracy is about solving collective problems. Decisions have to be made and action has to be taken. *Just* listening is not enough. When it comes to making a collective judgment or taking collective action, citizens are expected to carefully take into account what others have to say.

The democratic listening act amounts to a recognition on the part of listeners that the voice of the speaker is relevant to their own thinking and behavior. Crucially, however, to carry democratic power, listening does not have to result in the adoption of the speaker's policy preferences or an endorsement of her perspective. To be democratically meaningful, listening does not mean that you will be swayed by another's story, or that you will change your mind or your behavior in response to what you hear. Instead, you are listening for the *possibility* that you will be influenced by what you hear.

4.2 Listening Act Theory

If we are to base our prospects for democracy on the quality of communicative encounters between citizens, studying the listening act is at least as important as studying the speech act. Listening is the necessary correlate of speech and unites the inputs of deliberation to the relevant audience, one's fellow citizens, so that what is shared can be considered. As I show, the intersubjective quality of deliberation depends on listening.

Here I take inspiration from communications theorist Doyle Srader's discussion of "performative listening."[11] Borrowing Austin's classification of speech acts, Srader applies them to the act of listening. In his essay, Srader focuses on the category of performative listening, or what he calls the "illocutionary listening act." Renaming and expanding Srader's categories, I use his initial account to develop a larger "listening act theory" that I then apply to democratic theory. Ultimately, I use this listening act theory to explain the various ways that listening contributes to deliberative democracy.[12]

Briefly, according to Austin, utterances can have *locutionary* force, *illocutionary* force, or *perlocutionary* force.[13] Habermas summarizes the differences between these kinds of speech acts, respectively: "to say *something*, to act *in* saying something, to bring something about *through* acting in saying something."[14]

As Srader reminds us, in answering the question "What time is it?" my response may have locutionary, illocutionary, or perlocutionary force. If

[11] Doyle W. Srader, "Performative Listening," *International Journal of Listening* 29, no. 2 (May 4, 2015): 95–102.

[12] Here, I examine not only Srader's illocutionary listening act, which I rename the "ilauditory listening act," but the auditory and perauditory listening acts as well. In his essay, Srader refers to "illocutionary listening acts" and "perlocutionary listening acts" even though, as he explains, "the semantic content of those morphemes mixes as poorly as different cleaning products." I offer an alternative set of terms for the three categories of listening acts: the auditory, ilauditory, and perauditory listening acts. Ibid., 96.

[13] Austin, *How to Do Things with Words.*

[14] Jürgen Habermas, *The Theory of Communicative Action*, vol. 1 (Boston: Beacon Press, 1984), 289.

I respond by saying it is eight o'clock in the evening, "My locutionary performance consists merely of eliminating the questioner's uncertainty about the time of day."[15] If, however, as the host of a dinner party, I respond by saying, "It's dinnertime," I "utter an *illocutionary* performative that changes the meaning and purpose of the gathering, granting permission to my guests to begin eating."[16] The perlocutionary *effect* of my utterance may vary depending on how my guests react, but "my *illocutionary* move of declaring the meal underway takes full effect regardless of their choice of response."[17] In other words, the utterance itself constitutes an act with the power to change lived reality, initiating the beginning of *dinnertime* no matter how others react to the utterance.

Informed by both Srader's and Habermas's use of Austin, I develop a broader listening act theory to illuminate the various ways that listening contributes to democratic deliberation. First is what I call the auditory act, wherein we listen to *something*. The auditory act of listening emphasizes the input, or *what* is heard. This part of the listening act is largely passive and amounts to receiving an input that is transmitted or made audible. Again, here, the emphasis is on the content of what is heard. On the other hand, we have the perauditory force of listening, which relates to the effects of listening, or what is brought about *through* acting in listening to something. Much like the perlocutionary effects of a speech act, these perauditory effects of the listening act vary, but might include reaching understanding, or even uncovering misunderstanding and disagreement. Listening can also have significant attitudinal, behavioral, and informational effects on both the person listening and the person being listened to.[18]

Finally, the *ilauditory* force of listening occurs somewhere between the auditory and perauditory listening episodes. This is what Srader calls "performative listening." The ilauditory listening act refers to how we act *in* listening to something, irrespective of any effects arising out of the listening act. Briefly, consider the legal hearing as a quintessential example of performative listening, or how we act *in* listening.[19] By listening to the accused, the

---

[15] Srader, "Performative Listening," 96.

[16] Ibid., 95.

[17] Ibid., 96.

[18] It's worth noting that the *per*auditory listening act is not the *per*formative listening act that I develop in greater detail in this chapter. *Per*formative listening refers instead to the ilauditory listening act. This prefix confusion is at least consistent with Austin's theory of speech acts, for which *per*locutionary acts are not the same as *per*formative utterances. Instead, Austin refers to illocutionary performative utterances. The Latin prefix "per" means *through*. And the perauditory listening act refers to what is brought about *through* listening.

[19] Srader, "Performative Listening," 98.

judge and jury might bring about certain desirable outcomes (perauditory effects), including knowledge of the truth. Still, the hearing—wherein those deciding the case listen to the defendant—itself constitutes an act and carries significance independent of the outcome.[20] This is the ilauditory force of the listening act.

According to Srader, listening research to date has focused primarily on what listening *is* as well as the *effects* of listening, or what I call, respectively, the auditory and perauditory listening episodes. Neglected, however, is this "*performative* listening episode," or listening as an act in itself. By considering this often-ignored element of the listening act, Srader wants to call attention to the ways that listening "completes its objective in its enactment not by yielding a product such as enhanced understanding or unmasking of deceit but rather by satisfying a duty or conforming to the dictates of a virtue."[21] And so when it comes to the ilauditory force of this listening act, the question is not so much whether listening was *effective*, but whether "it succeeded in fulfilling the threshold duty of calling the relationship into existence."[22] Performative listening is distinct from both "*active* listening" and "*critical* listening," both of which involve "*mining the message* for goods."[23]

With this theoretical framework, I hope to expand and refine our understanding of how listening contributes to the democratic functioning of a deliberative system. In the discussion that follows, I place existing accounts of the democratic power of listening within the framework provided by listening act theory. Accordingly, I distinguish *what* we hear in listening to our fellow citizens, from what is brought about *through* acting in listening, and lastly, how we act *in* listening to someone and so move deliberation closer to the democratic ideal of fair consideration. Table 4.1 shows how my listening act theory compares to Austin's speech act theory.[24]

Studying these three elements of the listening act, I explain how each relates to democratic deliberation. While the auditory listening act ensures

---

[20] To say that the ilauditory force is achieved independent of outcomes is not to say that outcomes are irrelevant to our assessment of that force. For example, while we cannot always determine the legitimacy of a hearing by looking at the outcome, certain outcomes could still raise red flags, causing us to doubt whether the ilauditory force of listening was achieved. More on this in Section 4.2.3 in this chapter. Simone Chambers, "Making Referendums Safe for Democracy: A Call for More and Better Deliberation," *Swiss Political Science Review* 24, no. 3 (2018): 306.

[21] Srader, "Performative Listening," 96.

[22] Ibid., 100.

[23] Ibid., 96, 99.

[24] For Srader, the auditory and perauditory aspects of listening are not unimportant, just better understood when compared to the ilauditory or performative listening act.

Table 4.1 Speech Act Theory Compared to Listening Act Theory

Speech Act Theory		Listening Act Theory	
Locutionary act	To say *something*	Auditory act	To listen to *something*
Illocutionary act	To act *in* saying something	Ilauditory act*	To act *in* listening to something
Perlocutionary act	To bring something about *through* acting in saying something	Perauditory act	To bring something about *through* acting in listening to something

*The ilauditory act refers to what Srader calls "performative listening."

inclusion, fair consideration is dependent on the ilauditory listening act, or what I call "performative democratic listening." What's more, in my discussion of listening act theory, especially the perauditory *effects* of listening, I identify outcomes that are undesirable at best and undemocratic at worst. Given that listening is essential to both inclusion and uptake and so the democratic functioning of a deliberative system, we must be mindful of these outcomes so that we can guard against them.

4.2.1 Inclusion and the Auditory Act

The auditory force of the listening act refers to hearing *what* another person shares, with an emphasis on the content of the message. When we listen, we hear *something*, and similarly when we do not listen, we miss that *something*. In democratic deliberation, the auditory force of listening would refer to citizens actually receiving the messages that others put into deliberation. This element of the listening act contributes to the intersubjective deliberative act by ensuring *what* is shared is ultimately heard. This simple listening is a crucial, but limited, first step in ensuring that the broad currents of public communication are generated in a discursive way.

Despite the use of the word "auditory," this part of the listening act should not be understood in an exclusively auditory way. In a democratic context, citizens can "listen," in the sense of receiving another's input, with multiple senses, for example, by reading a person's testimony, watching an interview on television, or scrolling through Twitter.[25] But while the auditory aspect of

[25] In American Sign Language, there are two signs for "to listen." One means to give attention with the eye, while the other means to give attention with the ear. "ASL Sign for: Listen," *Handspeak*, https://www.handspeak.com/word/search/index.php?id=1285 (accessed June 1, 2018).

democratic listening is incidental, its intersubjective nature is essential. We listen to others. As I show, when realized, the auditory force of the listening act plays a crucial and distinct role in expanding inclusion in deliberative democracy.

In *Listening for Democracy*, Dobson identifies two main goals of deliberation, both of which rely on what I call the "auditory force" of the listening act. First, listening allows for the possibility that citizens will be swayed by what Habermas calls the forceless force of the better argument. As Dobson explains, we obviously cannot "know what 'the better argument' is if we haven't listened to all the other ones."[26] Simple listening, then, allows us to hear various arguments so that we can then consider them. We do not know what is at stake in a particular debate or decision unless we listen.

Second, and more to Dobson's point, listening contributes to "deliberative democracy's other central objective," namely, inclusion.[27] He points out that a citizen has not been included if that person has not been heard. Meanwhile, inclusion is necessarily expanded when citizens "listen *out* for voices that may not have been heard before."[28] In other words, Dobson focuses on hearing *what* is shared, specifically, a particular argument or perspective that we may or may not find compelling.[29] He is most concerned with the exclusionary consequences of someone's voice not being heard.

In order to make deliberation more inclusive, Dobson argues we must find ways to institutionalize listening.[30] Indeed, according to Dobson, the "pay-off of isolating listening as the key component in achieving recognition and inclusion" is that "there are ways of improving listening."[31] By way of

---

[26] Andrew Dobson, *Listening for Democracy: Recognition, Representation, Reconciliation* (Oxford: Oxford University Press, 2014), 12.

[27] Ibid.

[28] Ibid.

[29] The stark line that Dobson draws between these two goals of deliberation—being swayed by the forceless force of the better argument on the one hand and inclusion on the other—seems untenable. Why else do we want inclusion if not to ensure that all relevant perspectives and inputs are brought to bear (through consideration) on democratic decisions? By inclusion, Dobson seems to emphasize the important *feeling* of being included. In other words, by inclusion, he refers, in part, to the concept of recognition.

[30] As I argued in Chapter 2, compared to uptake, inclusion is more amenable to institutional guarantees. Dobson focuses especially on listening in formal political settings, including "face-to-face contact between elected politicians and the people they represent," interactions between "politicians themselves," and finally, the relationship between "the government and the people." Dobson, *Listening for Democracy*, 170–96.

[31] Ibid., 174.

example, he discusses the Occupy Wall Street movement's use of the "human microphone" as a tool for ensuring voices were heard. As he explains, this technique "enabled unusual levels of inclusion in noisy environments."[32] But a closer look reveals that this example of institutionalized listening refers more to the amplification of a particular input than its reception.

In other words, instead of focusing on whether messages are received, Dobson here focuses on the question of "access" or whether voices are audible.[33] As such, this account of how to institutionalize listening relates primarily to giving people the opportunity to hear a message. Making a message audible gets us closer to but cannot guarantee even the auditory force of the listening act. If a hearing person walks by Occupy Wall Street protestors who are making use of the human microphone, she does not have to listen. To avoid hearing their message, she may cross the street or turn up the volume in her earphones.

Alternatively, consider Texas House Bill 15, which requires women seeking an abortion to receive a sonogram at least twenty-four hours before the procedure. During the sonogram the doctor is required to display the sonogram images and make "audible the heart auscultation for the pregnant woman to hear."[34] The woman, however, is not required to actually listen. While hearing might be the default for a woman with use of that sense, she can still opt out and avoid it. In fact, the law permits a hearing woman to cover her ears if she does not want to listen.[35] While it's true that a message cannot be heard unless it is made audible, making it audible will not guarantee others will actually listen to it. It seems, therefore, that institutionalizing even simple listening is not as straightforward as Dobson suggests.

Moreover, as I explain further, the democratic significance of the listening act goes beyond simply ensuring that what is shared is received by one's fellow citizens. To be fair, in his discussion of "listening out," Dobson puts a more active spin on the listening act. Still, according to Dobson, if dialogue is understood as a transaction between two subjects, then a speaker

[32] Ibid., 180.

[33] Though Dobson calls attention to the need to go beyond what we typically understand to be inclusion in order to consider whether messages are received, his treatment of listening nonetheless reproduces the overburdening of inclusion typical of most deliberative models of democracy. See Chapter 2 in this volume for more on the overburdening of the concept of inclusion.

[34] Texas House, *Relating to informed consent to an abortion*, H.B. 15, 82nd Legislature, Regular Session, as enrolled, May 3, 2011, https://www.capitol.state.tx.us/tlodocs/82R/billtext/pdf/HB00015F.pdf#navpanes=0.

[35] Zain Shauk and Todd Ackerman, "Sonograms Evoke Strong Reactions as Mandate Takes Effect," *Houston Chronicle*, February 8, 2012.

gives and the listener receives.[36] Even "active listening," the kind of listening often encouraged in a classroom, for example, is seen as a way to signal one's receptivity. Ultimately, the value Dobson places on listening relates primarily to its ability to capture discrete messages that are transmitted in deliberation.

Importantly, listening also has the potential to influence what is or is not offered in the first place.[37] In other words, we cannot necessarily assume the existence of a discrete message that either will or will not be heard and therefore included (and ultimately considered). Just as our own preferences and perspectives may change as a result of listening to others, the very perspective we offer may be influenced by practices of listening themselves.[38]

Research in communications, for example, has found that the quality of an audience's listening can shape the speaker's message.[39] Specifically, experiments in autobiographical storytelling show that "narrators change stories for inattentive listeners" by "changing the content they narrate, offering different interpretive content, and altering story structure."[40] In my own classes, I have adjusted a lecture when confronted with what appeared to be a tired or uninterested group of students. And in our own everyday conversations and personal interactions, we often find ourselves more eager to share a story or opinion if we believe someone is really listening.[41] This dynamic relationship between speaking and listening has important implications for inclusion, as listening can affect the very content of what people share in deliberation. And yet, only by attending to the perauditory effects of listening, discussed shortly, can we capture this dynamic relationship between speaking and listening.

[36] Dobson, *Listening for Democracy*, 171–72.

[37] Such a dynamic view of listening has the added benefit of allowing for the possibility of a disciplinary effect of knowing one is being listened to, which I discuss in Section 4.2.2 in this volume.

[38] Deliberative democratic theory's accommodation of a dynamic view of preferences is seen as an improvement over aggregative models of democracy, which assume citizens have fixed preferences.

[39] Heather Noel Fedesco, "The Impact of (In)effective Listening on Interpersonal Interactions," *International Journal of Listening* 29, no. 2 (2015): 103–6; Monisha Pasupathi and Jacob Billitteri, "Being and Becoming through Being Heard: Listener Effects on Stories and Selves," *International Journal of Listening* 29, no. 2 (2015): 1–18; Srader, "Performative Listening."

[40] Pasupathi and Billitteri, "Being and Becoming through Being Heard," 73.

[41] In political contexts too, knowing that someone is listening seems to have positive effects on individuals' willingness to deliberate. Neblo and colleagues found that invitations to have a discussion with one's representative motivates participation in deliberation precisely among those people who, demographically speaking, are less likely to participate in traditional ways, including voting. Michael A. Neblo, Kevin M. Esterling, Ryan P. Kennedy, David M.J. Lazer, and Anand E. Sokhey, "Who Wants To Deliberate—And Why?," *American Political Science Review* 104, no. 03 (2010): 566–83.

Thus, as we learn from listening act theory, it would be a mistake to equate the full effect of listening to simply hearing, and therefore receiving, a discrete message. The full democratic effect of listening goes beyond even the successful reception of a discrete message to be considered in our decision-making process. Ultimately, the auditory listening episode, which relates to *what* is received, is just one of the ways that listening contributes to the democratic nature of deliberation. To expand our understanding of the democratic function of listening, I turn in the next section to a discussion of the various consequences or effects brought about *through* the listening act. The listening act carries different outcomes for those listening compared to those being listened to. And as I show, these perauditory effects carry their own democratic significance, though not always positive.

4.2.2 Perauditory Listening Outcomes

The perauditory listening episode refers to what is brought about *through* listening rather than to the content of *what* we hear when we listen. These outcomes include not only the oft-mentioned learning, understanding, and agreement for the listener (or decoder) but also feelings of empowerment, shifts in attitude, and even changes in political behavior for the encoder (or the one being listened to). Here, I do not offer a complete inventory of all of the outcomes of listening but instead focus on what I take to be the most democratically significant ones. I draw special attention to outcomes of listening that often go unnoticed, including those that do not necessarily boost our democratic prospects. As I show, we should expect listening to bring about a variety of outcomes that will affect the democratic functioning of a deliberative system for better and worse.

As I mentioned earlier, the quality of listening can have an effect on what people are willing to share in conversation. If I sense that people are not really listening, I may "save my breath," so to speak. Still, more listening does not always lead to more conversation. Recognizing the dynamic relationship between speaking and listening also reveals those moments or contexts when attentive listening can have a chilling effect on conversation. This perauditory effect of the listening act goes untheorized in the literature. For example, while Dobson talks about the democratic value of encouraging the powerful to "listen *out*" for the voices of the relatively powerless, he misses the political effects of the powerful "listening *in*" on others.

We know, however, that "Big Brother" may be listening as much as he is watching.[42] And fear of being listened to is likely to have the same disciplinary effect on the object of "the audit" as fear of being watched has on the object of the gaze. These effects include feelings of powerlessness, anxiety, and exposure. Consider the pedagogical technique of walking around or "patrolling" the classroom when students are engaged in small-group work. This technique employs listening to ensure that students' small-group discussions stay on topic. Importantly, then, feeling as though you are being listened to is not always the empowering experience that Dobson suggests.[43] Indeed, we may have good democratic reasons for wanting to ensure that citizens, especially those with relatively little political power, have the opportunity to share, plan, or organize, out of earshot of those in power.[44]

Of course, in discussing listening as an essential feature of democracy, Dobson is undoubtedly referring to the power of being listened to precisely when one wants to be heard. Still, the reverse is also true and worth noting. Being able to choose when not to be heard (especially by one's political opponents or those with more power) is itself a kind of political power and one that is not shared equally. In other words, the democratic value of listening does not extend to instances when a person might prefer not to be heard. Indeed, successful organizing and consciousness raising likely require space where individuals can speak to friends and allies without being heard by either those in power or unlike-minded individuals.

Nonetheless, in order to make a political impact, the positions built up through "enclaved deliberations" eventually need to be expressed in an inclusive public sphere where they will be heard and considered by all citizens. Mansbridge describes the need for "some mixture of protection and publicity in the early stages of a deliberative process, but maximum feasible publicity

[42] James Bamford, "Big Brother Is Listening," *Atlantic Monthly*, April 2006, https://www.theatlantic.com/magazine/archive/2006/04/big-brother-is-listening/304711/.

[43] Dobson explains throughout his book that his aim is to ensure that the "experience of the power of being listened to is the rule rather than the exception." Dobson, *Listening for Democracy*, 177.

[44] Jane Mansbridge, "Everyday Talk in the Deliberative System," in *Deliberative Politics: Essays on Democracy and Disagreement*, ed. Stephen Macedo (Oxford: Oxford University Press, 1999), 221. This insight regarding the power of not being heard is borne out in research on "enclaved deliberation." As Cass Sunstein has shown, enclaved deliberation, or deliberation among like-minded people, leads to greater mobilization and is essential to "the development of positions that would otherwise be invisible, silenced, or squelched in general debate." Cass R. Sunstein, "The Law of Group Polarization," *Debating Deliberative Democracy* 10, no. 2 (2002): 190. Maija Setälä, "The Public Sphere as a Site of Deliberation: An Analysis of Problems of Inclusion," in *Deliberative Democracy: Issues and Cases*, eds. Stephen Elstub and Peter McLaverty (Edinburgh: Edinburgh University Press, 2014), 149–65.

in the final stages."[45] All else equal, we do want to encourage listening to those who want to be heard. If, when speaking in public spheres, members of oppressed groups are heard as a matter of course, it becomes harder to ignore their concerns.[46] The absolute democratic value of listening, in other words, amounts to the ability to be listened to when one wants to be heard and to not be listened to when one does not want to be heard.

Besides these potential disciplinary effects, the listening act can have attitudinal and informational effects as well. For example, the act of listening across political divides can foster trust or cooperation between members of otherwise adversarial groups. And Dobson celebrates the positive attitudinal shifts that occur when members of societal outgroups are afforded the opportunity to share their experience with members of dominant majority groups *who listen*.

In one study, Palestinians were given the chance to share their stories with Israelis.[47] This study found that the listening act had positive perauditory effects for both the listeners as well as those being listened to. Interestingly, however, while being listened to prompted an attitude change among Palestinians, it was the act of listening that brought about an attitude change among Israelis.[48] With these attitudinal changes, we see potential democratic benefits of getting those with relative power and privilege to listen to the relatively less powerful and privileged.[49]

But again, the Palestinian participants' attitudes toward Israelis also changed as a result of being heard, becoming more positive than they were before the listening encounter. And in this particular experiment, researchers were able to differentiate the effects of intergroup interaction as such from interactions marked specifically by listening on the part of the

[45] Mansbridge, "Everyday Talk in the Deliberative System," 221; Jon Elster, "Deliberation and Constitution Making," in *Deliberative Democracy*, ed. Jon Elster (Cambridge: Cambridge University Press, 1998), 117.

[46] I am reminded of a quote attributed to Zora Neale Hurston that I read in an article about the death of Sandra Bland: "If you are silent about your pain, they'll kill you and say you enjoyed it." Kristen West Savali, "#SandySpeaks: 'I'm Here to Change History,'" *The Root*, July 22, 2015, https://www.theroot.com/sandyspeaks-i-m-here-to-change-history-1790860601.

[47] Emile G. Bruneau and Rebecca Saxe, "The Power of Being Heard: The Benefits of 'Perspective-Giving' in the Context of Intergroup Conflict," *Journal of Experimental Social Psychology* 48, no. 4 (2012): 855–66.

[48] The authors refer to this as the power of "perspective giving," as opposed to "perspective taking." Here, the authors seem to be using "taking" in a sense other than imagination, but actually taking as in receiving another's perspective in dialogue. If someone gives, the other takes. But here, the "taking" is done through listening.

[49] Dobson claims that there is power in the simple experience of "being listened to." As I mentioned earlier, Dobson's goal is to ensure "that the less powerful experience the power that is *being listened to* as a matter of course rather than as an exception." Dobson, *Listening for Democracy*, 15.

dominant group. Interestingly, the positive attitudinal effects did not hold for Palestinians in the "control condition," who were able to share their experience without necessarily being listened to.[50] The authors conclude that these differentiated effects illustrate "the critical role of *being heard*."[51]

It's worth noting that these positive attitudinal shifts could actually be the result of people *feeling* heard. The democratic value of deliberation, however, is not satisfied by people *feeling* like their voices have been heard. Instead, a deliberative system achieves its democratic function when citizens' perspectives, grievances, and demands are fairly considered by their fellow citizens in discursive processes of collective opinion and will formation.[52] Thus, as democratic theorists, we ought to be concerned if, in another case, members of an oppressed group were to experience a positive shift in attitude toward a dominant and potentially oppressive group owing simply to feelings of being heard.

We would likely find it disturbing, for example, if employees' attitudes toward an exploitative employer improved simply as a result of their having the opportunity to be heard by their manager and without any corresponding promise that their feedback would be used to improve working conditions. How might these attitudinal shifts, brought about by the powerful listening to the less powerful, shield an otherwise undemocratic or unjust status quo from criticism or reform? It's easy to imagine, for example, how a positive shift in attitude brought about as a result of being listened to, but independent of any effort to take corrective action, might make it harder to facilitate costly collective action in the face of injustice. Among other things, these attitudinal shifts brought about through listening alert us to the possible strategic uses of listening.[53]

These attitudinal shifts brought about *through* listening are often accompanied (if not driven) by important informational benefits for the listener, including greater understanding of one's opponent as well as a recognition of the stakes of political discourse.[54] In her 2006 book, *Hearing the Other*

---

[50] Bruneau and Saxe, "The Power of Being Heard," 854.

[51] Ibid.

[52] Importantly, feelings of being listened to may reduce the critical edge of some claims of injustice. Another possible pathology of listening pertains to the uneven burden that listening as a practice of democratic citizenship imposes on some members of society. For example, listening to hateful sexist or racist speech is likely more challenging for those at whom it is directed.

[53] For more on the strategic use of listening, see Carolyn M. Hendriks, Selen A. Ercan, and Sonya Duus, "Listening in Polarised Controversies: A Study of Listening Practices in the Public Sphere," *Policy Sciences* 52, no. 1 (2019): 137–51.

[54] Here, the use of "opponent" would connote a horizontal rather than a vertical relationship.

Side: Deliberative versus Participatory Democracy, Diana Mutz finds that listening to those with whom we disagree, what Mutz calls "exposure to cross-cutting views," makes people both more aware of rationales for oppositional viewpoints and more tolerant.[55] She also finds, however, that hearing opposing views can actually lead listeners to withdraw from politics.[56] The perauditory force of listening in contexts of political difference, then, would seem to include not only increased knowledge and higher levels of tolerance, but also demobilization when it comes to traditional forms of political participation, including voting.[57] In other words, the informational and attitudinal benefits of listening are often enjoyed alongside a less welcomed behavioral cost.

These behavioral changes have both epistemic and social sources. For example, Mutz finds that hearing the other side can "lower the certainty with which we hold our views."[58] This uncertainty, in turn, decreases the chances that we will vote. Meanwhile, socially speaking, even if we remain confident in our position, we are often "too afraid of offending our friends and neighbors" and so may opt out of political involvement.[59]

But is it really so bad, democratically speaking, if those individuals with relative privilege—pushing, say, to dismantle the social safety net—are demobilized as a result of listening to those who rely on Medicaid? Dobson might defend against the threat of demobilization by pointing to the specific need for the powerful to listen to the relatively powerless.[60] As Tanja Dreher

[55] Mutz measures tolerance as "support for civil liberties *in spite of* ongoing negative attitudes towards groups." Diana C. Mutz, *Hearing the Other Side* (Cambridge: Cambridge University Press, 2006), 66.

[56] To measure political engagement, Mutz considers voting, donating to a campaign, attending a rally, and other activities related to campaigns and elections.

[57] Tolerance was measured according to the respondents' support for civil liberties for their "least-liked" group. Participation was operationalized in more of a partisan than deliberative way. By this I mean that opportunities to participate revolved around support for a particular candidate or political party. Across two surveys, Mutz measured a respondent's participation according to the following self-reported behaviors: intending to vote in a presidential election, trying to convince someone to support a particular candidate, volunteering for a party or candidate, attending rallies, displaying a yard sign, or donating money to a party or candidate. Diana C. Mutz, "Cross-Cutting Social Networks: Testing Democratic Theory in Practice," *American Political Science Review* 96, no. 1 (2002): 116; Diana C. Mutz, "The Consequences of Cross-Cutting Networks for Political Participation," *American Journal of Political Science* 46, no. 4 (2002): 854.

[58] Mutz, *Hearing the Other Side*, 109.

[59] Ibid. In the next chapter, I discuss the need for citizens to cultivate a greater acceptance of conflict in political life. This could help mitigate the demobilizing effect of listening across difference.

[60] Seraina Pedrini, André Bächtiger, and Marco R. Steenbergen, "Deliberative Inclusion of Minorities: Patterns of Reciprocity among Linguistic Groups in Switzerland," *European Political Science Review* 5, no. 3 (2013): 483–512.

argues, a politics of listening must be "power sensitive and responsive to the inequalities and conflicts that shape speaking and listening relationships."[61]

Being sensitive to the power always operating in our relationships and conversations, however, does not mean that practices of listening should be one-sided. Even if we wanted to use listening to "undo privilege" and challenge "taken-for-granted comforts and security," the idea that we could, prior to the act of listening itself, determine who is and is not owed listening is unworkable for a variety of reasons, which I discuss in greater detail in Chapter 7.[62] For now, I just note that when it comes to constituting democratic political power through deliberation, listening is owed to all citizens equally. In other words, we do not get to choose who listens to whom. Democracy requires a two-way listening relationship. As such, we have to be prepared for the possibility that listening across difference could demobilize those working to achieve justice for the politically marginalized and powerless.

Consider, for example, that supporters of civil liberties in the United States who live near the US-Mexico border are particularly well placed to oppose racist, inhumane, or unconstitutional policies targeting immigrants, including the separation of immigrant children from their families. But if their communities are politically diverse, we might fear, given Mutz's findings, that listening in such a cross-cutting environment could take the wind out of their resistance sails, so to speak. And while we would count it as a gain for democracy if white supremacists were deterred from taking political action as a result of "hearing the other side," what happens if, through the course of that listening act, staunch opponents of racism become less confident in their position or otherwise unwilling to speak out against their racist neighbors?[63] What happens if the white and racially privileged residents of Charlottesville are demobilized or otherwise deterred from taking action against Nazi protestors as a result of listening to members of the alt-right?

Relatedly, another worrisome perauditory outcome is the potential for acts of listening to normalize and legitimize abhorrent views that potentially

---

[61] Tanja Dreher, "Listening across Difference: Media and Multiculturalism beyond the Politics of Voice," *Continuum* 23, no. 4 (2009): 452.

[62] Ibid.

[63] This case provides a good example of when enclaved deliberation serves an important democratic purpose. Going back to the disciplinary effect that being listened to can have—especially being listened to by those in power, one's political adversaries, as well as those who may have a privileged position in an unjust status quo—we have good reasons to carve out spaces where conversations will not be heard beyond members of a particular outgroup.

threaten our democracy. It's possible, for example, that listening to a known misogynist could be interpreted by others as a sign that you take his ideas to be within the realm of political possibility. *Through* our listening, then, we might unintentionally lend credibility to a set of ideas we wholeheartedly oppose. In a more direct sense, robust listening practices could very well provide the oxygen needed for the flames of hate and prejudice to spread.

With this discussion, to which I return in Chapter 7, I mean to show that the perauditory outcomes brought about *through* listening are varied in their democratic value. As such, before adopting a listening approach to deliberation, we might be tempted to weigh the democratic benefits against the costs, much like we did with the empathy approach in Chapter 3. But such an analysis, I argue, would be premature.

In addition to the auditory and perauditory dimensions of the listening act, there is the crucial ilauditory listening episode or how we act *in* listening. Specifically, *in* listening to our fellow citizens we move our deliberation in the direction of greater democracy. Without listening, we cannot achieve the deliberative ideal of fair consideration. As such, given a commitment to deliberative democracy, we cannot trade listening for some other democratic benefit. And we cannot dispense with listening even to avoid certain undemocratic effects of its practice, including demobilization. The normative core of democratic deliberation would prohibit us from accepting less listening for greater mobilization.

Yet even if we accept that listening is owed to all citizens, the undemocratic outcomes I discussed above cannot be ignored and should worry even the most committed deliberative democrat. The indispensable nature of listening for democracy makes it all the more important that we be mindful of the potentially undemocratic perauditory outcomes of the listening act. Still, accounting for these perauditory outcomes must be taken as part of a mitigation strategy, rather than a cost-benefit strategy.[64] Understanding these consequences helps us guard against the undemocratic outcomes and maximize the democratic ones. For example, as I discuss in the next chapter, to avoid demobilization brought about through listening across difference, we ought to civically educate people in the ethos of a democratic citizen,

---

[64] To mitigate the undemocratic consequences of listening, we might adopt strategies already in use by members of marginalized groups who routinely listen *up*, in other words, listen for what is not said, listen for the dog whistle, and listen even for enmity. As I discuss in Chapter 7, listening has long been a tool of the powerless, used to help anticipate the whims of the powerful and to detect deceit or veiled threats.

teaching them that a good democratic life may be one with some level of controversy and contestation.

By overemphasizing the consequences of the listening act, we tend to overlook the way we act *in* listening.[65] In the next section, I turn to the ilauditory listening episode or the performative listening act to explain how *in* listening we move our deliberation in the direction of greater democracy.

4.2.3 Performative Listening and the Deliberative Ideal

The major advantage of studying democratic deliberation within the framework of listening act theory is that we get a more complete view of how listening impacts politics. To date, "empirical research on listening has focused on the measurement of listening comprehension and on perceived listening effectiveness."[66] Respectively, these approaches put the content or the outcome of listening ahead of the act itself. Correcting for this oversight, Srader invites us to think about how we act *in* listening. Specifically, with his concept of performative listening, he differentiates the act of listening both from *what* is shared in the encounter and what is brought about *through* listening. Especially when it comes to democratic deliberation, the normative weight of which is predicated on uptake, rather than either inclusion (input) or influence (output), we have good reasons not to equate listening with *what* is heard or the understanding, agreement, or behavioral response we hope to bring about *through* listening. In what follows, I examine and hone Srader's concept of performative listening—what I call the ilauditory listening episode—and then apply it to deliberative democratic theory.

Srader acknowledges that the ilauditory and perauditory dimensions of listening are closely connected, but insists that a distinction is "not beyond retrieval."[67] To develop this point, he offers three examples or categories of ilauditory listening acts where the objective is completed *in* listening itself and not in what is brought about as a result of listening. They include "listening toward *relationship*," "listening toward *leadership*," and "listening toward *fairness*."

---

[65] Srader, "Performative Listening," 96.
[66] Peter C. Fontana, Steven D. Cohen, and Andrew D. Wolvin, "Understanding Listening Competency: A Systematic Review of Research Scales," *International Journal of Listening* 29, no. 3 (2015): 148.
[67] Srader, "Performative Listening," 98.

In listening toward *relationship*, "the listener invokes a relational bond *in the act of listening*."[68] Put differently, the listener "listens *because* she or he belongs to the relationship, and not for the purpose of bringing a designed response in the encoder [speaker] via the investment of listening resources."[69] As discussed in the previous section, "investments" in listening, even when made strategically, can and do bring about positive relational benefits in interpersonal as well as political contexts. For example, listening on the part of one's therapist can induce feelings of trust, while being listened to by one's political adversary may reduce feelings of antagonism. Still, Srader contends that, in listening toward relationship, we can distinguish these (perauditory) outcomes from the ilauditory force whereby the relationship is constituted *in* listening. When it comes to listening toward *relationship*, our listening may fulfill the duties of a particular relationship, or even call that relationship into existence.

Listening toward *leadership* is like listening toward relationship, only the relationship is specified as one of leader to constituent or follower. Politically speaking, the relationship of representative and constituent is both formed and fulfilled *in* the act of listening. Certainly, a representative has strategic reasons to listen (or at least to appear to listen) to those who will vote in his election, but he also has an obligation to listen to those whom he represents. Therefore, if my representative does not listen to me and my neighbor, he is failing to fulfill the duties associated with his office.[70] On the other hand, *in* listening to someone, even if he is not responsible for representing them, he constitutes the relationship of representative and constituent. For example, if a member of Congress is listening to organized interests, then we ought to recognize that lobby as a relevant constituent.

And again, though a leader may have strategic reasons for listening, including to "empower a follower, or defuse the follower's resentment of an adverse decision," still, "those results are distinguishable from the leader's behavior; the leader creates an observable relationship for the duration of the listening performance, and that relational event is not fully enmeshed with its consequences."[71] In these cases, although the listening may, indeed, improve the relationship, it is executed in the first place because of the relationship.

---

[68] Ibid., 97.
[69] Ibid.
[70] The constitutive element of listening toward *leadership* has interesting implications for the role of lobbyists and private interests in a representative democracy.
[71] Srader, "Performative Listening," 98.

Lastly, Srader presents listening toward *fairness,* bringing us back to the paradigmatic example of a legal hearing. According to Srader, the success of a "hearing" is not based on any particular outcome, but instead on whether we are able to "inject listening into the *process* whereby the decision is crafted."[72] He explains that "when a judge, administrator, parent, or other decision maker agrees to a party's request to be heard, to 'hear me out,' a bid for listening toward fairness has been granted."[73] Even before a decision is made, something in the world changes *in* our listening to this person. In the case of a legal hearing, the hearing itself brings about the fulfillment of a duty.[74] Specifically, "A hearing in which one accused of misconduct is allowed to answer the charges infuses any following decision, whether adverse or redemptive, with legitimacy it would not have otherwise."[75] The ilauditory force of a legal hearing is not tied to any particular outcome. Even if our listening to the accused did not bring about knowledge of the truth, it would still have moved the hearing toward greater fairness. The hearing is one example, according to Srader, where listening is "entirely sufficient to fulfill duties and/or create relationships."[76]

But while the ilauditory force of listening is not *based* on the outcome of the listening act, outcomes may still be relevant to our assessment of the ilauditory listening act. For example, if a system's legal hearings resulted in a disproportionate number of guilty verdicts or uneven sentencing for members of an ethnic minority, we would have reason to question whether the judge or jury was listening toward fairness—in other words, whether their listening was successful in achieving the ilauditory force.[77] Crucially, however, even if the outcome of a hearing is relevant to our assessment of its ilauditory force, the outcome is not responsible for the ilauditory force of the listening act. It is still *in* listening to the defendant that we fulfill a demand of justice.

Though performative listening has been overlooked in democratic theory, a careful examination of the literature reveals latent references to the ilauditory force of listening. Without listening act theory to help situate these references, however, they have, at times, confused more than they

---

[72] Ibid., 99.
[73] Ibid., 98.
[74] Ibid., 100.
[75] Ibid.
[76] Ibid., 95.
[77] For more on the relationship of process and outcome in democratic theory, see Chambers, "Making Referendums Safe for Democracy."

clarified. In *Listening for Democracy*, for example, Dobson seems to hit on the ilauditory force of listening when he explains that the insight animating his book as a whole is that there is undeniable "power in being listened to."[78] His pro-listening intervention into deliberative democratic theory is motivated by what he sees as "the relationship between listening and power."[79] But rather than develop this ilauditory force of the listening act, or the power *in* listening, Dobson moves quickly to talk about the desirable outcomes achieved *through* the powerful listening act. For example, he focuses primarily on getting "the powerful to listen so that the less powerful experience the power that is *being listened to* as a matter of course rather than as an exception. . . ."[80] In this telling passage, and others like it, Dobson conflates the power of listening itself with what is brought about *through* listening. The feeling of being listened to is a powerful feeling indeed. And there are surely democratic benefits to expanding this experience *through* listening. But the democratic force of listening goes beyond this perauditory effect.[81]

For the most part, then, Dobson overlooks the ilauditory force of the listening act. While the perauditory outcomes Dobson discusses and which I reviewed in the preceding section are democratically significant, he misses what we accomplish *in* the listening act itself.[82] This oversight leaves us with an incomplete account of the democratic significance, indeed the democratic power, of listening. But more importantly, it also leads us to discount or forget what is at stake in deliberation: democracy. Feeling listened to is not the primary goal of the political listening act, though it might be for listening in a therapeutic or interpersonal context. We want the powerful to listen to the less powerful not so that the latter simply experience the power of being listened to, but so that they may realize democratic autonomy, by being included in the authorship of the laws to which they are held. In the next chapter, I show how *in* listening we move our deliberation in the direction of greater democracy.

Bickford also implicitly appeals to the ilauditory force of listening or how we act *in* listening. Notably, she suggests that *in* listening to our fellow citizens, we endow our decisions with a certain democratic quality they previously lacked. For Bickford, this democratic endowment seems to occur

---

[78] Dobson, *Listening for Democracy*, 16.

[79] Ibid., 15.

[80] Ibid.

[81] And as I explained in Section 4.2.2, this effect of feeling heard can also have undemocratic effects of placation and demobilization.

[82] Dobson, *Listening for Democracy*, 177.

independently of any of the outcomes of the listening act. Specifically, in *Dissonance of Democracy*, Bickford ties the democratic nature of citizens' deliberation to the "presence of listening" instead of the possibility of consensus. Given a world of difference, asking citizens to orient themselves toward consensus is not only unrealistic, but undesirable.[83] Optimizing for the possibility of consensus requires what Bickford calls the "purification of social action," so that we eliminate any and all suspicions of strategic action.[84] Listening, on the other hand, "does not require the purification of motives or abstracting from our identity, nor does it involve empathy for one another or a strong sense of community."[85] If listening is the goal of deliberation, then I need not share your concerns or sentiments in order to engage productively and democratically with you.

As such, practices of listening provide an avenue for achieving democracy in the presence of difference and disagreement and in the absence of empathy. The difference-accommodating function of listening recommends it as a useful standard for assessing the democratic nature of deliberation. Asking citizens to orient themselves toward listening is less burdensome than asking citizens to orient themselves toward reaching consensus. We can listen in spite of differences and in the absence of full understanding.

Still, as Bickford acknowledges, when it comes to making decisions across difference, in contexts of deep disagreement, and in the presence of scarce resources, it is not always easy to listen.[86] Thus, we still face the challenge of motivating citizens to listen in contexts of social division and ethical-political disagreement, precisely when they might prefer to tune out those with whom they disagree. In emphasizing the advantages of listening-oriented deliberation as compared to consensus-oriented deliberation, we have to be careful not to underestimate the challenges of achieving even listening in a political context, where high-stakes decisions need to be made in the presence of disagreement.

Moreover, unlike Bickford, who argues that the democratic nature of our decisions depends on the presence of listening, I still maintain that uptake is what carries the normative weight of deliberation. Nonetheless, listening is

---

[83] As I explained at the beginning of this chapter, I do not interpret Bickford's emphasis on listening to represent a departure from Habermas or deliberative democratic theory in general. Consensus achieved through means others than communication (which necessarily requires listening) would fail to carry democratic weight even according to Habermas's model of deliberative democratic theory.

[84] Bickford, *The Dissonance of Democracy*, 18.

[85] Ibid., 19.

[86] Ibid., 68.

an essential element of uptake. As I develop further in Chapter 5, *in* listening to our fellow citizens, we acknowledge that they are rightful participants in the decision-making process. Recognizing your input as pertinent is a necessary first step in my considering it. And as I explain, listening becomes "listening toward democracy" when citizens understand the act of listening to be, itself, an expectation of democratic citizenship and thereby accept the relevant normative framing of the listening encounter.

4.3 Conclusion

With my account of listening act theory, I have unpacked the multiple and varied ways that listening contributes to deliberative democracy. Specifically, I compared the auditory, perauditory, and ilauditory listening acts. As I have shown, listening amounts to more than simply hearing *what* is said. And it is not only valuable for its ability to *bring about* something like consensus or mutual understanding. In fact, listening can also bring about undesirable outcomes, including demobilization, or lead to disciplinary consequences that would go against important democratic values.

By offering a more complete view of the listening act, I have tried to improve our understanding of the democratic force of citizen listening in their everyday political talk. Ultimately, the full democratic power of listening is not captured in the existing literature, which tends to focus either on how listening makes deliberation more inclusive or on the outcomes of listening.

Importantly, the democratic significance of listening goes beyond merely hearing *what* someone says (i.e., the auditory listening act) and it cannot be equated with what is brought about *through* listening (i.e., the perauditory effects of listening). Indeed, I showed that we also act *in* listening. Using the insights of performative listening, the next chapter explains more specifically how listening helps constitute the deliberative act, ensuring that speakers' messages connect up with their relevant audiences. If the auditory force of listening contributes most directly to inclusion, then the ilauditory force of listening moves us toward fair consideration.

Further developing the concept of "listening toward democracy," Chapter 5 shows how our achieving the deliberative ideal of fair consideration depends more on the disposition of citizen listeners than on any particular outcome of their listening, including consensus or agreement. I turn now to the force and conditions of performative democratic listening.

5

Listening toward Democracy

Building on my account of listening act theory from the previous chapter, I turn my attention now to the ilauditory listening act and its relation to deliberative democratic theory. With the category of performative democratic listening, I mean to show that we do something *in* listening to our fellow citizens that has heretofore gone unrecognized. *In* listening to our fellow citizens, we perform a willingness and desire to take up what they have to say. *In* listening, we acknowledge that they have a rightful say in the decisions we make collectively.

The goal of this chapter is to explain how, exactly, this act of listening moves our deliberation in the direction of greater democracy. Pushing back against the tendency of deliberativists to shy away from any strong theories of citizenship, I argue that the source of the ilauditory force of listening is the disposition or ethos of the citizen listener.[1] Under the right conditions, specifically with the right affective-cognitive disposition, citizens can "listen toward democracy." A democratic listener listens to her fellow citizens so that their perspectives may be brought to bear on the formation of a collective opinion and will. This act of listening changes lived reality, equipping deliberation with democratic force.

Appealing to the democratic power of the ilauditory listening act, I argue in favor of taking a listening-centered approach to democratic deliberation. Adopting such an approach, democratic theorists would focus on the act of listening for the purpose of both improving and evaluating the democratic functioning of a deliberative system.

Importantly, not all acts of listening will carry the ilauditory force of performative democratic listening. Furthermore, while the ilauditory listening act is an essential component of fair consideration, uptake is not necessarily

---

[1] I follow Owen and Smith in turning toward questions of citizen capacity. David Owen and Graham Smith, "Deliberation, Democracy, and the Systemic Turn," *Journal of Political Philosophy* 23, no. 2 (2015): 213–34.

Beyond Empathy and Inclusion. Mary F. Scudder, Oxford University Press (2020). © Oxford University Press.
DOI: 10.1093/oso/9780197535455.001.0001.

entailed by even those listening acts that do rise to the level of performative democratic listening. Still, while not the same as uptake, performative democratic listening occurs on the way to uptake and so is a key feature of meaningfully democratic deliberation. This chapter goes on to address how we might encourage citizens to listen to one another, proposing strategies to help ensure that their listening achieves the ilauditory force of performative democratic listening.

To defend a listening approach to democratic deliberation, I begin with a discussion of the nature and source of the ilauditory force of performative democratic listening (5.1). Next, I consider the cultural and institutional conditions that I expect would encourage citizens to practice democratic listening (5.2). I then go on to identify empirical markers to use in our assessment of listening and in determining whether uptake has been achieved (5.3). The chapter concludes with a discussion of the challenges of relying on listening in political contexts of difference, disagreement, and inequality, which I develop further in Chapter 6.

5.1 Performative Democratic Listening

My goal here is to explain how *in* listening we can fulfill certain duties of democratic citizenship, or put differently, how we might *listen toward democracy*. To demonstrate the force of performative democratic listening, I want to return briefly to the distinctiveness of *deliberative* democracy as presented in Chapter 3. There I explained the crucial role that actual communication among citizens plays in realizing the promise of *deliberative*, as opposed to *deliberate*, democracy. Specifically, I showed that according to deliberative democratic theory, inclusive and considerate deliberation not only improves democratic decision making but is actually responsible for conferring a democratic quality on those collective decisions in the first place. Here I argue that listening plays an analogous role in deliberation: listening not only improves deliberation, but is actually responsible for conferring a deliberative quality to political communication. Listening, in other words, is constitutive of deliberation.

We speak in deliberation with the expectation that our fellow citizens or representatives will take what we say into account when forming their opinions and making decisions. As Doyle Srader explains, however, "Any speaker is in danger of speaking into the air in the same sense that it is possible to throw a ball into an empty field."[2] Importantly, then, "a listener completes a transaction in the same way one who catches the ball turns the throw into a game."[3] In catching the ball, you create a game of catch. Similarly, in listening to a fellow citizen, you call the deliberative act into existence. Our listening is what ensures a person's inputs connect up with the relevant audience. When we listen to our fellow citizens, we ensure that they are not "speaking into the air."[4] The ilauditory listening act, or what Srader calls "performative listening," changes lived reality. This change is brought about *in* our listening and occurs independently of the outcomes of listening.

In listening to our fellow citizens, we grant a bid for democratic autonomy or democratic self-rule. Recall that democratic autonomy is achieved when citizens see themselves as both the addressees and authors of the law. Going back to Rousseau, democratic autonomy means that in obeying the law, citizens obey only themselves.[5] But when it comes to coordinating action in large pluralistic societies, it's inevitable that some people will be on the losing side of a decision or judgment. As such, these groups or individuals will not see their own will reflected in the collective will that emerges from deliberation (and an eventual vote). But even if they do not support the decision taken (or just importantly, not taken), these people can still see themselves as having participated in the lawmaking authority so long as their perspectives were included and fairly considered.

As I explained in Chapter 2, Habermas reinterprets democratic autonomy intersubjectively, such that the self of the self-ruling autonomous self is found in the subjectless forms of communication circulating in the public spheres. Democratic autonomy is achieved when citizens participate in the lawmaking authority, having their inputs included and taken up in public debate. With this understanding of autonomy, Habermas shows us how we might achieve democratic self-rule in large pluralistic societies wherein even the most inclusive and considerate deliberation will not always result in an agreement or compromise that all can endorse. Performative democratic listening moves our deliberation in the direction of greater democracy by helping satisfy the conditions of this intersubjectively achieved autonomy.

---

[2] Doyle W. Srader, "Performative Listening," *International Journal of Listening* 29, no. 2 (May 4, 2015): 98.

[3] Ibid.

[4] Ibid.

[5] Jean-Jacques Rousseau, *The Social Contract and Other Later Political Writings*, ed. Victor Gourevitch (Cambridge: Cambridge University Press, 1997), 51–52.

In listening to our fellow citizens, we acknowledge that their perspectives are germane to any decision we might take. Performative democratic listening, therefore, amounts to people giving their fellow citizens the hearing they are owed. This listening ensures that speakers have an opportunity to shape collective decisions by allowing them to meaningfully participate in deliberative processes of opinion and will formation. Importantly, performative democratic listening fulfills this function even if the listening act is not ultimately "successful" in the sense of leading to agreement or ensuring understanding. This is what I mean when I say that the democratizing force of performative listening is independent of the outcomes of listening.

But even if the democratizing force of performative listening is achieved independent of the outcomes of listening, outcomes are still relevant to our assessment of whether that democratizing force was, in fact, achieved. As Simone Chambers explains in her critique of the idea of "outcome-neutrality" in democratic politics, "Even if the problem is traced back to faulty procedures, the red flag is triggered by the undesirability of the outcome and that in turn is premised on substantive normative commitments that are not entirely procedural."[6] Applied to the idea of performative democratic listening, we see that even when a problematic outcome can be traced back to a failure of listening, the undesirability of the outcome is what allowed us to identify the democratically deficient listening in the first place.

Democracy is about solving problems and making decisions. Despite offering a procedural conception of justice, deliberative democratic theory is not, in fact, outcome neutral. Deliberativists value deliberation precisely for its ability to improve the quality of collective decisions. If deliberative outcomes were consistently unmoved by listening and instead systematically reflected the pre-listening will of members of a politically dominant group, then we would have reason to doubt that the perauditory force of listening had actually been achieved.

The democratic power of the ilauditory listening act comes from the expectation that what is heard will be incorporated into the process through which we make collective decisions. If, in deliberation, listeners simply go through the motions, refusing to take on and deal with what their fellow citizens are saying, their listening cannot move us toward democracy. After all, as I explained in Chapter 2, it is having one's inputs considered (and not just

---

[6] Simone Chambers, "Making Referendums Safe for Democracy: A Call for More and Better Deliberation," *Swiss Political Science Review* 24, no. 3 (2018): 306.

heard) in the course of a decision-making process that ensures democratically legitimate outcomes.

The democratic force of listening is similar to the legal force of having an authentic hearing. A hearing in a sham trial whose decision was predetermined would necessarily lack the ilauditory force of listening toward fairness. If the listening act had no bearing on the outcome of the trial, it could not satisfy the conditions of listening toward fairness.

In this way, I depart from Srader, who argues that the ilauditory force of listening holds independent of all considerations of outcome. At the very least, outcomes matter for performative democratic listening in the sense that they must be open to the influence of the listening act. The crucial point remains, however, that these outcomes are not what actually move our deliberation in the direction of greater democracy. The act of performative democratic listening itself carries important normative weight.

Following the tradition of speech act theory, however, Srader argues that the ilauditory force of listening holds independently not only of the consequences but the quality of the listening act. He explains that "in the same way articulation of a promise consummates a redeemable obligation, an episode of performative listening entirely fulfills a duty regardless of the quality of its execution."[7] Recall that if a couple mumbles through their wedding vows, they are still married. The illocutionary force of their utterance is not dependent on its quality.

By downplaying the relevance of listening quality, however, Srader likely obscures the *source* of the ilauditory force of listening. Consider his own example of listening toward fairness. It seems obvious, for example, that a judge "listening" to the accused while surreptitiously reading the newspaper or watching television would fail to grant a bid of listening toward fairness. While this low-quality listening act might bring about certain perauditory effects, including the inducement of (underserved) feelings of trust in an unjust process, it would fail to achieve the ilauditory force Srader describes.

Mere listening, or what I have called "simple listening," cannot move our deliberation toward democracy. Similarly, perfunctory listening does not carry the ilauditory force of the listening act as I have described it. We would not consider a hearing person to be fulfilling even a minimal expectation of democratic citizenship simply by virtue of not covering her ears when another person spoke. And on this point, I think Srader would agree. Srader

[7] Srader, "Performative Listening," 100.

likely overstates the ways in which the ilauditory force of listening holds independent of quality in an effort to show that we act *in* listening. As Srader explains, "More than just bringing about ethically satisfying conditions, 'listening to others *is* an ethical good, part of what it means to have just and fair dealings with other people.'"[8]

According to my account, however, the ilauditory force of listening comes from the listener accepting the normative significance of the listening encounter. In the case of performative *democratic* listening, the ilauditory force of the listening act depends on the listener's willingness to attend to what her fellow citizens have to say, to let their input enter into her judgment. Only when citizens accept the relevant normative framing of the interaction—that is, when they recognize it as an interaction of co-citizens who are equally entitled to have a say in the laws to which they are held—can their listening have the ilauditory force of listening and thus move their deliberation in the direction of greater democracy.

In sum, the power of democratic listening to change lived reality comes from a citizen's willingness to listen for nonstrategic reasons. In other words, when citizens listen for the purpose of taking into account what others have to say, they *are listening toward democracy*. In contrast, listening that amounts to simply allowing another's voice to wash over you, so to speak, does not carry the ilauditory force of performative listening. Still, the ilauditory force of listening is independent of outcomes in the sense that in order for listening to move us toward democracy, interlocutors need not reach agreement or consensus. *In* listening to our fellow citizens, we acknowledge their moral equality, not the moral validity of the substance of their input. As such, the ilauditory force of democratic listening can be achieved even in contexts of deep difference and disagreement. Still unclear, however, is how, practically speaking, we can facilitate performative democratic listening among citizens in large pluralistic societies.

As we have seen in the foregoing, there are stakes to democratic listening. Recognizing or accepting the stakes of democratic listening makes it at once more meaningful and more difficult to achieve. Listening for the sake of coming to a political decision that has winners and losers and material consequences carries risks. In listening, we risk being proven wrong. We risk being offended, attacked, tricked, or deceived. We risk being indicted

---

[8] Ibid., 99. Here Srader is quoting Michael P. Nichols, *The Lost Art of Listening* (New York: Guilford Press, 2009), 307.

and blamed. And so, if people do not want to take these risks, if people do not want to be held accountable to, triggered by, or otherwise influenced by another's message, they can just refuse to listen. To avoid being persuaded or troubled by what the other person says, I may simply go through the motions to feign listening, refusing to really consider that person's message. Alternatively, I may use the listening act as an opportunity to "re-load," or prepare my counterargument or response.[9]

On a normative theoretical level, we know that these instances of listening would fail to initiate performative democratic listening. Still, practically speaking, in order to achieve the ilauditory force of listening, we need to find ways to motivate citizens to take on the role of democratic listener even when engaging with political adversaries. Getting citizens to not only listen but to listen for the sake of taking what they hear into consideration is a challenge, especially in contexts of difference and deep disagreement.

As we devise a workable strategy for a listening approach to deliberation, we have to be mindful of the possibility that our listening will fall short of the performative threshold needed for it to bring us toward democracy. Democratic listeners listen, not because of what will be brought about as a result of their listening, whether the appearance of open-mindedness or the reduction in partisan animosity. They listen, rather, so that they can take others' input into account. They listen so that their fellow citizens' perspectives can be brought to bear on the laws and priorities that we set for ourselves collectively. An important question in need of answering, then, is how we might motivate citizens to adopt the affective-cognitive disposition of a democratic listener when engaging with others. I turn to this question in the next section.

5.2 Conditions of Democratic Listening

While we can design formal procedures to help ensure auditory listening, the ilauditory force of listening defies procedural guarantees. Listening toward democracy has an essential dispositional requirement. In order to bring

---

[9] Andrew Dobson, *Listening for Democracy: Recognition, Representation, Reconciliation* (Oxford: Oxford University Press, 2014), 52.

about full and fair deliberation that meaningfully contributes to the democratic nature of our political system, we have to look beyond procedural design to consider the capacities and dispositions of citizens themselves.[10]

Empirical research relating to deliberative mini-publics and other discrete face-to-face deliberative encounters has shown that individual dispositions play an important role in determining the quality of deliberation. Take, for example, James Fishkin's research on deliberative polling, or the practice of assembling a random, representative sample of the public to deliberate and form a collective opinion on a particular topic. In this work, Fishkin has found that quality deliberation relies in large part on the dispositions of participants. While certain features of quality deliberation, namely those relating to inclusion (what Fishkin identifies as information, balance, and diversity) can be ensured through institutional design, "conscientiousness" and "equal consideration" rely on the "*dispositions* of the participants in how they engage in dialogue."[11]

Deliberative democratic theory, however, has tended to shy away from any strong theories of citizenship. Take, for example, the recent systemic turn in democratic deliberation. While Mansbridge originally presented the systems approach to deliberation as a way to put "citizens at the center" of democratic theory, it has mostly failed to do so.[12] Lamenting deliberative democracy's turn away from individual-level analysis in favor of a structural functional one, Owen and Smith have proposed reintroducing certain expectations of democratic citizenship.[13] Specifically, Owen and Smith argue that a democratic system should be judged according to whether it encourages and enables citizens to adopt what they call a "deliberative stance."[14]

Owen and Smith describe the stance as "a particular type of orientation; one that is challenging and fragile."[15] In their view, a deliberative stance involves "a relation to others as equals engaged in the mutual exchange of reasons oriented *as if* to reaching a shared practical judgment."[16] Only when

---

[10] This accords with my speculation in Chapter 2 that uptake, unlike inclusion, defies procedural guarantees.

[11] James S. Fishkin, *When the People Speak: Deliberative Democracy and Public Consultation* (Oxford: Oxford University Press, 2009), 160.

[12] Jane Mansbridge, "Everyday Talk in the Deliberative System," in *Deliberative Politics: Essays on Democracy and Disagreement,* ed. Stephen Macedo (Oxford: Oxford University Press, 1999), 212; Owen and Smith, "Deliberation, Democracy, and the Systemic Turn," 229.

[13] Owen and Smith, "Deliberation, Democracy, and the Systemic Turn," 221.

[14] Ibid., 229.

[15] Ibid.

[16] Ibid., 228.

citizens adopt such a stance can their communication be considered deliberative and, as a result, democracy enhancing. Owen and Smith argue that
to evaluate the deliberative quality of a political system, we should consider
how certain cultural, institutional, economic, and social features "sustain or
undermine the conditions for taking up a deliberative stance."[17]

While Owen and Smith do not fill in the details of what it means to adopt
a deliberative stance, or relate to "others as equals engaged in the mutual exchange of reasons," I would argue that any adequate notion of a deliberative
stance would have to include an orientation toward democratic listening.[18]
In what follows, I describe what such an orientation entails. Specifically,
I show that in order for our listening to move deliberation in the direction
of greater democracy, citizens must listen seriously, attentively, and humbly.
These affective-cognitive dispositional qualities of a democratic listener are
at odds with a listener who is insincere, distracted, or presumptuous.

You'll note that empathy is not included as part of the affective-cognitive
disposition required for performative democratic listening. In light of my
critical treatment of empathy in Chapter 3, this omission is unlikely to come
as a surprise. Indeed, I take the three qualities of the democratic listener to
be in contrast not only to the insincere, distracted, and presumptuous listener but the empathic listener as well. And as I explain further in Chapter 6,
the democratic power of listening can actually be weakened when we listen
either *for* or *with* empathy. Resisting the temptation of empathy, this section
considers an alternative set of affective-cognitive qualities to use in motivating citizens to listen toward democracy.

Democratic listeners approach the listening act with a certain level of *seriousness*. The serious listener recognizes the stakes of the listening act—that
they could disagree with their fellow citizens and thus not get their way—and
listens nonetheless. But the seriousness of a democratic listener is not just
about ensuring she will accept that others have a stake and thus should be
heard. Importantly, this dispositional quality also ensures that the listener
is sufficiently critical and discerning when listening to others' inputs. The
seriousness of a democratic listener keeps her from accepting what others
say uncritically, while also preventing her from assuming the worst of her
interlocutors.

[17] Ibid., 229.
[18] Ibid., 228.

The *attentive* listener gives time and energy to the listening act, trying her best to hear what the other person is saying and to understand what he means by what he says. This attentiveness also carries with it an assumption of intersubjectivity. The attentive listener attends to *others*, recognizing that she can only access a particular person's perspective by listening to him express it. Importantly, even if a listener does not fully understand what she hears, her attentiveness allows for the conversation to continue. As I will explain further in the next chapter, the democratic stakes of the listening act rely on citizens paying attention to others even when understanding is out of reach—for example, even if I do not understand why or how a person believes what she does.

Lastly, a *humble* or modest listener does not assume to know where the conversation will lead. The humble listener has modest and realistic expectations regarding the listening encounter and does not expect that all disagreement will be resolved or perfect understanding achieved. Here, a disposition of humility would entail adopting the principle of hermeneutical charity when listening to and interpreting what others have to say. This humility, coupled with attentiveness, means that citizens are willing to try to listen even while recognizing that it may be hard to reach an agreement. Importantly, democratic listening marked by an *initial* humility allows listeners, once they have heard and considered others' input, to challenge and even reject it. Again, performative democratic listening does not demand that we accept all perspectives and beliefs as having equal worth. Instead, it requires that we recognize others as our democratic peers and therefore as being equally entitled to having and voicing their beliefs.

Listening with seriousness, attentiveness, and humility is crucial in any context where coordination is required across social distance, including across power asymmetries. Listening with this disposition is especially important when one is an "outsider" in regard to a particular topic, policy, or injustice. As I develop further in Chapter 7, this disposition is also essential for citizens with relatively little political power, as it allows them to listen critically and even defensively for what is unsaid or implied.

In sum, listening toward democracy requires the cultivation of a particular disposition, one of seriousness, attentiveness, and humility. Being sensitive to the ontological realities of identity/difference, however, I recognize that understanding (and so uptake) can evade even the most generous listener. In large pluralistic societies, democratic listening occurs in what is necessarily a context of difference and social distance. Whether listeners accurately understand the precise meaning of someone's words is not determined by the listener's disposition alone. Still, listening with the appropriate disposition can help ensure that deliberation will continue even in the absence of agreement, consensus, and understanding. And as I go on to explain in Chapter 6, listening has resources internal to its practice that help guard against the possibility of selective or superficial listening and failed uptake. Moreover, instances of limited uptake that result from our best efforts to listen can still confer democratic benefits on deliberation, as when a listening encounter helps a person understand not the other but instead "networks of privilege and power and one's own location within them."[19]

Building out my preferred listening approach to democratic deliberation, in what follows I consider how diverse citizens might be motivated to occupy the posture necessary to listen toward democracy. The strategies we take for promoting listening toward democracy vary depending on the deliberative context. For example, we can look to a moderator to help facilitate performative democratic listening within deliberative mini-publics or other face-to-face interactions. But when it comes to promoting listening in broad and diffuse public spheres, we would need to look to system-wide cultural and institutional conditions.

To enhance the democratic quality of a deliberative system, we need to encourage citizens to listen to others in their everyday interactions. People must listen to the perspectives of colleagues they encounter through work, family members, and neighbors, as well as to those perspectives they might encounter only in a documentary or a published interview. Here I focus on promoting listening in informal deliberation or everyday talk that occurs in diffuse public spheres, rather than deliberation in formal institutional settings or deliberative mini-publics. As Owen and Smith explain, "the rituals and structures that inculcate and cultivate the deliberative stance are likely to be less resilient" in the everyday than in formal institutional settings.[20]

In what follows, I present an account of the cultural and institutional preconditions needed to sustain listening toward democracy and explain how these conditions differ from those we currently experience in a large pluralistic polity like the United States. I explain how these conditions would

[19] Tanja Dreher, "Listening across Difference: Media and Multiculturalism beyond the Politics of Voice," *Continuum* 23, no. 4 (2009): 451.
[20] Owen and Smith, "Deliberation, Democracy, and the Systemic Turn," 229.

work to foster the affective-cognitive disposition of a democratic listener and thus encourage citizens to consistently be willing to take on that role.

The cultural and institutional preconditions required for a listening approach to democratic deliberation include, first and foremost, a commitment to democratic self-rule. As I explain, such a commitment alerts citizens to the stakes of the listening act, making them more likely to take the encounter seriously. Second, we ought to formally institutionalize the expectation of listening. Such efforts are essential for cultivating attentiveness among citizen listeners. Lastly, to promote the necessary humility of performative democratic listening, citizens need to be educated about the legitimacy of disagreement within large complex democracies. Specifically, citizens must come to both expect and accept a fair amount of conflict and contestation as part of living an active democratic life.

5.2.1 Fostering a Cultural Commitment to Democracy

A listening-centered approach to democratic deliberation relies on citizens sharing a commitment to democratic self-governance. Specifically, citizens need to be educated as to the stakes involved in collective decision making, namely autonomy. Only then will they recognize their fellow citizens as people to whom they should be listening seriously.

It's worrying, then, to encounter evidence suggesting that democracy has gone down in popularity over the last century among American (and European) citizens.[21] In a recent survey, 70 percent of American respondents born in the 1930s answered that it is "essential" to live in a country that is governed democratically. But only 30 percent of respondents born in the 1980s gave that same answer. The authors of an article analyzing these survey results argue that this is a "cohort" effect rather than an "age" effect. As the authors explain, "Not so long ago, young people were much more enthusiastic than older people about democratic values."[22] Now democracy appears less essential, if not less popular, among younger generations. And it does not appear that millennials will necessarily warm toward democracy as they

[21] Roberto Stefan Foa and Yascha Mounk, "The Signs of Deconsolidation," *Journal of Democracy* 28, no. 1 (2017): 5–15.
[22] Roberto Stefan Foa and Yascha Mounk, "The Democratic Disconnect," *Journal of Democracy* 27, no. 3 (2016): 8.

get older. According to the authors, this ambivalence toward democracy has been coupled with growing support for populist strongmen.

Support for democracy, however, is threatened not only by populism but also by a "growing doubt, expressed more in private than in public, about the people's capacity to govern themselves."[23] Indeed, in conversations with my students I perceive a certain level of skepticism toward giving citizens more democratic control. An informal survey at the beginning of my "Democracy and Its Critics" course tends to reveal that most, if not all, of my students favor democratic governance. But when I ask more specific questions about the kind of power they are comfortable giving their fellow citizens and neighbors—whether they should be in control of setting policy priorities, and so forth—many students start to push back. Can we trust average citizens to make the right decisions? Is that kind of popular control really necessary for a democracy? Are we not, after all, a *representative* democracy? In my experience, a person's commitment to "democracy" does not always translate into a commitment to giving one's neighbors a meaningful say in the laws to which they are held. And this disconnect can be traced back to a poor understanding of *what* democracy is and what it has to offer citizens in large, complex societies.

Due to a poor understanding of democracy's nature and value, citizens are often presented with a false choice between populist demagoguery on the one hand and antidemocratic elitism on the other. Going back to Plato's equation of democracy with mob rule, the real meaning and value of democracy are often left behind.

An antipopulist cartoon from the January 9, 2017 *New Yorker* illustrates how the false choice between populism and elitism can degrade support for democracy.[24] The cartoon depicts a man on an airplane. He is standing up, midflight, addressing his fellow passengers. Asking for a show of hands, he says, "These smug pilots have lost touch with regular passengers like us. Who thinks I should fly the plane?" With this caption, the cartoon's creator criticizes the populist idea that any common person can substitute his or her judgment for any expert's judgment and do this in the name of democracy no less. But besides critiquing a populist approach to politics, the cartoon also seems to imply that the average citizen is as unfit to rule himself as the

---

[23] William A. Galston, *Anti-Pluralism: The Populist Threat to Liberal Democracy* (New Haven, CT: Yale University Press, 2018), 117.

[24] Will McPhail, "These smug pilots have lost touch with regular passengers like us . . . ," *New Yorker,* January 9, 2017.

average passenger is to fly a plane. And with this, we see the makings of a false choice between elitism and populism.

Even if we maintain the comparison between politics and piloting and accept the need for experts and representatives in government, it is indeed a serious problem if political elites lose touch with regular citizens. The necessary corrective for this problem from a committed democrat's perspective, however, is not to demand that average citizens—here the passengers— literally steer the ship of state. It is vital, however, that they be given a say in its destination.

All this is to say that we need not only encourage a cultural commitment to democracy, but also civically educate citizens as to the nature of democracy in the first place. I find that many of my students implicitly take an epistemic approach to democracy and are happy to support it to the extent that they expect it to produce epistemically superior outcomes. What they often miss, however, is the *moral* value of democracy. In the classroom, teaching Rousseau's *Social Contract* is usually effective in highlighting the moral reasons for wanting to give citizens a greater say in their own (collective) lives. The question, then, is how we might incorporate this lesson of moral autonomy into broader civic education efforts.

Of course, autonomy or self-rule is a fundamental American ideal. But citizens often see autonomy as a private, not a public issue. In fact, the primary association that Americans make with autonomy and political life is assuming that the latter poses a threat to the former. The assumption is that autonomy, freedom, and liberty are threatened by "the government." Without an understanding of public autonomy, or collective self-rule, citizens struggle to see the essential role that democracy plays in allowing them to lead self-directed lives.

Emphasizing democracy's role in helping citizens achieve autonomy can also be useful in combating populist threats to democracy. By focusing on the importance of autonomy, citizens are reminded that simply imposing the majority's preexisting preferences on their fellow citizens is as unacceptable, from a liberty standpoint, as having elites dictate personal choices. Reminding citizens that they are not guaranteed to have their will reflected in the laws, but rather to have a say, can help curb some of the dangerous populist sentiments currently on the rise.

For a listening-centered approach to democracy to succeed, we need citizens to understand what a commitment to democracy entails. Civic education, therefore, should emphasize democracy's relationship to autonomy or self-authorship. I would recommend having these kinds of conversations as early as elementary school and creating opportunities for democratic self-governance in schools beyond the standard student government representative model. This could be as simple as having students discuss and then decide, as a class, where to go for a field trip or what book to read. These sorts of exercises would alert children to the moral equality of each person's voice, eventually helping them recognize their fellow citizens as democratic peers, even if not epistemic peers.

Ultimately, in order for citizens to want to listen to their fellow citizens, they have to recognize them as having something worthy to say. If we teach democratic norms and the value of democracy, then people may be more likely to understand their fellow citizens as deserving of having their voices heard and their proposals considered. Efforts aimed at reinvigorating democratic education and ideals are essential for fostering the serious disposition required of a democratic listener.

5.2.2 Formalizing the Expectation to Listen

In adopting a listening-centered approach to democratic deliberation, we would also want to find ways to institutionalize and formalize the practice of listening. Note, however, that efforts to institutionalize listening cannot guarantee either the auditory or ilauditory components of the listening act. Nonetheless, these efforts can have an indirect effect on promoting democratic listening insofar as they draw citizens' attention to its importance. If we, as democrats, citizens, or political theorists, want to promote listening, at the very least we have to signal that it is a practice we value. Thus, in addition to fostering a commitment to democracy itself, another way to help bring about the democratic benefits of a listening-centered approach to deliberation would be to formalize the expectation that people listen to one another. By formalizing the expectation of listening, we emphasize the importance of citizens being attentive to their fellow citizens.

Continuing on the theme of education from the previous section, consider the ways that a teacher or professor might formalize expectations of student listening. In any classroom setting where participation is evaluated, we ought to clearly include listening to one's fellow students in that assessment. In all seminar-style courses that I teach, I have students fill out a self-assessment survey halfway through the semester and then again at the end of the term.

In the survey, I ask students to evaluate their class participation on a variety of criteria, indicating how strongly they agree or disagree with a particular statement. In addition to asking students whether they have completed the readings and are consistently on time to class, I also ask them to assess the extent to which they "listen attentively to other members of class." Formalizing and communicating this expectation helps students recognize how integral attentive listening (to their fellow students and not just to their instructor) is to having a productive discussion.

In *Listening for Democracy*, Dobson offers several examples of how we might do a better job emphasizing the importance of listening in formal political relationships. For example, he proposes instituting listening training for members of Congress. After all, if listening is something that we expect of our representatives, then it seems only right that we give them some kind of training on how to do so effectively. As a model, Dobson suggests adopting elements of professional training used for counseling psychology students.[25] Importantly, this professional training would make clear the expectation that representatives will, in fact, listen to their constituents and each other. Formalizing elected officials' role as elected listeners would, at the very least, remind representatives and citizens both that listening to their constituency—rather than to, say, donors or lobbyists—is an essential part of their job, and indeed a relevant standard with which to assess their performance during elections.

Of course, we know that clearly stating expectations does not ensure that others will necessarily meet them. This is as true for representatives as it is with students. Still, communicating the expectation of listening, specifically when and to whom someone should listen, is not trivial. In the classroom setting, students who are trying their best to be active participants often focus on speaking as much as possible. These students are disappointed when their participation grade does not reflect their sincere efforts. By elevating the act of listening to the same status as speaking we could teach well-meaning students what makes a positive contribution to the learning environment. Making this expectation clear on rubrics as well as self- and peer-evaluations reminds instructors to pay attention and to find ways to give credit to those, perhaps quieter students, who contributed to the class discussion through their attentive listening.

[25] Dobson, *Listening for Democracy*, 176; Jongpil Cheon and Michael Grant, "Active Listening: Web-Based Assessment Tool for Communication and Active Listening Skill Development," *TechTrends* 53, no. 6 (2009): 24–34.

Now, while Dobson sees these strategies as actually institutionalizing the listening act itself, I understand these efforts to be directed at cultivating a disposition toward democratic listening. This distinction is important insofar as it reminds us that these efforts do not guarantee that ilauditory listening is taking place, or that listening is actually moving our deliberation or associations in the direction of greater democracy. But while these efforts to institutionalize the expectation of listening are not sufficient, they would help facilitate listening toward democracy by bringing much-needed attention to the importance of listening.

Michael Neblo, Kevin Esterling, and David Lazer's recent book on building a directly representative democracy offers further insight into how we might formalize the expectation that elected representatives will listen to their constituents.[26] The authors' stated aim is to reinvigorate American democracy by creating "effective channels of communication between citizens and their government" so that citizens can participate in democratic politics "*as citizens*, rather than just as consumers."[27]

To that end, Neblo et al. developed a system of online "deliberative town halls."[28] In a series of experiments, participating members of Congress hosted "specially designed, online deliberative town hall meetings with randomly assigned, representative samples of their constituents, discussing some of the most important and controversial issues of the day—immigration policy and terrorist detainee policy."[29] The authors recognize, however, that creating opportunities for representatives to listen to their constituents cannot guarantee they actually will, nor can it ensure that this listening will have any real impact.[30]

As Neblo et al. explain, however, these town halls not only created an opportunity for members of Congress to listen to constituents, but actually incentivized them to do so. As the authors explain, "The elected officials knew that they were interacting with an unusually representative cross-section of their constituents who had been provided background materials on immigration policy."[31] The design of the town halls thus created strong incentives for representatives to listen to the citizens participating in the town hall.

---

[26] Michael A. Neblo, Kevin M. Esterling, and David Lazer, *Politics with the People: Building a Directly Representative Democracy* (Cambridge: Cambridge University Press, 2018).
[27] Ibid., 3.
[28] Ibid.
[29] Ibid., 18.
[30] Ibid., 21.
[31] Ibid., 104.

Creating more opportunities for citizens to interact directly with their representatives can initiate a virtuous cycle where constituents, knowing they will be heard, inform themselves on a particular issue, and representatives, knowing they are engaging with informed citizens, actually listen.

Looking beyond deliberation in empowered spaces like Congress and town hall meetings, we also have to work to formalize the expectation that citizens will listen to each other in their everyday lives. Grassroots efforts to promote political listening among citizens have proliferated since the 2016 election. Dozens of organizations have dedicated themselves to creating opportunities for citizens with divergent perspectives and values to come together in casual, but facilitated, conversations. These organizations are concerned primarily with the apparent growing incivility of political discourse. They include, among others, the Listen First Project, Living Room Conversations, All Sides, Bridge USA, Bridge the Divide, American Listening Project, Civic Dinners, Civil Conversations, and Make America Dinner Again.

By providing opportunities for citizens to listen across difference, these organizations help formalize an expectation of listening to one's fellow citizens. Despite the promise of these efforts, however, many of these groups make claims about the proper functioning of democracy that cut against the arguments that I have made in this book. An investigation of these groups' websites and mission statements reveals assumptions about the power and purpose of listening that are largely untenable. Specifically, these organizations tend to promote listening as the *cure* to our political ailments, which these groups assume are rooted in the presence of conflict. And while these groups refer to the power of listening itself, they are actually championing listening primarily as a means to more understanding, empathy, and even friendship. Listening is a way to "bridge" divides among citizens. In their own words, these organizations that make up the "listen first coalition" are united in "collaboratively promoting and practicing listening first to mend the frayed fabric of America by bridging divides one conversation at a time."[32]

As I explain in the next section, rather than assuming listening will resolve conflict between citizens, we are better off trying to encourage citizens to accept and become more comfortable with political conflict. Listening is

---

[32] "Who We Are: Listen First Coalition," *Listen First Project*, http://www.listenfirstproject.org/listen-first-coalition/, accessed April 25, 2018.

hard, especially listening to those with whom we disagree. Indeed, citizens may even be *less* likely to join in political conversations regarding contested political issues like immigration reform or abortion if they believe that these conversations are supposed to produce some resolution or compromise, or empathy for those with whom they deeply disagree.

Listening to people who express views that conflict with your own is just as likely to uncover deeper divisions as it is to bridge them. As should be evident by now, a listening-centered approach to deliberation does not value listening for its ability to promote consensus, empathy, or even civic friendship. Instead, I contend that the practice of listening is valuable precisely because it can make room for difference and disagreement. But it can only make room for difference if we are careful not to equate political listening with empathy or even understanding. A democratic polity, especially one that is listening across difference, is bound to have misunderstanding and conflict. Citizens should not expect their listening to always *resolve* these conflicts. Therefore, in formalizing listening expectations, we ought to be clear in regard to what we are and are not trying to achieve through listening. As I discuss in the next chapter, if we are to have any hope of achieving uptake in large pluralistic societies, we have to encourage citizens to listen not only in the absence of empathy but also in the absence of understanding.

Finally, remember that for many, listening is not a choice, nor is it done for the benefit of the other. For those with relatively little power, listening attentively is always serious business and not simply a courtesy extended to others. People who are dependent on the caprices of others have no choice but to pay attention to those who wield power over them. As I mentioned in the previous chapter, there is power in *not* having to listen. But for those who have relatively little power, perhaps because of the contingent nature of their job or their citizenship status, listening attentively is a necessity, even an act of self-preservation.

While we would not want to democratize these feelings of powerlessness for the sake of facilitating more attentive listening, the experience of the relatively powerless still has an important lesson for anyone seeking to encourage more listening among citizens. Namely, it shows us the need to both formalize the expectation of listening and highlight the ways in which everyone depends on their fellow citizens for the attainment of public autonomy. Together, these efforts can remind even those with relative power that listening is a moral necessity, if not a material one (for them).

5.2.3 Cultivating a Greater Acceptance of Conflict among Democratic Citizens

For a listening approach to democratic deliberation to work, we need citizens to grow comfortable with or at the very least accept the fact of conflict and disagreement in political life. A goal of civic education, therefore, should be to educate people in the ethos of a democratic citizen engaging in collective decision making, helping them recognize that a good democratic life must admit of some controversy and contestation. Democracies should not aim to eliminate that conflict, but to find ways to handle it democratically.

As Teresa M. Bejan discusses in her 2017 book, *Mere Civility: Disagreement and the Limits of Toleration*, the Latin origin of "civility," *civilitas*, means the "art of good citizenship or government."[33] But the term has come to mean something much more specific, relating to politeness and courtesy. Charges of "incivility" are often wielded like a sword against one's political adversary. And in contemporary American politics, claims of incivility are now found at the center of false equivalencies, as when President Trump accused counterprotestors of the Unite the Right rally in Charlottesville of being uncivil in their vociferous defense of democracy against its Nazi enemies.

In her compelling treatment of civility, Bejan takes a close look at how modern philosophers approached the issue of toleration in a diverse society. While Hobbes, so worried about the damage conflict would do to society, favored the practice of "civil silence," Locke defended an ethic of "mutual civility."[34] For the sake of keeping the peace, Hobbes favored making certain topics off-limits. Civility was achieved by silencing disagreement. For Locke, on the other hand, it was important to cultivate a minimal kind of respect for the views of those with whom you disagree.

As Bejan notes, even today it is often taken for granted that, as Rousseau said, citizens cannot live and make politics with those whom they believe to be damned.[35] Accordingly, political theorists have argued for civic education initiatives aimed at promoting civic friendship and greater empathy.[36] Bejan, however, challenges common conceptions of civility that have long favored

---

[33] Teresa M. Bejan, *Mere Civility: Disagreement and the Limits of Toleration* (Cambridge, MA: Harvard University Press, 2017), 8.

[34] Ibid., 98–106, 129–38.

[35] Rousseau, *The Social Contract and Other Later Political Writings*.

[36] Danielle Allen, *Talking to Strangers: Anxieties of Citizenship since Brown v. Board of Education* (Chicago: University of Chicago Press, 2009); Michael E. Morrell, *Empathy and Democracy: Feeling, Thinking, and Deliberation* (University Park: Pennsylvania State University Press, 2010).

the Lockean view. As she explains, by "*equating* civility with mutual respect, theorists necessarily move the discussion to an aspirational realm of ideal theory in which the kinds of problems civility is needed to address *do not even arise.*"[37] In other words, "respect for others" is not so much an answer to the problem of deep disagreement as it is a denial of that problem in the first place. This Lockean conception of civility offers nothing in the way of guidance when it comes to living with people whose ideas we cannot bring ourselves to respect.

Turning to religious radical Roger Williams, Bejan unearths and defends the idea of "mere civility," which is compatible with disagreeableness as well as a lack of respect for the ideas expressed by others. According to Bejan, "The virtue of mere civility lay in its ability to coexist with and even communicate our contempt for others' most fundamental commitments while continuing the conversation."[38] The only limit that mere civility imposes on citizens is to prevent disagreement from devolving into persecution and violence.

Bejan notes that "while we are stuck in the same boat with people we hate, we had better learn to make the most of it. There is no reason, however, to think that this will make us respect or like each other more. It is usually the opposite."[39] This observation provides important lessons for a listening approach to deliberation. While I argue we ought to listen to our fellow citizens, there is no guarantee that this listening will not strain relationships even further. What we need, therefore, is a conception of citizenship that prepares citizens to deal with this reality.

In her 2019 book, *Disrespectful Democracy: The Psychology of Political Incivility*, Emily Sydnor studies how people's individual conflict orientations shape their political behavior and patterns of media consumption. She finds that people who are conflict-approaching have an inclination "to confront those with whom [they] disagree, to publicly engage in arguments, and to be excited about the prospect of debate."[40] They tend to participate more in politics, even "when it gets nasty."[41] Those who are conflict-avoidant tend to participate less in politics, especially when marked by disagreement or

---

[37] Bejan, *Mere Civility*, 161.
[38] Ibid., 159.
[39] Ibid., 81.
[40] Emily Sydnor, *Disrespectful Democracy: The Psychology of Political Incivility* (New York: Columbia University Press, 2019), 141.
[41] Ibid., 154.

perceived incivility, as they find "disagreement and argument uncomfortable and anxiety inducing."[42]

Given the conflictual nature of contemporary politics, Sydnor argues that "effective democratic citizens could benefit from" developing "a conflict-approaching orientation."[43] Specifically, she advocates for "think[ing] about ways in which the conflict-avoidant could be encouraged to overcome their aversion."[44] To do this, we would want to focus on teaching people specific skills for overcoming anxiety in the face of conflict. Sydnor compares such a strategy with efforts aimed at helping students deal with anxiety in the face of public speaking.[45]

But the first step in helping citizens become more comfortable with disagreement and political conflict is to teach the legitimacy of that conflict in the first place. Civic education initiatives focused on teaching the acceptability of conflict would be in stark contrast to what is typically promoted in both popular culture and political science. As I mentioned, it is often assumed that civic education should aim at promoting civic friendship and greater empathy. But for a listening approach to democratic deliberation to work, people have to be prepared and willing to accept continued misunderstanding and disagreement even after their best efforts to engage. Accepting these more realistic outcomes of listening would encourage citizens to enter deliberation with greater humility in regard to what they expect to accomplish in their conversations with others.

The grassroots efforts to promote listening discussed in the preceding section, however, often miss this point. For example, the Listen First Project defines "listening" as "personally attentive and responsive communication that leads to awareness, understanding, and empathy."[46] According to this view, listening becomes a nearly impossible task. Not only do I have to hear my opponents out, but now I have to empathize with them and even be willing to share a meal with them. Especially in contexts of deep difference and disagreement, these kinds of expectations can deter citizens from listening to

---

[42] Problematically, Sydnor finds that the conflict-avoidant are "more likely to be less educated, members of minority groups, and women." She concludes, therefore, that variation in conflict orientation could exacerbate political inequality. This is even more reason to try to bridge the gap between those who are conflict-avoidant and those who are conflict-approaching. Ibid., 29.

[43] Ibid., 141.

[44] Ibid., 155.

[45] Ibid.

[46] Graham D. Bodie, "What Is Listening?," *Listen First Project*, 2018, http://www.listenfirstproject.org/listen-first-academy/, accessed July 1, 2018.

those with whom they disagree. But these expectations of listeners are not just too high, they are also normatively unnecessary.

Such a conception of listening is especially problematic and even dangerous when applied to contexts of historic injustice. For example, in April 2018 Listen First sponsored an event in Charlottesville, Virginia, intended to support "healing and reconciliation."[47] This initiative was criticized by local community members who interpreted the event as prioritizing "civility over justice."[48] In response to critics, Listen First clarified that "the abject racism and anti-Semitism on display in Charlottesville in August 2017 voids the privilege of a Listen First response."[49] In other words, listening is unnecessary in this case, as "we need not respect or normalize the belief."[50]

I would contend, however, that it is a mistake to equate listening with a sign of respect for or validation of any belief. According to the listening approach I have laid out here, we listen for the purpose of considering what someone says. In listening, we show respect for the equal status of the person speaking, not for that person's ideas. Once we make this distinction between listening and showing respect, it is no longer necessary (or appropriate) to make exceptions in regard to the question of who deserves to be heard. Every person is owed fair consideration and thus listening. Moreover, as Charlottesville community members pointed out, listening is neither the cause of nor the solution to the racism and violence of the Unite the Right rally. Ultimately, I would contend that a politics of listening has more to learn from Charlottesville than Charlottesville has to learn from a politics of listening. In other words, unlike the Listen First group, I do not consider Charlottesville to be a case that demonstrates the need for more listening. Instead, Charlottesville offers an example of contemporary political life that tests our intuitions about the democratic value of listening.

As we see in the case of Charlottesville, the expectation that citizens will listen to and take up the inputs of their fellow citizens creates uneven burdens for those who are personally targeted by a group's hateful or offensive speech. As Bejan carefully notes, her conception of mere civility "shifts much of the

[47] "Listen First Charlottesville," *Listen First Project*, 2018, accessed April 20, 2018 http://www.listenfirstproject.org/listen-first-in-charlottesville-event/.
[48] Solidarity Cville, "Listen First Is Coercive. Some Say 'Listen' When They Actually Mean 'Comply,'" *Medium*, April 19, 2018, https://medium.com/@solidaritycville/now-hear-this-listen-first-is-coercive-787312856114.
[49] "Frequently Asked Questions," *Listen First Project*, accessed July 1, 2018 http://www.listenfirstproject.org/faqs/.
[50] Ibid.

burden of civil conversation from the speaker to the listener, requiring the latter to cultivate, among other things, insensitivity to others' opinions and an identity separate from that immersed in debate."[51] Importantly, however, these burdens are not experienced evenly across all listeners. It's vital, therefore, that we continually search for ways to alleviate the mental and emotional load that a politics of listening imposes more on some than on others. I discuss strategies for doing just this in Chapter 7. At the very least, we should avoid increasing these burdens unnecessarily by insisting that citizen listeners also respond respectfully to what they hear. According to the listening approach defended here, a respectful response is not required in order for citizens to listen toward democracy. It's also important to remind citizens that the listening act need not go on forever.

Assuming, as the Listen First coalition does, that divides will be bridged through listening, implies that the listening act is not successful or even *complete* until common ground has been found. This assumption, however, goes against the claims I have laid out here. Indeed, having listened seriously, attentively, and humbly to a racist speaker, citizens can confidently and democratically put an end to the conversation without finding common ground. And citizens who are more comfortable with unresolved conflict in democratic politics will likely be more empowered to do precisely that.

Therefore, besides encouraging listening, a listening approach to deliberation must also find ways to empower people to respond to and even reject what they hear. When it comes to the issue of listening to undemocratic inputs, we have to constantly be searching for ways to empower people to respond critically and forcefully to inputs they find unacceptable or dangerous. In the case of neo-Nazis in Charlottesville, instead of claiming—as the Listen First group does—that these people can be dismissed out of hand without first being heard, the residents of Charlottesville can legitimately say, "We have listened to you, and we reject you." Charlottesville's residents who were bombarded with the messaging of white supremacists in the weeks and months leading up to the Unite the Right rally could say with full democratic legitimacy that they reject the white supremacists' input.[52] Indeed, what strengthens the counterprotestors' swift rejection of the white supremacists'

[51] Bejan, *Mere Civility*, 162.
[52] Laura Vozzella, "White Nationalist Richard Spencer Leads Torch-Bearing Protesters Defending Lee Statue," *Washington Post*, May 14, 2017.

rhetoric on August 12, 2017, is precisely that it *was* taken up before being rejected.[53]

Moreover, by cultivating a greater acceptance of conflict among democratic citizens, we might also alleviate one of the troubling perauditory effects of listening I discussed in Chapter 4. There, I explained the concern that an expectation of listening might normalize and legitimize the input of racists, misogynists, and other enemies of democracy. If, however, we accept that democratic engagement is not necessarily about finding common ground and bridging divides, then citizens will be less likely to interpret others' listening as a sign of approbation or legitimation for the content of what is spoken.

Ultimately, the goal of listening is not to transform political adversaries into friends who can sit down for a communal meal and a friendly chat. Instead, the much more modest goal is to ensure that all are treated fairly as equal citizens and, thus, are allowed to have a say in the laws to which they are held. Therefore, on a normative level, we do not necessarily have cause for concern if and when listening fails to bridge divides between citizens. Still, practically speaking, people are often uncomfortable when deliberating across disagreement. Thus, for a listening approach to move citizens' interactions toward democracy, listeners have to be prepared for their interactions to uncover profound and incompatible differences.

Fostering a cultural commitment to democracy, institutionalizing formal expectations of listening, and cultivating a greater acceptance of political conflict are essential to a listening-centered approach to deliberation. I have tried to show how these conditions would help encourage citizens to adopt the serious, attentive, and humble disposition of a democratic listener. Moreover, I have reasons to expect that these background conditions of democratic deliberation would also help reduce some of the more troubling perauditory listening outcomes discussed in the previous chapter. There, I pointed out that even when listening is achieved across difference and disagreement, it is still possible for that listening to produce certain undemocratic consequences, including demobilization and the normalization of hate. But a commitment to democracy, formal expectations of listening, and a greater comfort with the presence of political conflict and disagreement could go a long way

[53] Consider, for example, that the decision that the Unite the Right rally was protesting—namely, the decision to remove the Robert E. Lee statue from the newly renamed Emancipation Park—was only made after months of inclusive public deliberation.

toward minimizing those undemocratic perauditory effects, helping to en-sure that listening across difference does not bolster in-group / out-group distinctions or denigrate a commitment to the ideal of inclusion itself.

Still, even if we secure the aforementioned cultural and institutional preconditions for democratic listening, there is no guarantee that citizens will, in fact, adopt the serious, attentive, and humble disposition needed for performative democratic listening. In order to confidently identify better or worse strategies for fostering listening toward democracy, we need a way of knowing if and when the ilauditory listening act occurs. Only then will we know if the interventions discussed above are effective at fostering better lis-tening. To this end, the next section offers empirical markers of democratic listening.

5.3 Empirical Markers of Listening

According to the theory of listening acts presented here, it is only *in* listening to our fellow citizens that we can achieve the deliberative ideal of fair con-sideration. Moreover, the power of listening to move our deliberation in the direction of greater democracy depends on the disposition of the listener, whether she is listening seriously, attentively, and humbly so as to take up what her interlocutor is saying. Therefore, in order to evaluate the demo-cratic quality of a deliberative system, we need some way of accounting for citizen listening. The problem of operationalizing listening, however, is a dif-ficult one. In the discussion that follows, I hope, at the very least, to highlight avenues for future empirical research on the topic.

Existing empirical indicators of listening come primarily from work on "micro deliberation," or the study of discrete, face-to-face deliberative encounters. For example, the "discourse quality index" (DQI), which aims to "operationalize the essentials of the Habermasian logic of communica-tive action" includes a measure for "respect (listening)."[54] The DQI's concep-tion of listening has some important theoretical limitations, which I discuss.

[54] André Bächtiger, Simon Niemeyer, Michael Neblo, Marco R. Steenbergen, and Jürg Steiner, "Disentangling Diversity in Deliberative Democracy: Competing Theories, Their Blind Spots and Complementarities," *Journal of Political Philosophy* 18, no. 1 (2010): 38; Jürg Steiner, *The Foundations of Deliberative Democracy: Empirical Research and Normative Implications* (Cambridge: Cambridge University Press, 2012), 269; Marco R. Steenbergen, André Bächtiger, Markus Spörindli, and Jürg Steiner, "Measuring Political Deliberation: A Discourse Quality Index," *Comparative European Politics* 1, no. 1 (2003): 21–48.

The DQI is also limited, empirically speaking, when it comes to assessing listening on a macro or systems level. We cannot get a complete picture of democratic listening in a deliberative system by adding up the amount of listening occurring in sites of micro-deliberation.[55] How we assess listening in deliberation will vary depending on the context—for example, whether we are evaluating unstructured deliberation in the broad public sphere or more formal deliberation in a mini-public or experimental setting.

When it comes to making a systems-level analysis, listening is best seen as "an emergent property which results from the effective working" of all parts of a political system.[56] In what follows, I begin by considering how to observe and measure listening in micro-deliberative settings before turning to the question of listening in a deliberative system as a whole.

5.3.1 Listening in Micro-Deliberation

There are significant challenges to observing performative democratic listening, even in small-scale face-to-face deliberation. Of course, we can measure the accuracy of someone's aural recall to figure out whether they heard *what* was said. And we can look for reactions and responses to what is heard in order to find out what listening might have *brought about*. Currently, however, we lack an account of how we might measure the act of listening itself. Given the democratic force effected *in* listening, as well as the variable effects of listening (perauditory outcomes), it is imperative that we improve our empirical measures of the ilauditory listening act.

In order for listening to reach the performative threshold needed to move our deliberation in the direction of greater democracy, citizens have to be listening *for* the sake of considering what others have to say. According to my theory of listening acts, the ilauditory force of listening depends on the disposition of the listener, whether he is listening seriously, attentively, and humbly so as to take up what others are saying. Admittedly, knowing for sure whether someone is listening for the "right reasons" is difficult.

While there are certainly behaviors with which a listener can signal his attention or his desire to hear, these are not universally valid.[57] What

---

[55] André Bächtiger and John Parkinson, *Mapping and Measuring Deliberation: Towards a New Deliberative Quality* (Oxford: Oxford University Press, 2019).

[56] Ibid., 45.

[57] Dobson, *Listening for Democracy*, 55.

constitutes "good" listening varies across cultures. For instance, in Spain it is common for a person to demonstrate attentive listening by interrupting and finishing a speaker's sentence, whereas in Scandinavia good listeners are those who pause even after a speaker has finished.[58] This variation in how we judge good listening poses challenges for researchers trying to assess the quality of listening in both informal and formal deliberation.

The transformation of opinion is a similarly unsuitable measure of the performative listening act, which I have shown to be distinct from the perauditory effects of listening. If a citizen has acted in listening to another person's perspective and has carefully considered it, then she would be justified even if she ultimately rejected it without shifting her opinion. Even "silence"—which is readily observable, and perhaps an obvious condition for and correlate of democratic listening—is just as likely to signify a withdrawal from discourse as it is meaningful engagement.[59] Given the distinction I draw between mere auditory listening and the ilauditory listening act, it would also be inappropriate to equate the act of listening with the opportunity to hear. How, then, might we proceed with our task of assessing the seemingly unobservable ilauditory listening act?

Given the observational challenges of measuring listening, it is no surprise that the DQI measures the variable of "respect (listening)" indirectly, by assessing the level of responsiveness in the content of a person's speech.[60] The DQI, which was originally developed for use in formal deliberative settings, including legislatures and other small-scale institutions, offers a scale for third-party researchers to code various indicators of quality deliberation, including "respect (listening)." A listening score is based on whether speakers (1) ignore arguments and questions addressed to them; if they do not ignore speech addressed to them, then the score reflects whether they (2) distort these arguments and questions or (3) engage them "in a correct and undistorted way."[61]

Similarly, in their own study, Mark Button and Jacob Garrett operationalize the act of listening as "a verbal acknowledgment of another participant or another participant's previous comment."[62] Button and Garrett apply this measure to formal deliberation in seven deliberative forums hosted by the

[58] Ibid.

[59] Susan Bickford, The Dissonance of Democracy (Ithaca, NY: Cornell University Press, 1996), 153.

[60] Steiner, The Foundations of Deliberative Democracy, 269.

[61] Ibid.

[62] Mark E. Button and Jacob Garrett, "Impartiality in Political Judgment: Deliberative Not Philosophical," Political Studies 64, no. 15 (2016): 42.

National Issues Forums. For Steiner as well as Button and Garrett, *speech*, and not listening, remains the unit of analysis. For both, listening is measured by observing the level of a person's responsiveness.[63]

A speaker's level of responsiveness is a helpful, though limited, measure for identifying whether performative democratic listening has been achieved. A response, even if only a rebuttal, helps render the intra-psychic and so largely unobservable act of fair consideration observable. As such, responding to others provides a relevant empirical indicator to which one can point in the event that others accuse you either of not listening or not listening with the right attitude.

Responding to what one hears can also be democratically useful. For example, responding to others can help avoid and uncover misunderstanding or failures of understanding that undermine effective uptake. As I discussed in Chapter 2, understanding, and so uptake, can elude even the most generous interlocutors. Interpreting another's meaning is not always straightforward. And a person's meaning can remain obscure even after others make a good-faith effort to hear and understand. Responding to what I hear, even if only to explain exactly *what* I reject when I reject a particular input, gives the speaker an opportunity to clarify and explain.

In the case of neo-Nazi groups, including those who have targeted college campuses in recent years with racist propaganda, continuing the conversation by offering a response would likely make their racist and sexist message that much clearer. A response by a fierce opponent might help to galvanize resistance to the group's antidemocratic politics and to weaken the power of dog-whistle politics. Furthermore, responding to even the most objectionable, undemocratic, or insulting kinds of speech can have strategic value insofar as it helps dispel baseless accusations of not "hearing someone out."

It is also possible that responding to an input I understand to be racist could reveal that the true meaning of the message had been misconstrued. Consider, for example, those white middle-class Americans who hear "Black Lives Matter," and sincerely understand it to have racist meaning. Their reply that "All Lives Matter" gives BLM protestors a chance to explain, as they have done in the past, that while all lives certainly matter, "We're focused on the black ones right now, OK? Because it is very apparent that our judicial system

[63] Pedrini et al. also use responsiveness as a measure for "reciprocity" in deliberation. Seraina Pedrini, André Bächtiger, and Marco R. Steenbergen, "Deliberative Inclusion of Minorities: Patterns of Reciprocity among Linguistic Groups in Switzerland," *European Political Science Review* 5, no. 3 (2013): 483–512.

doesn't know that [they matter]."[64] This response from BLM protestors might help a person recognize the racist implication, even if not intent, of their own "All Lives Matter" reply. Still, according to my interpretation of the deliberative ideal of fair consideration, it is not incumbent upon BLM protestors to make this response.

And so, while responding to others' inputs can be democratically useful and even relevant to our assessment of the ilauditory force of listening, we should be careful not to equate listening with responsiveness. The perauditory outcomes of the listening act, including a person responding to what she hears, are not essential for the ilauditory force of the listening act to take effect. In other words, a listener's response is not what carries the normative weight of listening toward democracy. Therefore, neither the absence nor presence of a response offers a clear indication of whether performative democratic listening or fair consideration has occurred.[65] By assessing listening *outcomes*, the current measures of listening run the risk of overlooking the part of listening, "listening toward democracy," that I contend is essential for enhancing the democratic quality of our deliberation.

What's more, by using responsiveness as a proxy for listening, we would likely underestimate the amount of listening (and so uptake) taking place. This underestimation would be especially glaring in the case of people who are listening more and speaking less in deliberation. Using responsiveness as the sole measure for listening also obscures important variations in listening outcomes. For example, is a lack of a response really indicative of a failure to listen, or does it indicate a withdrawal from conversation as a result of listening to an input that was, say, offensive or combative? These two cases have different implications for democracy, yet extant measures for listening do not allow us to differentiate between them.

Despite the real challenges to operationalizing the act of listening itself, as opposed to listening outcomes, there is one way we might try to peek inside the deliberative black box, so to speak. Building on, rather than replacing, existing accounts of listening as responsiveness, I propose considering the perception of speakers themselves, whether they *feel* as if others have listened to them. This measure would be most easily used in discrete deliberative encounters, including experimental settings and deliberative mini-publics. In these small-scale deliberative contexts, this approach would involve

[64] Ishaan Tharoor, "Black Lives Matter Is a Global Cause," *Washington Post*, July 12, 2016.
[65] Remember, fair consideration can still elude the performative democratic listener insofar as the meaning of a person's input is not understood. For more on this, see Chapter 6.

asking participants to report the extent to which they agree or disagree with the statement that their input was given a fair hearing. As I discuss later in this chapter, this measure could be adapted for the sake of assessing the quality of listening in a deliberative system as a whole.

Crucially, the reason that we—that is, citizens, representatives, and democratic theorists—should care about whether someone feels like they have been heard is not that feeling heard is the goal of deliberation, though it may still be a good in and of itself. Thus, contra Dobson, the goal here is not to democratize the feeling of being heard.[66] Instead, we care about feelings of being heard insofar as they provide a relevant piece of information for assessing the quality of deliberative uptake, and thus the extent to which citizens have had a meaningful say in the laws to which they are held. Of course, these perceptions still only offer an indirect indicator of democratic listening. Importantly, however, they allow us to get an idea of whether listening has occurred without collapsing the categories of listening and responsiveness and without using speech as the unit of analysis.

Here, once again, the parallel between speech acts and listening acts is instructive.[67] According to speech act theory, in judging whether someone has made a real promise to me, I have to judge the speaker's credibility or sincerity.[68] As Bickford notes, "There are no transcendent grounds by which to prove the claims to truth, sincerity, and appropriateness that are implicit in speech. Such claims can only be 'redeemed'—or challenged—through more speech."[69] The same goes for listening acts. In other words, to know whether a listener has really acted *in* listening, the speaker must judge the credibility of the listening act.

---

[66] Performative listening, or the ilauditory listening act, connects the inclusion of actual voices to the uptake or fair consideration by their fellow citizens. It is not enough, then, to merely *feel* like we have been listened to. If the listening is perfunctory and not tied to any real consideration, it cannot confer legitimacy on the process. For example, people feeling like an authoritarian dictator has listened to them should be of little consolation to citizens or subjects. The value of democratic listening is not that it makes people *feel* like their voices have been listened to, but that it helps ensure that their perspectives, grievances, and demands are considered equally when making binding decisions. Black Lives Matter protestors want to be listened to, yes. But they also want to provoke *change* and *action*, which will only come as a result of the careful consideration of their claims. Dobson, *Listening for Democracy*, 174.

[67] According to Srader, it is up to the speaker to assess whether someone has, indeed, acted *in* listening, and therefore performed the ilauditory listening act. He explains that in the case of performative listening, "If the encoder [speaker] is satisfied, there is little left to wish for in the listening encounter." Still, I hesitate to accept Srader's claim that the satisfaction of the speaker is all that is required. I discuss this further in Section 5.3. Srader, "Performative Listening," 99.

[68] Srader, "Performative Listening," 100. See also Bickford, *The Dissonance of Democracy*, 157.

[69] Bickford, *The Dissonance of Democracy*, 158.

Indeed, most of us have a sense of when someone is really paying attention to us versus merely going through the motions or reloading her next argument (or response). As Bickford explains, " 'Being listened to' *is* an experience we have in the world."[70] Anyone who has given a lecture has probably noticed when a student (or two) tunes out. Even when students perform active listening, feigning rapt attention, professors can usually tell whether they are actually paying attention or surfing the internet.

Still, relying on subjective feelings of being heard poses problems for deliberative democratic theory. In the case of an especially skilled dissembler, feigned listening could appear to others as an authentic ilauditory listening act. In this case, a speaker may report feelings of being heard, even if the listening was done strategically and, thus, for the "wrong reasons." Take the case, discussed in Chapter 4, of the manager who asks for feedback from her employees without any intention of considering what they have to say. The manager may simply want to give the impression that she cares about her employees' concerns. The employees who have the opportunity to share their grievances may, as a result, *feel* heard and empowered. And the opportunity to provide input may induce more positive feelings toward the manager. But in this case, the employees' feelings of being heard would reflect their having been deceived, as the manager's listening would have failed to move that relationship toward greater democracy. In other words, perfunctory listening that is not aimed at consideration might induce feelings of being heard without actually conferring legitimacy on the deliberative process.

Still, when it comes to detecting insincere listening, there's no reason to think that a measure based on participants' perceptions would fare worse than existing measures based on the perceptions of outside observers. In the end, we cannot "prove" whether listening has occurred, except through further engagement and ensuing courses of action. For example, it's likely that these employees' feelings of being heard might fade over time if the manager refuses to take corrective action. Alternatively, someone might leave a deliberative encounter with the impression that others were *not* listening but then realize, in the course of further interaction, that they were. Consider the case of a student who feels that her professor did not really listen to her input in discussion. But then, a week later, the student changes her assessment after receiving a follow-up email revealing that the professor had been carefully

[70] Ibid., 157.

considering the question ever since, trying to find a better way to explain a difficult concept.

As I discuss further in the next section, there will of course be times when individuals claim (unpersuasively) that their voices have not been heard when, in fact, their perspectives were heard, considered, and simply rejected. But while imperfect, these perceptions, which are currently left out of assessments of discourse quality, can help capture the democratically relevant construct of "listening toward democracy" and thus help citizens and democratic theorists uncover patterns of failed uptake.

Ultimately, when we act in listening, we enact our intersubjectivity. As such, we should look beyond subjective feelings of being heard for intersubjective standards to use in identifying whether performative democratic listening has occurred. For this reason, rather than replacing the measure of listening through responsiveness, I would recommend adding participant perceptions to the existing DQI.[71]

Therefore, one way to operationalize listening in discrete deliberative encounters would be to use a composite measure. The goal here would be to use multiple observable features of listening to determine whether an unobservable, performative democratic listening episode had occurred. First, we would collect participants' perceptions of being heard. Second, we would consider participants' perceptions of the extent to which *they* listened to others.[72] Specifically, we would ask participants deliberating in experimental settings or small-scale institutions to report the extent to which they agree or disagree with the statement that they listened to and fairly considered the inputs of their interlocutors. Lastly, we would include the current DQI measure of "respect (listening)" used by third-party observers to gauge the level of responsiveness from a would-be listener. These distinct measures

---

[71] As Dryzek points out, the DQI is a comparative measure. In other words, while it can help us determine whether a particular deliberative encounter is more or less deliberative than another, it has a hard time telling us "whether the deliberation in any of the cases analysed is actually good enough by any theoretical standards." Adding to the DQI speakers' perceptions of being heard could help address this issue by building the normative standard of performative democratic listening into the measure. If all citizens reported feelings of being heard, we would have reason to believe the deliberation had reached a normatively relevant threshold to be deemed democratic. John S. Dryzek, "Theory, Evidence, and the Tasks of Deliberation," in *Deliberation, Participation and Democracy: Can the People Govern?*, ed. Shawn W. Rosenberg (New York: Palgrave Macmillan, 2007), 244.

[72] In the case of ongoing interactions, asking participants to report the extent to which they listened to others might have a priming effect, thus actually inducing them to listen better the next time. Testing for this effect would have implications for the strategies of formalizing expectations of listening discussed earlier, including implementing a mandatory listening training for newly elected members of Congress and asking students to assess the quality of their listening in the classroom.

could then be aggregated, with each assigned a particular weight, into a single composite indicator of democratic listening.

Employing this composite measure, it would be interesting to compare self-perceptions of listening to others' perceptions of being heard. In other words, do perceptions of listeners match the perceptions of speakers? Relatedly, is there much variation in people's perceptions of their own listening, or do most people generally self-report being good listeners? And while I would expect feelings of being heard to be driven, in part, by the level of responsiveness from listeners, it is still valuable to distinguish these observations and begin to consider what, if not careful listening, drives variation in responsiveness. Using this composite measure would likely reveal the extent to which these measures co-vary and, interestingly, the conditions under which they do not. Preliminary observations would allow us to adjust and refine these measures going forward to correct for redundancy or endogeneity.

5.3.2 Listening in a Deliberative System

The foregoing was an attempt to think through how we might use the normative standard of uptake, and the performative democratic listening on which it is predicated, to assess the democratic quality of actual face-to-face deliberation. Making a macro-level judgment regarding the quality of listening across an entire deliberative system presents a different set of challenges, which I consider in the remainder of this chapter.

In their 2019 *Mapping and Measuring Deliberation*, André Bächtiger and John Parkinson declare that "the days of developing an overall index of deliberative quality are over."[73] Instead, the empirical study of deliberative democracy is best served by a variety of methods and empirical approaches. The tools developed for micro-deliberation will only go so far in our assessment of listening in the overall deliberative system. Indeed, according to Bächtiger and Parkinson, much theoretical and empirical confusion has come from the application of micro-level measures to the assessment of macro-level deliberation and vice versa.

The crucial point is the need for researchers to choose the *right* tools and methods for the particular level of analysis they are pursuing. In other words,

---

[73] Bächtiger and Parkinson, *Mapping and Measuring Deliberation*, 132–33.

it's not enough to observe and add up discrete instances of listening among citizens or between citizens and their representatives. Uptake is not simply the byproduct of all the moments of listening taking place at various sites within a system.[74] Learning from systemic approaches, we should understand uptake more as "an emergent property which results from the effective working of all [a system's] parts."[75]

To that end, Bächtiger and Parkinson discuss various ways for researchers to assess the quality of a deliberative system as a whole, including the development of "computer-linguistic tools to trace deliberative practices and their interplay in a democratic system."[76] Specifically, we might use these tools to trace the emergence of formal policy proposals and agenda items to see if they originated organically in debate among citizens. Studying the "discursive shifts over time" in debate around a particular topic would allow us to determine the extent to which the arguments for and against proposals can be traced back to the perspectives and positions expressed in broad and unstructured public spheres.[77] Bächtiger and Parkinson also discuss the possibility of studying "official narratives of decisions," found in white papers, speeches, and so on and comparing them to citizens' discourses on social media in an effort to reveal continuities and discontinuities between them.[78]

These methods offer promising ways for empirical researchers to study "deliberative transmission." Recalling Habermas's two-track model of deliberative democracy, transmission is what allows the two tracks to talk to each other. It is through transmission, arguably a kind of system-wide listening, that the broad currents of public communication connect up with formal decision-making institutions. But when it comes to assessing the democratic quality of a deliberative system, we need to know more than *that* the transmission occurred. We also have to account for the discursive quality of the informal and everyday conversations occurring in the diffuse public spheres of the first track.

Here we see, once again, the empirical value of paying attention to citizens' perceptions of being heard. These perceptions of being heard can shed light on the quality of listening not only in discrete deliberative encounters but also

[74] Dryzek makes this point in regards to what he calls "deliberative inclusion." John S. Dryzek, "The Forum, the System, and the Polity: Three Varieties of Democratic Theory," *Political Theory* 45, no. 5 (2017): 620.

[75] Bächtiger and Parkinson, *Mapping and Measuring Deliberation*, 45.

[76] Ibid., 132–33.

[77] Ibid., 138.

[78] Ibid., 137–38.

in diffuse and informal deliberation that is neither structured nor decision-oriented. Feelings of being heard can be a useful indicator of listening and uptake on a systems level precisely because these feelings are themselves a reflection of a variety of factors and interactions across time and space. As such, when it comes to assessing system-wide listening and the conditions for uptake in broad and diffuse public spheres, we should pay attention to groups and citizens who claim to have been ignored or otherwise not given a fair hearing. To this end, researchers conducting a broad survey of the general population might include a question asking citizens to report the extent to which they feel "heard" by their fellow citizens and representatives when it comes to particular issues. Additionally, researchers could study discourses and practices of exclusion and look out for *repeated* complaints of "not being heard" that are expressed by individuals and groups.[79]

Importantly, when people are asked to report the extent to which their perspectives and preferences on a particular issue have been considered by their fellow citizens and representatives, their response will rarely be a function of a single conversation, and may not even arise from their own personal experiences. Instead, individuals' general feelings of being heard (or ignored) are likely rooted in numerous observations and interactions, some of which they did not even participate in directly, as well as the outcomes of those interactions.[80] Consider, for example, how a sexual assault survivor might feel in the wake of US Supreme Court Justice Brett Kavanaugh's Senate confirmation hearing in 2018. This person might report feelings of not being heard as a result of the Senate's hurried treatment of the credible allegations of sexual assault brought against Kavanaugh. These feelings would represent a valid complaint against the democratic system as a whole, insofar as they reveal the system's failure to fairly consider Christine Blasey Ford's testimony.

---

[79] See Terri Elliott, "Making Strange What Had Appeared Familiar," *The Monist* 77, no. 4 (1994): 431.

[80] This approach to measuring listening on a system-wide scale would suggest that individuals' perspectives could be taken up in a deliberative system without their actually voicing them in deliberation. Does this understanding of systems-level listening undermine the communicative core of deliberative democratic theory like the empathy approach I criticized in Chapter 3? If imaginative perspective-taking is democratically problematic because it misses the actual communicative element of deliberation, wouldn't this operationalization of democratic listening be guilty of a similar oversight? I argue that we can avoid the antideliberative tendencies of the empathy approach so long as we ensure that individuals always judge *for themselves* whether or not their interests or perspectives map on to those already being discussed in public spheres. In other words, while it's acceptable for people to refrain from *speaking* in deliberation because they feel like their own perspectives on a particular issue were authentically captured by others, it's unacceptable for people to refrain from *listening* in deliberation because they feel like they have adequately captured the would-be speaker's perspective.

They might also reveal problems with the polity's treatment of allegations of sexual assault and gender equality more generally. The crucial point is that by tracking citizens' feelings of being heard or ignored, we gain insight into the "complex interactions of many practices and institutions" within the broader deliberative system.[81]

Importantly, participant perceptions will not always be reliable, especially under conditions of "gross ideological domination."[82] In order to generate more reliable reports of being heard or ignored, we would want to work on educating citizens "in the everyday practices of deliberation," so that they can "spot and accept" the ways in which their inputs are transformed, improved, and adapted in the process of being taken up.[83]

Still, citizens' claims of not being heard can provide important information regarding the democratic functioning of a deliberative system even if we sometimes have reasons to doubt them. Such claims can uncover not only instances of failed listening but can also reveal ideological rigidity or a lack of commitment to democracy on the part of the complainants themselves. This may be evident, for example, when a person with relative privilege interprets advances in equality to be evidence of his own oppression.

As I noted in Chapter 2, when it comes to knowing whether uptake has occurred, there are no unambiguous behaviors or signs to which we can point. Instead, evidence of uptake emerges over time through the ongoing deliberative process. The same goes for listening, on which deliberative uptake is predicated.

Despite the difficulty we have assessing the level of listening and uptake on a systems level, framing claims of injustice according to the ideal of uptake can still have a direct democratizing effect on discourse insofar as it reminds us what we owe and are owed according to the expectations of democratic citizenship. While citizens are owed more than inclusion, uptake does not guarantee you will "get your way." The ideal of uptake and a politics of listening it endorses reminds citizens that the principles of democracy do not guarantee influence, nor the right to dictate political outcomes. Indeed, even when an individual or group convincingly highlights failures of uptake, it does not follow that their preferences and demands are themselves worthy of implementation. Rather, it means that they are worthy of our consideration.

---

[81] Bächtiger and Parkinson, *Mapping and Measuring Deliberation*, 1.

[82] André Bächtiger, Simon Niemeyer, Michael Neblo, Marco R. Steenbergen, and Jürg Steiner, "Disentangling Diversity in Deliberative Democracy: Competing Theories, Their Blind Spots and Complementarities," *Journal of Political Philosophy* 18, no. 1 (2010): 57.

[83] Bächtiger and Parkinson, *Mapping and Measuring Deliberation*, 131.

5.4 Conclusion

When we listen to our fellow citizens' input for the sake of taking it into consideration, we move our collective decision-making process in the direction of greater democracy. But while listening has the power to move us toward democracy, it will not always bring us closer to consensus or friendship. And that is okay. Indeed, according to the deliberative conception of democracy, feelings of empathy and friendship are not essential for democratic self-governance. We turn to deliberation for the purpose of achieving democracy in large pluralistic societies like the United States precisely when these feelings are out of reach. Crucially, then, the democratic value of listening does not come from its ability to bridge divides or promote empathy. Instead, by decentering these goals, a listening-centered approach to deliberation makes room for difference and disagreement in democracy.

Still, listening to those with whom we disagree, especially people who support policies that threaten our values or our ability to survive and thrive, is not always easy. Thus, the question remains: Can listening succeed where inclusion and empathy failed—in realizing meaningfully democratic deliberation in a world where individuals are constituted by deep differences? In the next chapter, I answer yes.

In what follows, I address the challenges of employing a listening-centered approach in contexts of difference and disagreement. The first challenge that a listening approach to deliberation faces in practice involves getting citizens to listen for the sake of considering what they hear, even amid disagreement and even when a decision with material consequences must be made. The second challenge involves how to proceed when performative democratic listening fails to achieve uptake, in other words, when even those citizens who listened toward democracy struggle to fairly consider what they hear.

In addressing these concerns, I articulate the strengths of a democratic listening approach to deliberation given the dynamics of identity/difference that constitute citizens' relationships in large pluralistic societies. As I explain, the advantage of a listening approach to deliberation is not that it can resolve the challenge of difference, but that it takes difference seriously. Moreover, I show how centering deliberation on the listening act not only makes room for difference in deliberation, but can actually put difference to work toward productive ends.

6
Listening for Difference in Democracy

In the foregoing, I have argued in favor of adopting what I call a "listening approach" to democratic deliberation. In adopting such an approach, our efforts to improve and evaluate the democratic quality of deliberation would center on the act of listening. The previous chapter identified the cultural and institutional innovations necessary for a listening-centered approach to deliberation to succeed. Specifically, I argued that taking a listening-centered approach would mean encouraging a more robust and informed commitment to democracy among citizens. Also, we should work to formalize expectations of listening among representatives and citizens. Lastly, we would want to support efforts aimed at cultivating a greater comfort with conflict and disagreement in political life. These cultural and institutional interventions would help support the affective-cognitive disposition of a democratic listener who approaches deliberative encounters seriously, attentively, and humbly. This disposition allows citizens to *listen toward democracy*.

Importantly, however, there is no guarantee that these efforts will necessarily translate into performative democratic listening. Furthermore, we have to entertain the possibility that uptake can fail even when our listening meets the threshold of performative democratic listening. As such, this chapter considers how the listening approach might fare in practice, specifically when citizens are listening to people with whom they disagree or to those whom they struggle to even understand. Can a listening approach to deliberation succeed in contexts of deep difference? If so, what would that success look like?

Centering deliberation on the act of listening is supposed to help us reclaim the democratic prospects of deliberation across difference. A listening approach to deliberation alleviates the pressure to force a consensus or resolution. Difference, disagreement, and even enmity are the conditions of inclusive deliberation in late-modern pluralistic democracies. Given those conditions, orienting ourselves toward listening is easier and less exclusionary than orienting ourselves toward agreement or even understanding.[1] But despite

---

[1] Susan Bickford, *The Dissonance of Democracy* (Ithaca, NY: Cornell University Press, 1996), 19.

Beyond Empathy and Inclusion. Mary F. Scudder, Oxford University Press (2020). © Oxford University Press.
DOI: 10.1093/oso/9780197535455.001.0001.

being a more attainable goal than, say, consensus, the listening approach to deliberation still faces important challenges in contexts of deep pluralism.[2] As Bickford explains, it takes courage to "make politics, not war, with [one's] enemies."[3]

In what follows, I show that the listening approach to democratic deliberation need not be undone by differences in the same way that I have argued the empathy approach is. As I explained in Chapter 3, empathy is out of reach—due to either an unwillingness to empathize or an inability to imagine other perspectives—precisely when differences, and so the threat of failed uptake, are greatest. In contrast to the empathy approach, a listening approach is well suited to contexts of difference and disagreement. By decentering even the seemingly desirable perauditory outcomes of agreement and understanding, performative democratic listening makes room for difference and disagreement in deliberation. But a listening approach not only makes deliberation more accommodating of difference, it can actually put difference to work toward productive ends. Specifically, I find that the listening approach to deliberation helps us achieve democracy in pluralistic polities not by overcoming obstacles to deliberation across difference but by drawing citizens' attention to the process of doing justice to those challenges.

This chapter begins with a discussion of the challenges of relying on listening for the sake of achieving uptake in political contexts of difference and disagreement (6.1). Here, I take seriously the possible objection that practices of listening are just as limited as practices of empathy when it comes to achieving fair consideration across difference. Responding to this challenge, however, I show that centering deliberation on the listening act not only makes room for difference in deliberation, essentially making it more inclusive, but actually allows those differences to aid in our attainment of uptake. Building on the work of Iris Young, I identify a heretofore unrecognized way that difference serves democracy, namely by highlighting the perspectival and incomplete nature of our own understanding, showing us that we have something to learn and so alerting us to the need to listen carefully to our fellow citizens (6.2).

[2] As I explained in Chapter 4, Bickford's emphasis on listening should not be seen as a departure from Habermas or deliberative democratic theory in general. Consensus achieved through means other than communication (which necessarily requires listening) would fail to carry democratic weight even according to Habermas's model of deliberative democratic theory.

[3] Bickford, *The Dissonance of Democracy*, 69.

I go on to argue that the prospects for democratic listening and fair consideration are improved when those deliberating recognize the inherent limits of their ability to understand each other (**6.3**). Here I also address the seeming contradiction in the claim that citizens' commitment to deliberation can be deepened by their recognizing its inherent limits. Specifically, I reinterpret Habermas's notion of the coordinating power of language in such a way that allows us to foreground the limits of mutual understanding and thus capture the democratic benefits of recognizing those limits.[4]

Through this discussion, I show that difference need not spell doom for a listening approach to deliberation. In fact, deliberative democrats would do well to design practices of listening that draw attention to differences, rather than focusing monologically on drawing out real or imagined commonalities between citizens (**6.4**). While the former would remind citizens of their underlying relation of identity and difference, the latter would discount it. As I show, when citizens encounter and grapple with differences in the listening act, they are not only alerted to challenges of deliberation but also to the need for greater attentiveness and careful consideration in light of those challenges. By encountering difference and resisting the urge to collapse it through appeals to empathy, the initial auditory listening act not only allows citizens to hear what someone says, but can also encourage them to carefully consider it. I conclude by explaining that the advantage of the listening approach to deliberation is not that it can overcome the challenges of deliberation across difference, but that it takes those challenges seriously in the first place (**6.5**).

6.1 Challenges to Listening across Difference

While listening may be essential to achieving full and fair deliberation, it is not yet clear whether a listening approach to deliberation can help address the issue of failed uptake in contexts of deep difference. When it comes to making a decision that will have an impact on our own lives, is it realistic to expect citizens to listen to people who present facts or arguments that are

---

[4] By the limits of "mutual understanding," I mean the limits to both our ability to reach an understanding, in the sense of coming to an agreement, as well as our ability to comprehend others, to understand their perspectives, where they are coming from, and the precise claims they are trying to make. Jürgen Habermas, *The Theory of Communicative Action*, Vol. 1 (Boston: Beacon Press, 1984), 287; Jürgen Habermas, *Between Facts and Norms: Contributions to a Discourse Theory of Law and Democracy* (Cambridge, MA: MIT Press, 1996), 18.

inconvenient or contradict their priorities or preferred policies? As Plato's Socrates in the *Republic* is reminded, if someone does not want to risk being persuaded by another's argument, the easiest thing to do is not listen.[5] Even when citizens do listen, they may be doing so for purely strategic reasons. Alternatively, they might pretend to listen, or listen without an open mind, with no intention of actually considering what they hear. What makes us think citizens will do the hard work of listening toward democracy? In this section, I consider the challenges of listening across difference.

First, the expectation that citizens will listen to one another is more burdensome when listening amounts to more than simply letting others speak in one's presence. Listening toward democracy, wherein we listen for the sake of considering the perspective of another—perhaps our political opponent—is much more difficult to achieve than mere auditory listening. Again, there are stakes to democratic listening. And recognizing or accepting those stakes makes performative democratic listening at once more meaningful and potentially more elusive.

Second, unlike the auditory element of the democratic listening act, which can be supported by formal procedures, the ilauditory force of democratic listening defies procedural guarantees. As I explained in Chapter 5, listening toward democracy depends on the disposition of the citizen listener herself.[6] Thus, providing opportunities for groups and individuals to speak in the presence of their fellow citizens is not enough. And while we can take certain interventions to foster the disposition needed for citizens to listen toward democracy, these interventions will not always ensure uptake.

Even when listening with the right disposition, citizens will not always understand what the other person is saying. Listening in large pluralistic societies takes place always already in a context of distance and difference. Understanding can evade even the most generous listener. What happens, then, if we listen seriously, attentively, and humbly for the sake of taking into consideration what others say, but we still do not understand another person's meaning? How can a listening-centered approach help us achieve uptake and thus meaningfully democratic deliberation if what we hear turns

---

[5] Plato, "Republic," in *The Collected Dialogues of Plato including the Letters*, ed. Edith Hamilton and Huntington Cairns (Princeton, NJ: Princeton University Press, 1969), 1.327c.

[6] And so here, I depart from Dobson's assessment that the advantage of a listening approach to deliberation is that "there are ways of improving listening" through "rules and formalities." Without recourse to listening act theory, Dobson misses the limitations of rules and formalities in institutionalizing listening, especially the ilauditory listening act. Andrew Dobson, *Listening for Democracy: Recognition, Representation, Reconciliation* (Oxford: Oxford University Press, 2014), 175.

out to be ambiguous or incomprehensible? What are we listening *for* if not understanding? How can listening in the absence of understanding move us toward fair consideration?

If it turns out that practices of listening are as limited by difference and social distance as practices of empathy, then at the very least we are left with the same problem with which we ended Chapter 2. Chapters 3, 4, and 5 provided a better understanding of the conditions of fair consideration, namely its reliance on listening rather than imagination. But if citizens struggle to adopt the disposition needed to listen toward democracy, or if their best efforts at listening still result in failed uptake, then it would seem that we are no closer to our goal of a democratically functioning deliberative system.

Here I consider whether the listening approach to deliberation can succeed where the empathy approach failed, namely, in helping us achieve meaningfully democratic deliberation in a world where individuals are constituted by deep differences. In what follows, I answer yes. Specifically, I contend that even in the absence of understanding and in the case of failed uptake, the democratic prospects of deliberation are still good so long as people remain committed to continuing the conversation. As I explained in Chapter 2, some level of misunderstanding may be inevitable in contexts of deep pluralism and can result from even our best efforts to understand others. But when these misunderstandings result from actual engagement with others as opposed to imagined perspective taking, they are more likely to be identified and diagnosed. Moreover, as I show, a lasting commitment to deliberation can come precisely from citizens taking a more realistic view of what communication can achieve—in other words, from citizens accepting the limits to their ability to understand one another.

And so, while the listening approach is not immune to the problems of misunderstanding that plagued the empathy approach, I argue that it need not be stymied by these misunderstandings. Indeed, as I show, recognizing the limits of mutual understanding can actually boost the prospects of achieving fair consideration insofar as it reminds citizens of the essential need for continued engagement. Ultimately, failures of understanding that result from communicative engagement may precipitate *more* engagement.

Importantly, I do not expect the listening approach will resolve all of the problems that make deliberation across difference difficult. It cannot. Instead, the advantage of the listening approach, especially when compared to the empathy approach, is that it takes the challenges of democratic deliberation seriously. Thus, when it comes to meeting the burdens of democratic citizenship, the listening approach that I propose does not try to minimize those burdens, but vivifies them. An awareness of the limits of our ability to fully understand our fellow citizens' perspectives and affective inputs sustains rather than degrades the serious, attentive, and humble disposition needed for democratic listening.

Centering deliberation on the listening act does more than simply offer some interpretation of how deliberative democracy might be compatible with deep differences. Crucially, the listening approach to democratic deliberation allows deliberative democratic theory to glean important lessons from acknowledging the ontological relationship of citizens divided and constituted by deep differences.

6.2 Difference and Democracy

In arguing that difference should be seen as a resource in a listening-centered approach to democratic deliberation, I follow others, especially Iris Young, who argued that the inclusion of difference is not just democratically necessary, but democratically useful as well.[7] In viewing difference as a resource for democracy, Young departed from a long tradition of democratic theory that understood difference to be an obstacle to democratic governance. Consider, for example, that for a democrat à la Rousseau, difference must always be annihilated for the sake of democracy. According to him, a divided citizenry will never discern the general will and therefore cannot achieve democracy and the autonomy it promises. In the name of freedom, factions, diversity, and dissent must be squashed, by force if necessary. Difference poses a fundamental challenge to a Rousseauian model of democracy—as he notes, "Everything which destroys social unity is worthless."[8]

But as I argued in Chapter 2, the same is not true for a Habermasian model of deliberative democracy. Habermas turns to deliberation, in the form of actual communication, when the pursuit of a Rousseauian general will would be too costly, for example, in the context of a large pluralistic society. The appeal of deliberation for someone like Habermas is precisely its ability to

---

[7] Iris Marion Young, "Difference as a Resource for Democratic Communication," in *Deliberative Democracy: Essays on Reason and Politics*, ed. James Bohman and William Rehg (Cambridge, MA: MIT Press, 1997), 383–406; Iris Marion Young, *Inclusion and Democracy* (Oxford: Oxford University Press, 2000).

[8] Jean-Jacques Rousseau, *The Social Contract and Other Later Political Writings*, ed. Victor Gourevitch (Cambridge: Cambridge University Press, 1997), 147.

help citizens achieve democratic self-authorship in the presence of disagreement and without relying on underlying commonalities. Habermas's theory
of democratic deliberation is, at the very least, aware of the challenges of democracy amid difference.

Agonistic democrat Chantal Mouffe, however, has criticized Habermas
and his fellow deliberative democrats for approaching difference as a problem
in need of solving in the first place. According to Mouffe, while "Habermas
and his followers do not deny that there will be obstacles to the realization of
the ideal discourse . . . these obstacles are conceived as empirical ones."[9] In
other words, Habermas rejects the possibility, but not the desirability, of us
somehow "leav[ing] aside all of our particular interests in order to coincide
with our universal rational self."[10]

By approaching our differences as mere empirical fact, deliberativists
leave open the possibility that we should, if we could, try to overcome them.
And, indeed, for some deliberative democrats, the answer to the problem
of deliberating across differences is, if not to eliminate differences, then to
overcome or sideline them. Take, for example, the limits of public reason
that John Rawls proposes in his endorsement of democratic deliberation.[11]
These limits of public reason are meant to ensure that differences in citizens'
comprehensive doctrines do not undermine the legitimacy of collective
decisions.[12] Perhaps paradoxically, Rawls maintains that in order to accommodate and respect the diversity of comprehensive doctrines among citizens,
these differences must be excluded from deliberation in the public political
forum.[13] Such attempts to resolve the "problem" of difference—exemplified
not only by John Rawls's limits of public reason, but also in recent appeals to
empathy—come at the expense of democracy itself.

Indeed, Mouffe argues that we cannot overcome differences without doing
damage to ourselves. Difference is constitutive of politics and therefore unavoidable. Mouffe goes even further in her defense of difference, arguing
that we ought to recognize not only the fact but the *value* of difference in
democracy.[14]

---

[9] Chantal Mouffe, "Deliberative Democracy or Agonistic Pluralism?," *Social Research* 66, no. 3 (1999): 748.
[10] Ibid.
[11] John Rawls, *Political Liberalism* (New York: Columbia University Press, 2005), 216.
[12] Ibid.
[13] Ibid.
[14] Chantal Mouffe, "Democracy, Power, and the 'Political,'" in *Democracy and Difference*, ed. Seyla Benhabib (Princeton, NJ: Princeton University Press, 1996), 246.

But while differences have political value according to an agonist like Mouffe, in her view they still ultimately pose an insurmountable problem for deliberation. In fact, Mouffe maintains that it is only by rejecting the (unattainable) goal of a legitimate, power-neutral agreement through inclusive deliberation that we preserve democracy.[15] According to this reading of difference and democracy, difference presents a devastating challenge to deliberative decision making. For Mouffe, deliberation is wholly incompatible with the ontological reality of deep constitutive differences between citizens. By pursuing inclusive, democratic, and legitimate decisions, we risk the same apolitical and exclusionary outcomes of the Rawlsian approach Mouffe rejects. Democracy requires that claims of legitimate agreement always be deferred in the presence of inevitable difference and resulting disagreements. Again, it is the very rejection of the ideal of deliberative argumentation and consensus that "constitutes an important guarantee that the dynamics of the democratic process will be kept alive."[16]

Ultimately, Mouffe concludes that difference and deliberation are incompatible. And so, in my reading, Mouffe may have more in common with someone like Rawls than she allows. For both Mouffe and Rawls, difference and deliberation cannot coexist. Democracy is not big enough for the both of them. Despite their opposite valuations, both Rawls and Mouffe see deliberation and difference as zero sum. But while Rawls cuts off difference for the sake of deliberation, Mouffe cuts off deliberation for the sake of difference.

In contrast, I argue that the challenge of democracy is finding a way to balance a politics of "consensualism" on the one hand with a politics of agonism on the other.[17] As agonist Bonnie Honig argues, democratic politics occurs precisely in the space created by the tension between what she calls "a politics of settlement and a politics of unsettlement."[18] This space is closed off when we try to resolve that tension through appeals to empathy. It is also endangered by the impulse to view politics as simply "the unrelenting struggle of friends and enemies."[19]

[15] Ibid., 255.

[16] Ibid.

[17] Stephen K. White, "Varieties of Agonism" in critical exchange "The 'Agonistic Turn': *Political Theory and the Displacement of Politics* in New Contexts," *Contemporary Political Theory* 18, no. 4 (2019): 656.

[18] Bonnie Honig, *Political Theory and the Displacement of Politics* (Ithaca, NY: Cornell University Press, 1993), 14.

[19] White, "Varieties of Agonism," 656.

Forging an alternative path to both Rawls and Mouffe, Young argues that a strong communicative democracy "needs to draw on social group differentiation, especially the experience derived from structural differentiation, as a resource."[20] Here, she is speaking about difference in terms of "social differences of gender, race, cultural age, ability, and so on."[21] Young recognizes that the inclusion of such difference will not necessarily make deliberation easier or more likely to result in agreement.[22] This fact, however, does not present a problem in her mind, as she would reject easily achieved consensus as the goal of deliberation. Young, in other words, affirms a view of justice that accepts the validity of deep contestation.

In interpreting difference as a resource in democratic deliberation, Young allows for the possibility of democratically legitimate instances of deep contestation, while still rejecting Mouffe's view of politics as contestation all the way down. From Young, we learn that accepting the dynamics of identity/difference, even at an ontological level, need not spell doom for reaching democratically meaningful outcomes through deliberation. Our differences, though partially constitutive of our identities and experiences, do not fully dictate our moral-political orientation, nor do they necessarily derail deliberation's democratic aspirations. Instead, a dynamic of identity/difference is seen as setting certain important background constraints on that deliberation. Importantly, Young shows us that we can admit the existence of deep differences and still turn to deliberation for the purpose of achieving democracy.

But Young's defense of difference in deliberation goes beyond this claim that it need not spell doom for deliberation's democratic ends. According to Young, the inclusion of differences in perspective serves two essential functions in deliberation. "First, it motivates participants in political debate to transform their claims from mere expressions of self-regarding interest to appeals to justice."[23] Through encounters with those who are different from oneself, a citizen's focus can shift from self-interest to the democratic project of just decision making.

---

[20] Young, *Inclusion and Democracy*, 83. Young's argument regarding the ways in which group differences serve as a resource in deliberation relies on the "concept of *structural*, as distinct from cultural group. While they are often built upon and intersect with cultural differences, the social relations constituting gender, race, class, sexuality, and ability are best understood as structural." Ibid., 92.

[21] Ibid., 82.

[22] Ibid., 119.

[23] Ibid., 115.

Second, differences in perspective improve the epistemic value of deliberative decisions. Including difference in deliberation increases the information available to citizens. We get a more complete view of our shared world when we piece together the diverse social perspectives available in our pluralistic polity.[24] Young argues, "Not only does the explicit inclusion of different social groups in democratic discussion and decision-making increase the likelihood of promoting justice because the interests of all are taken into account. It also increases that likelihood by increasing the store of social knowledge available to participants."[25] As Young explains, "Pooling the situated knowledge of all social positions can produce" an "objective understanding of the society."[26] Note that this objective understanding of the world is not achieved by bracketing, excluding, or even imagining these differences. Instead, the communication of differences helps correct biases that occur when we consider only one point of view or perspective.[27]

Importantly, however, expanding the pool of knowledge available to citizens is only valuable if those citizens actually drink of its waters. Moreover, what makes a person's perspective so valuable to public discourse according to Young—namely that it adds something *new* and *different* to our collective knowledge—is precisely what makes it difficult for others to hear and consider. While these concerns are not unanswerable from Young's perspective, they go largely unaddressed. Thus, much like her related discussion of inclusion, Young's account of difference as a resource in deliberation is weakened by an inattention to the question of uptake or fair consideration.[28] Building on Young's work, I consider another way that difference might serve as a resource in democratic deliberation: by empowering listening.[29]

Like Young, I aim to put the tension between difference and deliberation to work, but this time I put it to work for the sake of democratizing uptake and not just input. While Young focuses on how difference operates on citizens

---

[24] Ibid.
[25] Ibid., 83.
[26] Ibid., 117.
[27] Ibid., 83.
[28] See Chapter 2, this volume.
[29] In identifying difference as a resource, however, I do not mean to suggest that differences can motivate a commitment to democracy in the first place. Thus, my appeal to difference as a resource is analogous to Morrell's and Krause's appeal to empathy as a resource. Like them, I am assuming a commitment to democracy in a world structured by the dynamics of identity/difference. Thus, similar to their claims regarding empathy, encounters with difference will not necessarily motivate citizens to *want* democracy. Rather difference serves as a resource by helping citizens committed to democracy actually achieve it. See Chapter 5 in this volume for a discussion of the cultural and institutional preconditions of a listening approach to democratic deliberation.

in their role as speakers, here I extend her analysis to consider how difference can serve as a resource for citizens in their role as listeners. Specifically,
I argue that in addition to expanding the pool of knowledge available to citizens and encouraging them to reframe their demands and preferences in
terms of justice rather than self-interest, difference also serves as a resource
in promoting the performative democratic listening that is essential for fair
consideration. Recognizing that others have a unique perspective that is not
captured by your own, even through your attempts to imaginatively broaden
your perspective, shows you the value and, yes, the risk of listening. By
foregrounding the dynamics of identity/difference and thus the limits of mutual understanding, encounters with difference remind citizens of the hard
work of democratic decision making. As I will discuss here, this attention
to the difficulty of deliberating across difference provides the listening approach to deliberation a strategic edge over the empathy approach discussed
in Chapter 3.

In her essay "Difference as a Resource for Democratic Communication,"
published three years before *Inclusion and Democracy,* Young actually lists
a third way that difference serves as a resource in deliberation, this time
gesturing toward citizens in their role as listeners. There, Young writes that
"confrontation with different perspectives, interests, and cultural meanings
teaches individuals the partiality of their own, and reveals to them their
own experience as perspectival."[30] Young continues to explain that such a
revelation "exposes their partiality and relative blindness" and "where such
exposure does not lead them to shut down dialogue and attempt to force
their preferences on policy, it can lead to a better understanding of the
requirements of justice."[31]

Importantly, as Young notes, we cannot simply *assume* that exposure to
one's own partiality and limited understanding will lead to more dialogue as
opposed to precipitating the end of dialogue. In fact, we should not expect a
single response from all citizens who encounter difference and disagreement
or experience misunderstandings when listening to others. Still, in what
follows, I offer reasons for being optimistic that, under the right conditions,

[30] While this language of the perspectival nature of our own views still appears in *Inclusion and
Democracy,* Young folds it into her discussion of the expanding the pool of social knowledge available to citizens (see pp. 115–16). As I show, however, this benefit is probably best understood as a
distinct outcome of encounters with difference. Young, "Difference as a Resource for Democratic
Communication," 403.
[31] Ibid.

listening to difference can, in fact, bring us closer to the deliberative ideal of fair consideration.[32]

As I explain, difference can serve as a resource in deliberation by sustaining a commitment to communicative engagement. Here, I invert the thinking I presented in Chapter 3. If empathy's emphasis on similarities distracts citizens from the need to engage, how might an emphasis on differences be a boon for deliberation, once we have fully comprehended what is required for truly fair deliberation?

It's telling that Rousseau did not see the benefit of having citizens deliberate before coming to a decision. Compare, for example, his rejection of deliberation with his endorsement of censorship, civil religion, and his preference for a small polity with limits on economic inequality.[33] Rousseau arguably sought to create the institutions and social conditions necessary for a kind of deliberation-free empathy to circulate among the citizens.

Unlike Rousseau's ideal general will, however, the deliberative ideal of fair consideration can actually be strengthened by encounters with difference. In what follows, I argue that difference alerts citizens to the limits of their ability to understand each other, thus showing them the need for communicative deliberation in the first place. Consider that if people were all the same, there would be little need for them to exchange ideas. In contrast, the value of speaking with others becomes more apparent once we recognize that our view may differ from theirs. Thus, in the same proportion that difference undermines our attainment of Rousseau's republican-communitarian ideal of democracy, it might actually help us achieve the deliberative ideal of democracy by drawing citizens' attention to the vital importance of engaging with one another. Meaningfully democratic engagement is propelled by the friction created by our desire to understand each other and our recognition of our inability to do so.

---

[32] Like Young, I focus on the power of difference to serve as a resource for someone already committed to democracy. As I show, difference is essential for helping committed democrats understand the full implications of what might be demanded of them in realizing that goal.

[33] Rousseau, *The Social Contract and Other Later Political Writings*.

6.3 The Democratic Value of Recognizing the Limits of Mutual Understanding

As I discussed in the previous chapter, listening to our fellow citizens will not always bridge divides that exist between us. In fact, listening is as likely to reveal deep incompatibilities as it is to reveal latent similarities. These revelations, however, need not derail meaningfully democratic deliberation. Instead, as I show, we should even expect certain democratic advantages in cases where listening uncovers or highlights differences that exist between people.

Specifically, I argue that differences serve as a resource in democratic deliberation by highlighting the limits of our ability to understand others. As I show, the prospects of democratic listening and fair consideration are actually improved when those deliberating are oriented toward the limits of mutual understanding. By the limits of mutual understanding, I mean not only the limits to our ability to reach an agreement but also the limits to our ability to fully understand others' perspectives. In other words, citizens should approach deliberative encounters with the acknowledgment that understanding may be beyond their reach.

With this discussion I intend to show how an ontology of identity/difference vivified through encounters with difference can actually offer a productive background for a deliberative democratic theory centered on the listening act. My goal in this discussion is to show not only that limits to understanding are real and unavoidable but that accepting them can be productive. Indeed, I argue that our conscious recognition of the potential limits in our ability to understand others can help sustain deliberation. As I show, even within Habermas's deliberative model of democracy, we can foreground the limits of mutual understanding and capture important democratic benefits in doing so.

6.3.1 The Limits to Mutual Understanding

To be sure, there is a seeming contradiction in employing the limits of mutual understanding to sustain deliberation *aimed* at understanding. How can playing up differences and the difficulty we have communicating in light of those differences work as a strategy for encouraging further engagement? Won't citizens have even less reason to engage in the hard work of democratic listening without the hope of understanding or reaching an agreement with one another?

In his critique of Iris Young's politics of difference, Lorenzo Simpson argues precisely this. Specifically, he contends that assuming from that start that some experiences or perspectives will remain beyond others' understanding has the unwanted effect of shutting down conversation.[34] Similarly, feminist philosopher Uma Narayan rejects what she calls the "unconveyability-of-insights" thesis, defending instead the "epistemic privilege of the oppressed."[35] Though herself a proponent of a politics of difference, Narayan argues that the belief that outsiders could never understand the experience of insiders "would make communication between member[s] of an oppressed group and sympathetic non-members pretty close to useless."[36] What is the point of even trying to communicate across difference if we do not expect it will lead to greater understanding? In contrast to the unconveyability-of-insights thesis, Narayan argues that the more modest epistemic privilege of the oppressed thesis is actually productive for deliberation as it helps us see that our understanding of particular others can only come from engaging with them.[37]

According to these critics, the unconveyability-of-insights thesis is not only counterproductive, it is simply not *true*. As Narayan points out, "Many of us would claim to know, say, a few men who are sympathetic to and understand a good deal about feminist concerns, or white people who are concerned with and understand a good deal about issues of race."[38] Similarly, Simpson argues that "the recognition that full transparency may be an unrealizable ideal does not make it unreasonable for us to hope and strive to allow some light to shine through a glass darkly."[39] Before jumping to defend the democratic benefits of recognizing the limits of mutual understanding, it's

---

[34] Lorenzo C. Simpson, "Communication and the Politics of Difference: Reading Iris Young," *Constellations* 7, no. 3 (2000): 440.

[35] Uma Narayan, "Working Together Across Difference: Some Considerations on Emotions and Political Practice," *Hypatia* 3, no. 2 (1988): 37.

[36] Ibid., 36. In explaining the benefits of recognizing the limits of mutual understanding, I have adopted Narayan's language of "insiders" and "outsiders," which she employs with respect to specific forms of oppressive social structures. This language of "insider" and "outsider" has the advantage "of reversing conventional ideas of what is central and what is marginal." Narayan acknowledges a disadvantage in employing the terms "insider" and "outsider" insofar as they "lack an explicit sense of hierarchy," which inevitably characterizes relations of oppression. For the purposes of this chapter, which highlights the importance of listening across all relations of social distance and not just those characterized by explicit power asymmetries, the words are particularly fitting. Ibid., 35.

[37] Ibid., 38.

[38] Ibid., 37.

[39] Simpson, "Communication and the Politics of Difference," 439.

worth considering whether these limits are even real. In other words, might a politics of difference *overstate* the limits in our ability to understand others?

Ultimately, the point I am trying to make in regards to the democratic value of recognizing the limits of mutual understanding is not inconsistent with Narayan's and Simpson's positions, nor does it require me to defend a stronger incommensurability thesis. I do not deny, for example, that "some light" can "shine through a glass darkly." Or that some sympathetic outsiders know a "good deal" about the concerns of insiders. My point is simply that we ought to recognize the dimness of that light and the mediated quality of that knowledge.

In other words, the democratic functioning of a large and diverse deliberative system is enhanced when people recognize the uncertain access they have to the perspectives, ideas, and experiences of others. More specifically, I aim to show that recognizing the ways in which our understanding of others can remain incomplete or imperfect despite our best efforts to understand has the power to actually keep conversations going.

In fact, Narayan's and Simpson's language is instructive here. Narayan, for example, describes sympathetic outsiders as knowing a "good deal" about feminist concerns. That qualification is important. While some insights can be conveyed to outsiders, others will likely be only partially conveyed. Indeed, given the way that social categorizations intersect, women of different races, classes, or religions would not necessarily share or recognize a set of "feminist concerns." Any sympathetic outsider, or insider for that matter, who claimed to know more than a "good deal" about feminist concerns would run the risk of shutting down further conversation (and as a result, further understanding too).

Tellingly, Simpson himself acknowledges that "there is no doubt a limit beyond which we cannot go, and our hermeneutic hubris and presumption should be chastened with humility."[40] Still, he opposes "our setting a limit at the outset" for fear it might undermine efforts to engage.[41] I argue, however, that by recognizing (not setting) the potential limits at the outset, we foster the very humility that Simpson acknowledges is needed to forestall "premature interpretative closure."[42] In other words, the tension between our desire

---

[40] Ibid., 440.
[41] Ibid.
[42] Ibid.

to understand and our recognition of the limits to our understanding can be democratically productive.

Before getting into exactly how the limits of mutual understanding can be incorporated productively into deliberative politics, allow me to call briefly on the aid of Socrates, whose commitment to philosophy offers some immediate support for the deliberative benefits of recognizing the limits of mutual understanding.

6.3.2 Socratic Citizenship

Socrates, arguably the most committed philosopher who ever lived (and died), accepted the worthlessness of human wisdom.[43] Students of Plato often wonder why Socrates dedicated his life to philosophy if he believed that its apparent purpose, gaining wisdom, was and would forever remain out of reach. As they learn, Socrates's epistemic humility, his acceptance of the limits of knowledge, fed rather than starved his curiosity. Crucially, he committed himself to the practice of philosophy, not in spite of his inexorable ignorance, but *because* of it.

The process of philosophy, a life examined through engagement with others, became more important as Socrates realized the destination could never be reached. Socrates's commitment to philosophy was a feature, not a defect, of his epistemic humility. In other words, his ignorance drove his philosophizing. And that's a good thing too, because as we know, Socrates's efforts in philosophy were not, ultimately, worthless. Though he never attained knowledge of the Truth in an absolute sense, at the very least, his philosophical inquiry helped him better understand the bounds of his knowledge, recognize what he knew and what he did not, and direct his further examination accordingly.

Democratic citizens, and deliberative democrats for that matter, have something to learn from Socrates. In the same way that Socrates's epistemic humility was integral to motivating his ongoing philosophical engagement, so too is the acceptance of the limits of citizens' ability to understand those who are most different from them essential to motivating a commitment to listening.

---

[43] Plato, "Apology," in *The Trial and Death of Socrates*, trans. G. M. A. Grube (Indianapolis: Hackett, 2000), 23a.

Importantly, citizens do not need to, nor should they, go as far as Socrates in believing that, in this case, their knowledge of the other is worthless. And it is worth noting the dark side of a Socratic model of democratic citizenship, especially in a deliberative context. After all, conversations with Socrates did not always inspire his interlocutors to follow him on the path of philosophical inquiry. Instead, these challenging conversations frustrated Socrates's fellow citizens so much that they chose to kill him rather than let the conversations continue.

Nevertheless, Socrates's ignorance-driven inquiry provides a useful example of how acknowledging the limits of our ability to understand others could help motivate or reinforce a commitment to democratic listening. And indeed, the fate that befell Socrates highlights the need for certain institutional and cultural background conditions if a listening approach to democratic deliberation is to succeed. Consider, for example, that Socrates's fellow Athenians were not exactly committed to the same robust conception of deliberative democracy that I discussed in Chapter 5. And the cultural context of the *polis* did not allow for the acceptance of difference and disagreement that I have argued is essential for a listening approach to democracy to work. Indeed, under the political and cultural conditions we currently confront in the United States, citizens who adopted the same contestatory approach to politics as Socrates would likely pay personal and professional costs.

Admittedly, the limitations of a Socratic model of citizenship are not only circumstantial but can be found in the character of Socrates himself. For example, at times, Socrates's epistemic humility appears to be directed as much toward others as toward himself.[44] Observing Socrates in dialogue, we get the distinct impression that he does not take all of his interlocutors seriously.[45] In democratic deliberation, however, citizens must not be dismissive of others, nor should they assume that a particular person's input will be meaningless or worthless. Instead, the presumption has to be that others have something relevant to say. As I explain below, I'm after an initial level of humility in regard to one's own ability to imagine or understand another person's perspective.

[44] Ibid., 23b.
[45] Plato, "Crito," in *The Trial and Death of Socrates*, ed. G. M. A. Grube (Indianapolis: Hackett, 2000).

6.3.3 Revisiting Mutual Understanding in Habermas

Returning now to the challenge raised earlier, how does an orientation to the limits of our ability to understand one another fit within the model of deliberative democracy I have outlined throughout this book? For example, given the normative weight that Habermas places on communication aimed at reaching understanding, it would seem that his model of deliberative democracy is at odds with an ontology of identity/difference that I want to argue can productively serve as the background to democratic theory today.

To comprehend fully this contradiction (and begin to find a way out of it), we must return to Habermas's *Theory of Communicative Action*. While *The Theory of Communicative Action* is a sociological work that predates Habermas's more explicit contribution to democratic theory in *Between Facts and Norms*, it would be a mistake to view these two pillars of his research program as unrelated.[46] Indeed, the connection that Habermas draws between democracy and discourse can be traced back to his theory of communicative action in which he harnesses the potential of everyday communication to validate claims intersubjectively. It makes sense, therefore, to see *Between Facts and Norms* as an extension of the larger research program Habermas introduced in his *Theory of Communicative Action*.

In that earlier work, Habermas identifies the power of language to coordinate action through persuasion rather than force or manipulation. According to Habermas, "reaching understanding is the inherent *telos* of

---

[46] Stephen White has made the case for understanding Habermas's *Theory of Communicative Action* as setting out a broad research program with both normative and empirical elements. The normative and empirical parts of this research program are interrelated. As I mentioned in Chapter 2, what makes Habermas's sociological theory of communicative action so distinct is that it seeks to explain not only the integration and reproduction of society, but also the breakdown of that reproduction. By thematizing the breakdown of social reproduction, Habermas introduces important normative considerations to his *Theory of Communicative Action*. For Habermas, ongoing communicative action only has the presumption of rationality if interlocutors are free and empowered to challenge validity claims they find problematic. As White shows, this move on Habermas's part alerts us to the need to always ask "how power relations in practices and institutions may be constraining the way that [a given] problem has emerged and developed." Building on these insights, White and Farr have shown the advantages of interpreting Habermas's deliberative democratic theory against the background of his theory of communicative action. Understanding *Between Facts and Norms* against the backdrop of *The Theory of Communicative Action* helps us develop a theory of deliberative democracy that is power-sensitive and relevant. Stephen K. White, "The Very Idea of a Critical Social Science: A Pragmatist Turn," in *The Cambridge Companion to Critical Theory*, ed. Fred Rush (Cambridge: Cambridge University Press, 2004), 319; Stephen K. White and Evan Robert Farr, "'No-Saying' in Habermas," *Political Theory* 40, no. 1 (2012): 32–57. See also Stephen K. White, *A Democratic Bearing: Admirable Citizens, Uneven Justice, and Critical Theory* (Cambridge: Cambridge University Press, 2017).

human speech."[47] We communicate in order to reach some understanding with one another. And for Habermas, this orientation toward mutual understanding is key to the coordinating power of language, which he develops into a central component of his discourse theory of democratic deliberation.[48] Language works to mediate a disagreement only if participants are oriented toward reaching mutual understanding. And so, the legitimating power Habermas attributes to discursive processes of collective opinion and will formation comes from deliberators being mutually committed to *trying* to understand one another.[49]

While the success of deliberation may not depend on the achievement of consensus or agreement, it does absolutely depend on citizens maintaining the "performative attitude of a speaker who wants to *reach an understanding* with a second person about something in the world."[50] As Romand Coles explains, for the most part, Habermas resists "ontological harmony claims."[51] He does not assume, for example, that consensus is a natural or automatic part of the human condition. Still, Habermas does maintain that "because our existence and coexistence are deeply communicative, we are ontologically and normatively characterized not by de facto agreement but by a mutual lived commitment (agreement) to coexist through efforts to agree."[52] For him, the orientation toward mutual understanding that sustains communicative action is built into the pragmatics of natural language. In other words, Habermas suggests that people will be motivated to adopt the attitude of someone oriented toward mutual understanding as a function of their capacity for language, given the intuitive pull of language's *telos*.[53]

The point I want to make here, however, is not about where such an orientation toward mutual understanding comes from or whether it is automatic or even real. Instead, with this discussion I mean to show how the very

---

[47] Habermas, *The Theory of Communicative Action*, 1:287.

[48] As White explains, "Ongoing communicative action is Habermas's account of unproblematic social interaction." Habermas's understanding of "discursive justification, both cognitive and normative," however, "is constitutively related to this intersubjective bond's becoming problematic in some way. In other words, communicative rationality has to be understood finally as a practice of *coping with* the emergence of *problems within a context of intersubjectivity*." White, "The Very Idea of a Critical Social Science," 319.

[49] Habermas, *Between Facts and Norms*, 103, 130, 269, 324–25.

[50] Ibid., 18.

[51] Romand Coles, *Rethinking Generosity: Critical Theory and the Politics of Caritas* (Ithaca, NY: Cornell University Press, 1997), 150.

[52] Ibid.

[53] But we do not need to accept Habermas's foundationalist claim regarding language's *telos* in order to make the coordinating power of language into a key component of democratic life. White, *A Democratic Bearing*, 61.

notion of mutual understanding at which Habermas's model of deliberation aims can be deceptive and self-defeating for Habermas's very goals. In contrast, a strategy that acknowledges the potential limits of even our best efforts to communicate allows us to recognize and foreground the full depth of how difficult mutual understanding is as an ideal. And yet, the goal that I am pursuing here is still a kind of understanding. But, crucially, the understanding at which I aim would sustain a democracy that takes difference seriously. I reject the idea that difference presents an empirical obstacle that—with difficulty—can be overcome by admirably motivated and empathetic citizens. The challenges of deliberating across deep difference and disagreement cannot always be overcome by people simply trying harder to agree or trying harder to want to agree.

While we have an obligation to try and understand what others are saying, we must also embody a sense of the deep limits to achieving that understanding. I argue that we are able to coordinate collective action legitimately through language rather than force or manipulation only when citizens are also oriented toward the limits of mutual understanding. Put differently, meaningfully democratic deliberation occurs in the space created by the tension between our desire to reach mutual understanding and our recognition of the limits of our ability to do so. It is democratically useful, therefore, to keep this tension alive. And encounters with difference that occur within the right institutional and cultural contexts can do precisely that.

In her discussion of deliberation in the aftermath of traumatic events, specifically political violence against women, Wendy Hui Kyong Chun argues that victims are owed listening. According to Chun, however, in these cases the commitment to listen must be "based on *lack* of comprehension."[54] She explains, "By emphasizing gaps in understanding, in refusing interpretations that reduce traumatic events to factors we can know, we may begin the encounter that may help us finally to stay together."[55] Unless we acknowledge the limits in our ability to understand others' perspectives, we continually run the risk of translating others' experiences, pain, and lives into something we can fully understand—and doing damage to their stories in the process. Importantly, when differences in experience make it difficult for me to understand you, my very attempts to understand you can actually stand in the way of my reaching a more adequate comprehension. In other words, the

---

[54] Wendy Hui Kyong Chun, "Unbearable Witness," *Differences: A Journal of Feminist Cultural Studies* 11, no. 1 (1999): 139.
[55] Ibid., 139–40.

opportunity to achieve understanding only arises when we give up on fully understanding the other.

Andrew Dobson, relying heavily on Chun's discussion of listening in the absence of understanding, introduces the category of *apophatic* listening to democratic politics, which he equates with "notions of empathy, of maintaining a distance between testifier and listener, and of the 'co-production' of meaning."[56] But Dobson's appeal to a "lack of comprehension" as both the "bedrock and guarantor" of political listening has more potential once we separate it from his calls for empathy.[57] As Dobson writes, "Any claim to 'understand' must be provisional and temporary."[58] But the provisionality of our understanding is emphasized only when we listen without trying to empathize. The limits of our ability to understand those most different from ourselves are concealed and devalued when we encourage citizens to listen for similarities or for the sake of imagining ourselves in another person's shoes.

In sum, linguistic encounters with difference should be seen as an asset instead of a liability for democracy, as they reveal to us the limits of mutual understanding. Feelings of deep difference—brought about through deliberative encounters with others—not only help citizens see the perspectival nature of their own beliefs but also encourage them to recognize their fellow citizens as having something meaningful, or at least distinctive, to contribute. An attention to difference thus offers a way to achieve meaningfully democratic deliberation in large pluralistic societies, one that does not follow the siren song of empathy. In recognizing that I may never fully understand my interlocutor's perspective, I also come to see that my interlocutor may never fully understand my own. This motivates a *minimal* or *nominal* kind of perspective taking, where I come to "understand myself as my Other's Other."[59] But importantly, the similarities that are revealed through this kind of perspective taking are relational, not substantive.

Despite these limits to communication, however, when we engage with others, we still do so for the sake of furthering our understanding. Light is shed on another person's perspective, experience, or feelings. We hear what

---

[56] Dobson, *Listening for Democracy*, 71.

[57] Ibid.

[58] By blending the concept of listening with empathy, however, I think Dobson undermines the contribution he is making. Such a move toward empathy is counterproductive, given empathy's tendency to defy humility and to obscure the limits to our ability to understand others. Ibid.

[59] Barbara Fultner, "Gender, Discourse and Non-Essentialism," in *Dialogue, Politics and Gender*, ed. Jude Browne (Cambridge: Cambridge University Press, 2013), 64.

they are saying. But when we recognize the potential limits in our ability to understand, let alone come to an agreement with our fellow citizens, we are made aware of both the challenges and the stakes of democratic listening. Importantly, we are more serious, attentive, and humble in our encounter, precisely because we recognize that our understanding is mediated through our (incomplete) communicative engagement with the other. This mediation means that some things may remain unknown and unknowable to us.

As I have argued throughout, there are real and often unavoidable limits to our ability to understand those who are most different from us. Here I am suggesting that accepting this basic truth can actually have democratically productive effects within democratic deliberation. In other words, differences and the ontology of identity/difference that they vivify for citizens can serve as a resource even in a Habermasian model of democratic deliberation.

6.4 Listening to Difference as a Strategy for Democratizing Deliberation

In this section, I explain what a listening-centered strategy for achieving uptake across deep difference might look like in practice. According to the account I have laid out above, to enhance the democratic functioning of a deliberative system, we should look for ways to encourage citizens to *just* listen to their fellow citizens. Importantly, citizens should listen to each other, not because mere listening, in and of itself, ensures the democratic functioning of a deliberative system. Recall that on its own, the auditory listening act or mere listening carries little democratic weight. Unlike interpersonal relationships, politics is about solving problems and making decisions. *Just* listening is not enough. Still, listening is essential if we are going to make politics and not war with those with whom we disagree.[60] Furthermore, listening without an agenda, and especially listening without immediately searching for similarities, allows citizens to better encounter differences. And these encounters with difference have the power to show citizens the limits to mutual understanding, and to do so to democratic effect.

---

[60] According to Bickford listening to one's adversaries—making "politics, not war," with one's enemies—takes courage. She cites the example of Yitzhak Rabin, who was assassinated by an extremist who opposed his participation in the Oslo Accords. Bickford, *The Dissonance of Democracy*, 68.

Through encounters with difference, the listener's assumptions, preconceptions, and prejudices can be challenged and bracketed (at least temporarily). Without these assumptions and expectations to fall back on, citizens are able to engage with one another in a more serious, attentive, and humble way, recognizing the stakes and normative parameters of their political talk. By helping to foster the affective-cognitive disposition needed for performative democratic listening, encounters with difference can transform mere auditory listening into something more meaningful, namely listening toward democracy.

Of course, these encounters must occur within a larger ethical-political framework, wherein citizens share a commitment to democracy itself. I do not contend, in other words, that encounters with difference will somehow make citizens more committed to democracy. Indeed, without the cultural and institutional conditions I discussed in Chapter 5, it is hard to imagine encounters with difference having the democratic impact I describe here. Under the right conditions, however, listening across difference can bring about a dispositional transformation among citizens by showing them the limits of their ability to understand one another.

Importantly, then, the auditory listening act provides an opportunity for difference to work on citizens' attitudes and dispositions in a democratically productive way. But for this to occur, we must discourage citizens from monologically mining these listening acts for commonality or sources of agreement. As I discussed in Chapter 3, supporters of empathy value imaginative perspective taking, in part, for its ability to reduce the distance between citizens, thus implying that such distance can and should be overcome in order to achieve productive deliberation. In contrast, the listening-centered strategy that I identify for achieving uptake in large pluralistic societies works in the absence of empathy and without relying on the underlying similarities or social proximity that produce empathy. Indeed, by focusing on the need to listen to our fellow citizens, this approach foregrounds difference, acknowledging from the start that we are not so alike that we can simply imagine the perspectives of others.

When encountering differences as such, and not as something to try and overcome by identifying underlying similarities, I recognize that my interests may actually be in competition with yours. As such, I come to realize that I may fail to convince you of my position, and thus may "lose" whatever might be at stake in our conversation. Acknowledging these stakes of deliberation, I am more likely to approach the deliberative encounter with the appropriate level of *seriousness*. Furthermore, encountering those with whom we disagree or those who offer a new perspective can help foster a certain level of seriousness insofar as it shows us that we are all limited in our ability to understand others and to make ourselves understood.

The recognition of difference also encourages citizens to see the other as having relevant information to share and so perk up for the purpose of hearing it. In showing me the perspectival nature of my view, encounters with difference can generate a certain level of curiosity among listeners who want to learn more about others' similarly unique perspectives. For example, the acknowledgment on the part of straight citizens that they may never fully understand or accurately imagine what it feels like to be discriminated against because of their sexual orientation is vital to ensuring that citizens pay attention to the perspectives that particular others actually communicate. By reminding citizens of these limits to our understanding, difference can also help generate the *attentiveness* needed for citizens to listen democratically.

When a citizen feels the deep difference that divides her from others, she recognizes the limitations of communication. As a result, she not only becomes more attentive to what others have to say, but she is also humbled. We are humbled in our encounters with difference as we recognize that our own knowledge is situated and perspectival. Encounters with difference can have a particularly productive humbling effect on members of social groups that have dominated political discussion and therefore may assume their experiences are "neutral and universal."[61] This *humility* can also help avoid certain well-worn reactions to claims of injustice that imply blame or privilege on the part of the listener and make them hard for some to take up. Listening to different perspectives shows us that our view of the world is never as complete as we tend to think. Mark Button defines democratic humility as "a cultivated sensitivity toward the incompleteness and contingency of both one's personal moral powers and commitments, and of the particular forms, laws, and institutions that structure one's political and social life with others."[62] Being confronted with ideas and perspectives that are different and even contradict our own shows us the insecure, tentative, and provisional quality of any mastery we presume to have over a subject or a decision.

[61] Young, *Inclusion and Democracy*, 144.
[62] Mark Button, "A Monkish Kind of Virtue? For and against Humility," *Political Theory* 33, no. 6 (2005): 851.

According to Button, humility is "supportive of cognitive/affective openness, a spirit of attentiveness and active listening."[63]

Humility on the part of citizen listeners helps them to understand that the need for engagement is never satisfied. Our understanding of the other is never complete, and even our incomplete understanding can only be realized through continual (and actual, not imagined) engagement. As Button explains, humility is "a window through which we allow that which is outside of the self or group to enter in and work upon us, at least for a time."[64]

By fostering seriousness, attentiveness, and humility among citizens, encounters with difference can help sustain performative democratic listening. As a result, the auditory listening act gives way to the ilauditory listening act, moving citizens' deliberation in the direction of greater democracy. Importantly, however, even when encounters with difference realize performative democratic listening, uptake will not always or necessarily follow. The specific claim that I wish to defend here, however, is that encounters with difference and disagreement *do* help citizens recognize the limits of mutual understanding. Moreover, this recognition can be democratically useful insofar as it alerts citizens to the difficulty of deliberation and the hard work of democracy itself, thus priming them to be more serious, attentive, and humble in their listening. In order to faithfully consider the opinions and perspectives of others, it is crucial to recognize that their experiences may be beyond your understanding. The realization of the limits of our ability to understand others in the presence of deep difference opens us more vividly to the ways in which we are inconspicuously limited in our opinions, our basic understanding of issues, and our relationship to the democratic community. This sort of engagement is less likely to occur if we imagine only our commonalities or assume that we can know or feel how another feels.

To demonstrate how deliberation among citizens who recognize the limits of mutual understanding would look compared to the deliberation of empathic citizens, consider reactions to Trayvon Martin's death in 2012. In the aftermath of his death, the phrase "I am Trayvon" was popularized in public discourse as a means for people to show their condemnation of Martin's killing as well as the acquittal of his killer, George Zimmerman. *Ebony*

---

[63] Button, "A Monkish Kind of Virtue?," 851.
[64] Ibid.

magazine, for example, printed several covers featuring famous black men wearing hoodies and posing with their sons under the title "We Are Trayvon."

Growing out of this rallying cry, however, was a countermovement of sorts that turned the original slogan on its head. The new rallying cry was, "I am NOT Trayvon Martin." This slogan has been used by white "allies" who, like many black Americans, are disturbed by the outcome of the Zimmerman trial. Claiming "I am NOT Trayvon" demonstrates an admission on the part of these individuals that they cannot imagine or fully understand the experience of black Americans. The white people who adopted this approach demonstrated a recognition of the limits to mutual understanding. The perspectival or experiential differences emphasized the need to listen seriously and attentively, as the listener would expect to hear something new and unfamiliar. Identifying and recognizing limitations of our understanding creates the space wherein white Americans can encounter, through listening, the concerns and demands of black Americans. These citizens also demonstrated humility, rejecting the presumption of fully understanding black Americans' perspectives and emotions related to events surrounding the death of Trayvon Martin. In saying, "I am NOT Trayvon," the white citizen accepts the limits of her own imagination and understanding as well as the risk that she might find out something that challenges her status or view of the world.

Under the right conditions, encounters with difference help citizens recognize the cultural, experiential, and communicative divides between themselves and others. Such an acknowledgment is especially important for members of politically or socially dominant groups and those who, depending on the particular context, may be "outsiders" or nonmembers of an oppressed group. When claims of injustice are being expressed, it is often hard for "outsiders" of oppression to understand or recognize them.[65] As a result, insiders of oppression are often easily dismissed or ignored in deliberation.

But an awareness of the limits of our ability to understand others is also needed *among* insiders of oppression.[66] The lines between insider and

[65] Narayan, "Working Together across Difference," 35.
[66] As Greta Snyder explains in her work on multivalent recognition, recognizing the differences and diversity that occur *within* groups is as important as recognizing the differences between groups. There is no "monovalent identity" shared by all women. Listening, then, is as crucial between men and women as between women of different races or socioeconomic status. Greta Fowler Snyder, "Multivalent Recognition: Between Fixity and Fluidity in Identity Politics," *Journal of Politics* 74, no. 1 (2012): 249–61.

outsider are continually redrawn, as someone can be an insider in regard to one form of oppression, by being a woman, while being an outsider in regard to another, by being white, for example.[67] As Narayan notes, "It is sad, but seems unfortunately true, that experience and understanding of one form of oppression does not necessarily sensitize one to other forms."[68]

Recognizing the limits of our ability to understand others through encounters with difference can help avoid dividing and then essentializing groups along stark lines. In regard to deliberation about the meaning and injustice of Trayvon Martin's death, for example, the categories of insider and outsider are not obvious. Do black women share the same insider status as black men? What about mothers? Each of us remains an outsider to the experience and particular perspective of others.

What I have just said does not imply that white Americans, for example, should not speak about race or that men cannot speak about sexism. As a resource for deliberative democracy, difference is valuable insofar as it can promote *more* engagement, not less. At the very least, encountering our differences through the auditory listening act can show citizens the importance of paying close attention to what others say. Moreover, these encounters foster a particular orientation to the conversation that originates in an acknowledgment of the limits of our ability to understand one another. Ultimately, recognizing the differences between ourselves and others can motivate citizens to reconsider their moral or political commitments, to engage in meaningful evaluation, and to begin to resist subtler aspects of power operating in political discourse.

Still, recognizing the limits of mutual understanding and the particularity of one's own perspective can contribute to any deliberation between subjects in relations of social distance, not just those that involve histories of oppression or lasting inequality. The listening approach represents an alternative to the empathy approach, offering its own a set of strategies for achieving meaningfully democratic deliberation in the face of deep differences. Whereas an empathy approach uses imagination to access inputs, and uses similarities between citizens to fuel their imaginations, the listening approach relies on actual communication to access inputs and employs differences to motivate the serious, attentive, and humble listening at the center of that communication.

[67] Narayan, "Working Together across Difference," 35.
[68] Ibid., 44.

6.5 Conclusion

A major goal of this book has been to find ways to achieve democracy in a world of difference and disagreement. And in looking for ways to make deliberative democratic theory more accommodating of deep differences, I found that difference can actually serve as a resource in a listening-centered model of deliberative democracy. Importantly, however, the opportunity for difference to serve as a resource in deliberation is missed and even foreclosed to us when we rely on empathy.

Practices of listening that downplay empathy and encourage citizens to resist putting themselves in another's shoes are more consistent with deliberative democratic theory. The listening approach assumes citizens will have trouble understanding one another, and yet expects them to engage nonetheless. In the end, deliberation is not improved by efforts to boldly overcome difference. Instead, greater space must be allowed for difference. And a democratic listening approach provides precisely the space for difference lacking in existing models of deliberative democracy. Accordingly, the listening approach to deliberation helps respond to the challenges raised by difference democrats who, as I discussed in Chapter 2, contend that deliberation's exclusionary tendencies undermine its democratic aspirations. Rather than trying to overcome these differences, I have shown how these differences can actually contribute to deliberation in a distinctive way. The listening approach thus helps achieve democracy across difference, not by overcoming challenges to deliberation, but by drawing citizens' attention to those challenges.

Here I have shown how the listening approach can be made compatible with the dynamics of identity/difference that characterize the relationships of citizens within large pluralistic societies. Finding ways to vivify our awareness of the relationship of identity/difference is especially important in these late-modern times when we are trying both to be robustly democratic and to seriously accommodate deep difference. By foregrounding difference and disagreement, a listening-centered approach can alert citizens to the potential limits of their ability to fully understand others, and the vital importance of serious, attentive, and humble listening in light of those limits.

But while listening with the right disposition is an essential component of meaningfully democratic deliberation, it is no guarantee that uptake will be achieved. In the end, no silver bullet exists for achieving uptake across difference. And in the event that the meaning of a particular input remains obscure, even after citizens listened toward democracy, we might conclude that uptake had failed, even if it was not necessarily denied. Alternatively, we might say that uptake was achieved in some sense, even if only partially. For example, perhaps my opposition to a certain policy was registered by my fellow citizens, but they misunderstood my specific concerns or they underestimated the strength of my opposition. Borrowing more of Austin's language, we might refer to this as a case of "infelicitous" uptake.[69] Importantly, these failures of understanding that follow from even the most serious, attentive, and humble listening can prevent a person from having a say in the laws to which they are held.

Still, by seeing listening as an end in itself, and not just a means to reaching consensus, the listening approach brings us closer to achieving uptake in democratic deliberation by emphasizing the need for continued engagement even when we may not immediately understand what is said or when we might disagree and therefore prefer to tune out. The challenges to democratic discourse in a pluralistic world are significant, given that it occurs always already in the presence of disagreement. Calling attention to the hard work of deliberative uptake, I argue, is a necessary first step in any effort to improve its practice.

[69] J. L. Austin, *How to Do Things with Words* (Cambridge, MA: Harvard University Press, 1962), 16.

7

Democratic Ideals in a Non-Ideal World

A major goal of this book has been to identify the normative conditions required of informal deliberation in order for it to confer democratic legitimacy on our collective actions. I have been interested in answering the question of how deliberation allows citizens to meaningfully participate in the authorship of the laws to which they are held, and so realize the promise of democracy. To that end, I analyzed the normative core of deliberative democracy, finding that fair consideration carries much of the democratic weight of citizens' deliberation.

My inquiry has been motivated by a particular interest in understanding the prospects for democratic autonomy in large pluralistic societies where "the people," constituted by deep differences, do not agree. Specifically, I have tried to address concerns over deliberation's inability to deliver on the promise of democracy in contexts of deep disagreement. Far from dismissing these concerns, I have shown that they are valid and will continue to undermine the democratic prospects of deliberation until we are able to guarantee uptake alongside inclusion.

I began in Chapter 2 by demonstrating the insufficiency of inclusion for ensuring the democratic functioning of a deliberative system. Simply amplifying the voices of relevant parties, or making processes of deliberation more formally inclusive or accommodating, cannot ensure that citizens' voices will be heard and their ideas considered. To achieve the democratic force of deliberation, especially in large, pluralistic societies and other contexts marked by difference or disagreement, we must go beyond inclusion to consider the extent to which citizens' perspectives are actually taken up by their fellow citizens and representatives. Importantly, the uptake or fair consideration required to recognize the moral equality of each citizen's voice does not demand equal influence, but equal *opportunity* to influence. So, while mere inclusion is not enough to ensure the proper functioning of a deliberative system, influence is too high of a standard. Uptake, which allows for influence but does

Beyond Empathy and Inclusion. Mary F. Scudder, Oxford University Press (2020). © Oxford University Press.
DOI: 10.1093/oso/9780197535455.001.0001.

not guarantee it, provides the appropriate normative standard with which to assess the democratic quality of a deliberative system and the decisions it makes.

As I went on to explain, however, given the dynamics of identity/difference that constitute and divide citizens in diverse societies, we cannot assume uptake will automatically follow from inclusive deliberation. Therefore, I went on to evaluate various practices for their ability to bring about fair consideration in contexts of deep difference and disagreement. For example, in Chapter 3 I explored the ways in which empathy could be used to support both inclusion and uptake in deliberation. Here, empathy referred to cognitive role-taking, or the process of putting oneself in another's shoes. This process can lead to feelings of concern for another person (affective empathy), or it can lead to empathic understanding (cognitive empathy), whereby you come to comprehend the feelings of another, even if you do not ultimately share them.

But in my analysis, I revealed the limitations and potential pathologies of relying on empathy as a strategy for achieving meaningfully democratic deliberation. Complicating recent accounts of empathy, I showed that not only are affective and cognitive empathy very difficult to achieve in practice, but even when the process of empathy results in these outcomes, it does not necessarily promote communicative uptake. The deliberative ideal of fair consideration is not served by either the imaginative component of empathy or its emphasis on uncovering similarities.

Offering an alternative to the empathic turn in deliberative democratic theory, Chapter 4 considered the essential role that listening plays in achieving full and fair deliberation. There, I introduced a theory of listening acts to explain the various ways that listening affects a deliberative system. With this listening act theory, I showed that instead of regarding listening as simply hearing what is said (i.e., the auditory listening act) or, conversely, as that which brings about something like consensus or mutual understanding (i.e., the perauditory listening act), we need to recognize that we also act *in* listening. *In* listening to our fellow citizens, we recognize their moral equality of voice. I called this ilauditory listening act "performative democratic listening."

Building on this category of performative democratic listening, or how we act *in* listening, Chapter 5 gave an account of the source of performative listening's democratic power. Specifically, I showed that mere auditory listening becomes "listening toward democracy" when citizens listen seriously, attentively, and humbly. Performative democratic listening, in other words, relies on the affective-cognitive disposition of citizens who listen to their fellow citizens for the purpose of taking up what they have to say.

Chapter 5 also identified key cultural and institutional conditions needed for citizens to achieve listening toward democracy across difference. These included a cultural commitment to democratic self-rule, formalized expectations of listening, and a greater acceptance of conflict as part of living an active democratic life. Nevertheless, I emphasized that listening, especially performative democratic listening, faces significant challenges in contexts of difference and disagreement. Still, even if citizens struggle as much to listen as they do to empathize with those most different from themselves, listening, unlike empathy, is necessary for fair consideration and so warrants the investment.

Moreover, in Chapter 6, I explained why I believe a democratic listening approach to deliberation would have more success in achieving fair consideration across difference and disagreement than an approach based on either inclusion or empathy. Again, the democratic power of performative listening comes from the disposition of citizens who listen for the sake of taking into account what others say. And this disposition can actually be grounded in the recognition of the limits to reaching mutual understanding. In other words, the prospects of democratic listening and fair consideration are improved when citizens recognize the limits of mutual understanding. In addition, I showed that this claim is not wholly inconsistent with Habermas's deliberative democratic theory.

Now, in this concluding chapter, I want to draw out more vividly the implications of using fair consideration, and the democratic listening on which it is predicated, as the relevant normative standard for assessing the democratic quality of our deliberation and the decisions that result from it. First, I examine the ways in which our efforts to promote uptake can be made sensitive to issues of power, inequality, and injustice (7.1). Here, I pick up my discussion from Chapter 2 regarding how best to deal with the inputs of democracy's enemies—for example, racists and authoritarians. Specifically, I show how uptake can be deployed defensively in deliberation to help citizens identify undemocratic inputs that should be denied influence on democratic decisions.

Next, I go on to examine how listening to the inputs of others, especially those with whom one disagrees, might corrode or at least challenge a citizen's commitment to democracy itself (7.2). Specifically, I entertain the possibility that listening to and even focusing on the distance between one's self and others might lead citizens to withdraw from further engagement. Finally, I explore how to deal with repeated failures of democratic listening and fair consideration (7.3). What practical value does the ideal of uptake have if our efforts to attain it inevitably fall short? If democratic listening, which I argue is essential to the attainment of democracy, is consistently denied, withheld, or beyond our reach, then we must consider what to do in its absence. Thus, in conclusion, I discuss the critical value of ideal theory in a non-ideal world.

7.1 Uptake in the Real World

Democracy, as I have envisioned it, is hard work. What's more, it may end up being harder for some than others. Remember, inclusive deliberation introduces the *demos* not only to the inputs and perspectives of committed democrats but of democracy's enemies as well, including white nationalists, misogynists, and authoritarians. Expecting all citizens—even those who are personally targeted by the hate and vitriol of these groups—to listen seriously, attentively, and humbly to these inputs seems unfair. In what follows, I consider how the ideal of uptake and a politics of listening can be pursued in a way that is sensitive to the non-ideal conditions we currently confront.

Does the expectation to fairly consider the inputs of others apply equally to members of a minority or marginalized group as it does to the relatively powerful and privileged members of society? According to Pedrini, Bächtiger, and Steenbergen, the answer is no. As I discussed in Chapter 2, they propose relaxing the expectation of deliberative "reciprocity" for minorities and the disadvantaged.[1] And as they rightly point out, it would be wrong to expect these groups to "always be responsive and respectful toward the privileged, especially if there has been inequality in the past or if their vital interests are at stake."[2]

Nonetheless, I have argued in these pages that according to the normative core of deliberative democracy, everyone is owed listening. I stressed, however, that to satisfy the ideal of uptake, listeners do not need to respond, let alone respond respectfully, to what they hear. In defending a universal

---

[1] Seraina Pedrini, André Bächtiger, and Marco R. Steenbergen, "Deliberative Inclusion of Minorities: Patterns of Reciprocity among Linguistic Groups in Switzerland," *European Political Science Review* 5, no. 3 (2013): 484.

[2] Ibid., 489.

expectation of listening among citizens, I understand democratic listening to be more than simply letting someone talk, but less than agreeing with or even showing respect for what you hear. Democratic listening means paying attention to what others have to say. And, as I argued in Chapter 2, only by attending to what others have to say can we identify dangerous inputs and determine which ideas and perspectives ought to be rejected.

Still problematic, however, are the uneven burdens that an obligation to fairly consider all inputs imposes on those individuals who are targeted by hateful or discriminatory speech and policy proposals. Meeting the requirement of fair consideration is less challenging for citizens who are in the majority or otherwise have a privileged position in society. If we are to accept uptake as a universal democratic ideal, we must continually search for ways to alleviate the uneven burdens that an expectation of fair consideration places on the less powerful and those individuals and groups who are targeted by hateful or abusive inputs.

Unfortunately, however, addressing these burdens is not as easy as letting certain citizens off the hook, so to speak. Even if a strategy of tuning out hateful speech was democratically permissible, it is not always a live option. Given the way that power operates in our relationships, paying attention to the inputs of others is not always a choice, nor is it necessarily done for the benefit of the other. Consider, for example, that many Charlottesville residents likely felt that their own personal safety depended on their paying attention to the neo-Nazis marching through their streets. Listening has long been a tool of the powerless, used to help anticipate the whims of the powerful and to detect deceit or veiled threats. Groups frequently targeted by democracy's enemies do not have the luxury of simply ignoring those who threaten them. Therefore, simply easing the formal expectation of uptake for structural minorities, disadvantaged groups, or anyone else who is saddled with an uneven mental or emotional load in deliberation may do little to actually reduce these burdens in practice.

Instead, we must direct energy and attention toward empowering citizens to respond critically and forcefully to inputs they find unacceptable or dangerous. As I noted in Chapter 5, we can begin these efforts by reminding citizens that, to be deemed fair, the consideration, and the conversation for that matter, need not carry on forever. Still, even after I have taken up and rejected a hateful and unpersuasive perspective, it is appropriate (and prudent) to check back in periodically to see what a particular group or individual is saying.

In such a case, I may rely on a trusted ally who is not personally targeted by hate speech to listen for me—in other words, to act as a liaison in future communicative interactions with any group or individual who targets me with inflammatory or discriminatory political speech or proposals. In practice, this might mean that white residents of Charlottesville take the lead in protesting the Unite the Right rally so that those whose vital interests are threatened by the neo-Nazis' ideology aren't carrying this burden on their own. It's worth noting, however, that the ideal of uptake does not require committed democrats to participate in the constant re-litigation of their rejection of white supremacy. Still, we need to listen to groups we suspect of advancing this ideology, at the very least so that we know that their ideas deserve to be rejected on the basis of our considered condemnation of white supremacy. In the end, citizens can actually use robust practices of listening to protect themselves and their institutions from dangerous and undemocratic ideas.[3]

I do not deny, however, that democratic deliberation requires a certain level of psychological robustness on the part of citizen listeners, especially those who are targeted by hate speech and other antidemocratic inputs.[4] Remember, however, that these unequal burdens are not imposed by the ideal of uptake itself, but by the structural inequalities, ideologies of domination, and social pathologies of privilege that plague contemporary democratic politics. Moreover, it is precisely by adopting the ideal of fair consideration that we can better understand and so begin to address these psychological burdens.

7.2 Challenging Democracy

The view of democracy I have presented here is admittedly a challenging one. In what follows, I examine the ways in which successfully achieving uptake across difference could actually have a dampening effect on citizens' willingness to pursue democracy in the first place. In other words, I ask how

---

[3] For a discussion of the democratic power of "adversarial listening" see Carolyn M. Hendriks, Selen A. Ercan, and Sonya Duus, "Listening in Polarised Controversies: A Study of Listening Practices in the Public Sphere," *Policy Sciences* 52, no. 1 (2019): 137–51.

[4] Teresa M. Bejan, *Mere Civility: Disagreement and the Limits of Toleration* (Cambridge, MA: Harvard University Press, 2017), 162.

listening to difference might weaken or otherwise strain citizens' very commitment to democratic self-rule.

Throughout this book, I have aimed to first identify the normative requirements of meaningfully democratic deliberation and then identify practical challenges that stand in the way of our meeting those requirements. Still, in my analysis I have assumed a world where citizens are, for the most part, motivated to *want* democracy in the first place. In other words, when talking about the practical challenges to achieving meaningfully democratic deliberation, I have generally assumed a commitment to democracy among citizens.

Thus, when I say that inclusion is not sufficient for moving deliberation in the direction of democracy, I am speaking specifically about the deliberation of committed democrats. The same goes for my critique of empathy. Essentially, my goal has been to show how even those citizens motivated to pursue justice can be misled as to what justice requires when they focus only on expanding inclusion or when they turn to empathy to sustain that inclusive deliberation. Similarly, when I argued that practices of listening are better suited to achieving meaningfully democratic deliberation across difference, I was referring specifically to listening between citizens who are already committed to a democratic process. In other words, in comparing practices of inclusion, empathy, and listening, I have, for the most part, held citizens' commitment to democracy constant.

Recall that in Chapter 5, I discussed particular cultural and institutional preconditions needed for a listening approach to democratic deliberation to work, including the need to cultivate a more robust commitment to and nuanced understanding of democratic self-rule. Even with such a commitment, however, it's possible that either the relatively demanding expectation that citizens listen to those with whom they disagree, or the experience of actually engaging across difference, could corrode real-world citizens' motivation to put in the work of achieving democracy.

In this section, I examine empirical evidence from political science research on the topic of difference, disagreement, and deliberation. To begin, I return to Diana Mutz's work, first discussed in Chapter 4, on the political effects of encounters with "cross-cutting views" or political diversity (7.2.1). While Mutz's findings regarding the demobilizing effects of deliberation across difference would seem to justify the concerns raised above, I offer reasons to be more optimistic. I go on to discuss another particularly relevant line of research in political psychology—affective intelligence theory (7.2.2).

With recourse to this theory, I show that the feelings we would expect citizens to have in the face of deep difference or disagreement do, indeed, carry the democratic potential I identify in this book.

7.2.1 Political Effects of Exposure to Cross-Cutting Views

In *Hearing the Other Side*, Mutz finds what she calls a "dark side of mixed political company," especially for people who are conflict avoidant.[5] Specifically, Mutz finds that exposure to difference turns citizens off from participation, traditionally understood. In fact, she concludes, "The greater the cross-cutting exposure in the person's network, the more likely he or she is to abstain from voting."[6] In measuring the effect that "hearing the other side" has on political engagement, Mutz goes beyond voting, actually *quantifying* participation by counting the number of discrete campaign and election-related activities in which an individual participates. She finds that, across multiple different measures of partisan political engagement, "cross-cutting exposure is negatively related to participation."[7]

What, then, should we make of Mutz's conclusion that "hearing the other side"—in other words, listening to difference—has a dampening effect on citizens' willingness to engage in democratic politics? As I explain here, I have reasons to doubt the applicability of Mutz's findings to my own account of the democratic benefits of listening to those with whom we disagree. Furthermore, building on discussions from Chapter 5, I present ways we might moderate any negative (perauditory) effects that do result from listening to difference.

First, I am suspicious of the causal relationship Mutz draws between the diversity of a person's social network (her independent variable) and his level of political participation (her dependent variable). In designing her research this way, Mutz finds that homogeneous social networks lead to more participation, while heterogeneous social networks lead to less participation. She then concludes that "hearing the other side" is causally responsible for the lower levels of participation. But it seems just as likely that the causal arrow

---

[5] Diana C. Mutz, *Hearing the Other Side: Deliberative versus Participatory Democracy* (Cambridge: Cambridge University Press, 2006), 89.

[6] Ibid., 112.

[7] Notably, even Mutz's nonvoting measures of participation all relate to partisan, electoral politics, including, "donating money to candidates and putting up signs." Ibid., 112–13.

points the other way. While it may be true that people who have more politically diverse social networks are less likely to be politically engaged as a result
of their cross-cutting exposure, it is equally plausible that a person's level of
political engagement and partisanship plays a role in determining the diversity of his social network.[8]

For example, citizens who are highly involved in partisan forms of participation might, as a result of their involvement, be more likely to have
homogeneous social networks. Consider, for example, the case of a person
who becomes estranged from her family or childhood friends over politics. Those who are uninterested in politics are probably less likely to choose
their social networks based on political affiliations. But those who are actively involved in partisan political action may avoid discussing politics (or
even interacting) with those with whom they disagree. Indeed, it's possible
that opposing partisans may avoid *them*. Research tells us, for instance, that
strong partisans discriminate against opposing partisans.[9]

This is all to say that the demobilizing effect Mutz attributes to cross-
cutting networks could actually reflect a self-selection bias. Rather than
cross-cutting social networks *causing* political (specifically, partisan) demobilization, maybe partisan demobilization or disinterest can explain
the existence of a cross-cutting network in the first place. In other words,
participation might influence a person's social network. Or perhaps a third
variable—say, strength of partisanship—is affecting both a person's level of
participation and the diversity of her social networks. Without an experimental design, Mutz is not actually measuring the "consequences of communication across lines of difference."[10]

Mutz does control for many of these potentially confounding variables,
and she acknowledges that she cannot rule out reverse causality.[11] In a sup-
plementary appendix, Mutz uses a statistical model explicitly designed to account for this type of selection effect. Although she finds no evidence of such

---

[8] There are reasons to doubt the applicability of Mutz's findings to our discussion of listening as
such. Mutz seems to be studying the effects of diverse social networks rather than the effects of actually hearing the other side. Furthermore, when we are talking about conversations occurring within
a person's own community, can it really be called "the other side"? In contrast, Bruneau and Saxe,
whose work I addressed in Chapter 4, study the effects of listening to members of a distinct outgroup
with whom an individual would have little interaction outside of the experimental treatment. Emile
G. Bruneau and Rebecca Saxe, "The Power of Being Heard: The Benefits of 'Perspective-Giving' in the
Context of Intergroup Conflict," *Journal of Experimental Social Psychology* 48, no. 4 (2012): 855–66.

[9] Shanto Iyengar and Sean J. Westwood, "Fear and Loathing across Party Lines: New Evidence on
Group Polarization," *American Journal of Political Science* 59, no. 3 (2015): 690–707.

[10] Mutz, *Hearing the Other Side*, 89.

[11] Ibid., 115.

184 BEYOND EMPATHY AND INCLUSION

selection dynamics, she notes that her model struggles to account for citizens' selection into heterogeneous and homogeneous social networks. This seriously "limited the conclusiveness" of her findings.[12] It is therefore impossible to rule out reverse causality based on these results alone.

If the correlation Mutz identifies is, as I suspect, driven partially by self-selection into partisan social networks, then her findings would not necessarily undercut my claim regarding the democratic benefits of encouraging citizens to listen across difference. Even if we accept that those people who tend to engage across difference are less likely to vote, this would not necessarily imply that those who previously failed to engage across difference, but were subsequently encouraged to do so, would exhibit the same patterns of behavior. For example, we should not necessarily assume that listening across difference would demobilize more politically motivated and active citizens. Furthermore, Neblo and colleagues have found that structured and mediated encounters with difference do not have the same demobilizing effects as spontaneous encounters with difference in one's social network.[13] These findings suggest that there may be specific strategies we could use to mitigate any possible demobilizing effects.

Still, even if we concede that exposure to cross-cutting views has a dampening effect on aggregative (as opposed to deliberative) forms of participation, there is additional empirical evidence suggesting that this exposure could actually further catalyze deliberation. For example, Neblo and colleagues find that "it is precisely people who are less likely to participate in traditional partisan politics who are most interested in deliberative participation. . . . People are attracted to such participation as a partial alternative to 'politics as usual.'"[14] Deliberative democracy actually provides "an outlet for those frustrated with status quo politics."[15] Thus, the very people who are turned off from partisan politics as usual, perhaps as a result of hearing the other side, express a desire and willingness to deliberate. And as I have shown, this willingness to deliberate has democratic value in its own right.

As the emphasis in her subtitle suggests, Mutz identifies a trade-off between participation and deliberation.[16] I would contend, however, that she

---

[12] Diana C. Mutz, "The Consequences of Cross-Cutting Networks for Political Participation," *American Journal of Political Science* 46, no. 4 (2002): 845.

[13] Michael A. Neblo, Kevin M. Esterling, Ryan P. Kennedy, David M. J. Lazer, and Anand E. Sokhey, "Who Wants to Deliberate—and Why?," *American Political Science Review* 104, no. 03 (2010): 566–83.

[14] Ibid., 567.

[15] Ibid., 574.

[16] Unlike John Hibbing and Elizabeth Theiss-Morse—who argue in *Stealth Democracy* that deliberation is problematic because it often fails to bring about its intended consequences, including

draws too stark of a line between participatory and deliberative modes of engagement. As Simone Chambers has argued, by dismissing "participation in civil-society organizations as 'apolitical,'" Mutz likely overstates the dampening effect that exposure to difference can have on democratic participation.[17] According to my understanding of democracy, those citizens hearing the other side are already engaging in democratically meaningful activity.

Furthermore, given the democratic power of listening that I have identified, the goal in hearing the other side is not to increase partisan levels of participation, but to achieve uptake. Thus, not only does Mutz take too narrow a view of what democratic participation entails, but she also misses one important way that we could measure deliberative "success."[18] According to the normative core of deliberation, the democratic value of cross-cutting deliberation is not to improve levels of partisan participation or even to increase tolerance for out-groups. Rather, the goal is to achieve fair consideration, which allows for citizens to meaningfully participate in the authorship of the laws to which they are held. And according to my listening act theory, the deliberative ideal of fair consideration can be achieved in our listening to our fellow citizens. With reference to the ilauditory force of listening, the trade-off between deliberation and participation becomes much less stark.

Citizens who listen to others in their diverse social networks are already participating in the political process, by helping to shape a collective opinion. And they are participating in a way that satisfies the normative core of deliberative democratic theory presented in Chapter 2. In setting up deliberation and participation as distinct political ideals, Mutz ignores the fact that deliberation, and specifically listening, is itself a form of political participation, albeit one that is more difficult to measure or track than voting, attending rallies, or making campaign contributions.

Engaging critically with Mutz's findings, Chambers has appealed to a systems approach to deliberation.[19] Rejecting the existence of a singular ideal of citizenship, Chambers insists it's okay, democratically speaking, for citizens to play different roles in politics. Accepting, for the sake of argument,

---

more tolerance—Mutz considers the downside of *successful* deliberation. John R. Hibbing and Elizabeth Theiss-Morse, *Stealth Democracy: Americans' Beliefs about How Government Should Work* (Cambridge: Cambridge University Press, 2002).

[17] Simone Chambers, "The Many Faces of Good Citizenship," *Critical Review* 25, no. 2 (2013): 206.
[18] Diana C. Mutz, "Reflections on Hearing the Other Side, in Theory and in Practice," *Critical Review* 25, no. 2 (2013): 260–76.
[19] Chambers, "The Many Faces of Good Citizenship," 200.

the trade-off between deliberation and participation, Chambers maintains that it is not necessarily cause for concern.[20] Every citizen need not embody both the deliberative and participatory ideals of citizenship for a system to be deliberative (and therefore democratic). Instead, Chambers argues that the responsibilities of citizenship can be divided. When taken as a whole, the various actions of different citizens combine to increase the overall democratic nature of a system. Like me, Chambers seeks to emphasize the important democratic work being done by more deliberative forms of participation.[21]

Still, even if we agree with Chambers in her rejection of a singular view of democratic citizenship, Mutz's finding that those individuals listening to diverse political views are rarely those who participate enthusiastically in aggregative politics is still potentially problematic.[22] In light of the role uptake plays in conferring democratic force on a deliberative system, the potential disconnect between those most likely to consider opposing viewpoints and those most likely to vote is troublesome. In order for uptake to contribute to the democratic quality of a deliberative system, we would want those who are fairly considering their fellow citizens' inputs to be formally involved in making decisions.[23] But if, as a rule, the citizens doing the considering are turned off from participating in the formal decision-making process, it's harder for their fair consideration to lend democratic legitimacy to the system and the decisions it makes.[24]

Thus, while a healthy democratic system can tolerate a division of labor in regard to various modes of citizenship, listening seems to be one labor

[20] Ibid.

[21] Ibid, 204.

[22] Mutz, *Hearing the Other Side*, 133.

[23] There are, however, ways other than voting and campaign contributions to have one's voice heard. As such, even if citizens were demobilized as a result of listening across difference, there are alternative ways for cross-cutting deliberations in the public sphere to connect up with formal decision-making bodies. Again, Habermas's model of deliberation occurs along two tracks: the informal communication dispersed across public spheres in which a collective opinion is formed, and the formal deliberation that occurs in official decision-making bodies like Parliament and Congress, from which emerges a collective will. First, communicative power is generated through discourse in public spheres, then it must be transformed into administrative power. The second track provides an institutional focus for what Habermas calls the broader "subjectless" communication of the first track. While elections provide one route for transferring communicative power into administrative power and thus ensuring "uptake" between the two tracks, transmission can also occur more informally. For Habermas, the normative weight of democratic deliberation "is grounded ultimately in the interplay between institutionally structured political will-formation and spontaneous, unsubverted circuits of communication in a public sphere that is not programmed to reach decisions and thus is not organized." (See Jürgen Habermas, "Three Normative Models of Democracy," *Constellations* 1, no. 1 (1994): 8; Habermas, "Popular Sovereignty as Procedure," 57.

[24] Selen A. Ercan, Carolyn M. Hendriks, and John S. Dryzek, "Public Deliberation in an Era of Communicative Plenty," *Policy & Politics* 47, no. 1 (2019): 19–36.

of citizenship that cannot be divided without undemocratic effects. For example, looking at the big picture, we might see some citizens speaking and others listening, and then (prematurely) conclude that the deliberative system is adequately democratic. But if some citizens *only* speak and others *only* listen, though the labor seems to be fairly divided, the deliberative system is not functioning properly. Consider, for example, another kind of system that thrives on a division of labor: a game of baseball. If we assess the functioning of the game as a whole (system), we see how different players contribute different skills. The game is actually improved when we encourage some to specialize in pitching and others to play in the outfield or don the "tools of ignorance" as a catcher. But in the end, if the teams do not alternate batting and fielding, we have no game. Playing defense and offense are two labors that cannot be divided perpetually. Just as players must take their turn fielding, citizens must take their turn listening.

This is not to say that we ought to advance a singular ideal of democratic citizenship, something that Chambers persuasively warns against. Rather, it is to say that we need to account for the capacities and dispositions that citizens must have in order for their deliberation to enhance the democratic force of a political system. Owen and Smith called this a "deliberative stance," and I have shown that this stance requires an orientation toward democratic listening.[25]

Therefore, it's imperative that we, first, find ways to encourage all citizens to listen to their fellow citizens, and, second, address the potential demobilizing effect that listening across difference may have on more formal types of participation, including voting. Fortunately, the demobilizing effects of deliberation across difference are not a given and could likely be reduced if, as I advocated in Chapter 5, we cultivated a greater acceptance of conflict among citizens.[26] As Mutz explains, the demobilizing effects of hearing the other side are strongest for those who are conflict avoidant.[27] Thus, to mitigate the troubling aspects of Mutz's findings, we likely need to distinguish citizenship—in its various forms—from the quiet life of a contented customer. While Chambers is right in arguing that "a healthy democracy requires that some citizens take up banners—but thankfully not all citizens,

[25] David Owen and Graham Smith, "Deliberation, Democracy, and the Systemic Turn," *Journal of Political Philosophy* 23, no. 2 (2015): 213–34.

[26] Emily Sydnor, *Disrespectful Democracy: The Psychology of Political Incivility* (New York: Columbia University Press, 2019).

[27] Mutz, "The Consequences of Cross-Cutting Networks for Political Participation," 851.

all the time," even those citizens embodying the more deliberative ideal of citizenship ought to try to cultivate a greater comfort with contestation.[28]

7.2.2 Affective Responses to Difference in Deliberation

Renewed closure in the face of differences and disagreement would certainly get in the way of our achieving the deliberative ideal of uptake. As such, this possibility deserves further investigation. In what follows, however, I point to empirical evidence suggesting that the affective response we would expect citizens to have in the face of deep difference would indeed carry the democratic benefit that I identified in Chapter 6.

Researchers in political psychology have studied the effect that various emotions have on a citizen's political behavior, including their willingness to participate in political activity and consider opposing views. Affective intelligence theory was originally developed as a way to understand voter behavior. It found "anxious voters pay more attention to politics, rely less on party identification and ideology, and consider candidate characteristics and policy preferences more carefully when deciding for whom to vote."[29] Importantly, however, the explanatory value of the theory of affective intelligence extends beyond voter behavior. The theory has also been used to explain a broader set of citizen behaviors, including information seeking. For example, in a 2010 study, MacKuen and colleagues used affective intelligence theory to better understand situations "where people who disagree about political goals are willing to listen to alternative viewpoints and seek common ground."[30] Now, as I have made clear throughout this book, there are good reasons for us to reject agreement or consensus as a sign of full and fair deliberation. Moreover, democratic listening, which is required for deliberation, does not entail any particular outcome, nor does it require us to seek common ground. But while the authors mention seeking common ground, the experiment they designed actually measured the affective drivers of people's willingness to simply listen to opposing views.[31]

[28] Chambers, "The Many Faces of Good Citizenship," 204.

[29] Eric Groenendyk, "Current Emotion Research in Political Science: How Emotions Help Democracy Overcome Its Collective Action Problem," *Emotion Review* 3, no. 4 (2011): 457.

[30] Michael MacKuen, Jennifer Wolak, Luke Keele, and George E. Marcus, "Civic Engagements: Resolute Partisanship or Reflective Deliberation," *American Journal of Political Science* 54, no. 2 (2010) : 442.

[31] More specifically, the researchers measured the number of web pages a participant visited that conflicted with their prior views. Ibid., 448.

Interestingly, the research suggests that the feelings one might have in the face of deep difference or disagreement may indeed help sustain the affective-cognitive disposition of listening toward democracy. For example, MacKuen and colleagues have shown that "anxiety," operationalized as having feelings of fear and unease, often in the face of "unfamiliar or uncertain circumstances," disrupts our ongoing perspectives and leads to greater open-mindedness.[32]

This research suggests that difference as novelty could work to disrupt our ongoing processing and assumptions, showing us the need for careful listening. Thus, the type of disruption caused by feelings of uncertainty may be foundational to meaningfully democratic deliberation. Without such a disruption, we assume that our worldview is definitive or adequate, in which case monologue becomes preferable to dialogue. In fact, according to MacKuen and colleagues' findings, we may not engage even in monological reflection if our reliance on political habits and heuristics is not disrupted.

These findings would seem to support Terri Elliot's assertion, "Seeing as strange what had appeared familiar is the beginning of any inquiry."[33] Insofar as encounters with difference necessarily involve that which is unfamiliar and, by my account, potentially unknowable, we have reason to believe that anxiety is not only deliberatively productive but indeed the *likely* response to difference. These findings regarding the ways in which novelty and difference sustain information-seeking behavior support my claim that orientating ourselves to the limits of our ability to understand those who are different can actually motivate the listening toward democracy on which deliberative uptake, and thus the promise of democracy, depends.

Still, another particularly relevant study in this line of research found that "aversion," a construct that measures "anger, disgust, contempt, and bitterness," while motivating participation, traditionally understood, did not necessarily promote more deliberation.[34] Specifically, researchers found that these emotions tended to "prepare people for the defense of convictions, solidarity with allies, and opposition to accommodation."[35] Anger, disgust,

[32] Ibid., 444, 455. Bethany Albertson and Shana Gadarian also find that anxiety leads to information seeking, but also find that anxiety can bias the type of information people prefer. Bethany Albertson and Shana Kushner Gadarian, *Anxious Poliltics: Democratic Citizenship in a Threatening World* (Cambridge: Cambridge University Press, 2015).

[33] Terri Elliott, "Making Strange What Had Appeared Familiar," *The Monist* 77, no. 4 (1994): 424.

[34] Nicholas A. Valentino, Ted Brader, Eric W. Groenendyk, Krysha Gregorowicz, and Vincent L. Hutchings, "Election Night's Alright for Fighting: The Role of Emotions in Political Participation," *Journal of Politics* 73, no. 01 (2011): 156–70; Groenendyk, "Current Emotion Research in Political Science," 457.

[35] MacKuen et al., "Civic Engagements," 440.

and bitterness, then, are powerful tools in the arsenal of citizens, especially when it comes to opposing injustice.[36] But such a defensive position would cut against the deliberative ideal of democracy if it impeded a willingness to even listen to what others had to say. Thus, we would not want citizens to develop feelings of aversion before or without fairly considering what others had to say.

Even so, I reject the implication that these sorts of reactions are necessarily problematic for achieving the deliberative ideal of democracy in practice. The deliberative democratic ideal does not require citizens to accommodate the preferences of their fellow citizens. Rather, it requires that they consider them. And if that consideration is fair, but results in feelings of anger and disgust and a refusal to compromise, then these reactions would actually be evidence of the democratic functioning of a deliberative system.

As I mentioned in Chapter 5, the value of bringing citizens together in conversation is generally assumed to lie in the reduction of partisan animosity or the bridging of divides between citizens.[37] Accordingly, political engagement across difference is often assumed to have failed if it does not lead to compromise or otherwise increase tolerance. But if we accept deep constitutive differences as an essential and legitimate feature of politics, then we must use alternative standards to judge the success of our deliberative encounters.

According to my interpretation of the deliberative ideal, we should assess the democratic force of political talk according to whether and how citizens listened to one another. Citizens could leave these conversations frustrated, confused, and even mobilized to shut down another's political efforts. But the interaction would still have contributed to the democratic nature of those actions so long as participants heard and considered what others had to say. Even if these conversations did not reduce partisan animosity, increase tolerance, or reveal common ground, they would still have accomplished the vital democratic goal of getting citizens to engage with one another. In the end, adopting the standard of fair consideration and thus pursuing listening toward democracy changes the way in which we approach and evaluate political talk.

Nonetheless, democratic deliberation centered on listening might fall short of the deliberative ideal in practice. Though essential, listening cannot guarantee citizens will achieve uptake. Especially in contexts of deep

---

[36] Katie Stockdale, "Losing Hope: Injustice and Moral Bitterness," *Hypatia* 32, no. 2 (2017): 363–79.
[37] Angel Quicksey, "Breaking Bread and Bridging Differences," *Civicist Civic Tech News & Analysis*, July 25, 2017, https://civichall.org/civicist/breaking-bread-and-bridging-differences/.

difference and disagreement, understanding and thus fair consideration can elude even the most generous listener. Despite good-faith efforts on the part of citizens and regardless of the intent of the listener, these failures of uptake still prevent a person from having a say in the laws to which they are held.

I contend, however, that even in the absence of understanding and in the case of failed uptake, the democratic prospects of deliberation are still good as long as people remain committed to continuing the conversation. Moreover, as I argued in Chapter 6, a lasting commitment to deliberation can come precisely from citizens taking a more realistic view of what communication can achieve—in other words, from citizens accepting the limits to our ability to understand one another. Still, in the next section, I consider what we ought to do in cases where the deliberative ideal of fair consideration is continually unmet.

7.3 What Do We Do When Ideal Standards Are Not Met or Repeatedly Violated?

In this book, I have argued that fair consideration or uptake, which must come after inclusion, is the relevant standard to use when assessing the democratic quality of our collective decisions. Furthermore, I have argued that practices of listening, not empathy, are best suited for helping us attain the deliberative ideal of fair consideration.

In the preceding chapters, I considered persistent challenges to improving our practices of listening and to ensuring that listening results in deliberative uptake. While I have proposed some interventions that might promote successful democratic listening, it is still possible for listening to fall short of the deliberative ideal. But even if practices of listening faced similar challenges to empathy, unlike empathy, listening is *necessary* for fair consideration (and therefore democracy) and so warrants the investment. *In* listening to our fellow citizens—not empathizing with them—we get closer to the deliberative ideal of fair consideration and so the promise of democracy. In other words, while these practical challenges deserve careful attention, it's worth remembering that my defense of the democratic listening approach to deliberation and my skepticism toward empathy-based approaches are fundamentally normative, not strategic.

If, in practice, citizens' listening did not meet the threshold needed for listening toward democracy, that would not necessarily undermine my claim that fair consideration is predicated on performative democratic listening. It is not my intention to grade democracy "on a curve," so to speak, lowering the bar to ensure it is achievable (or observable, for that matter). Thus, any skepticism regarding citizens' ability to adopt the disposition of a performative democratic listener when deliberating with others would not speak against listening's validity as an essential practice of full and fair deliberation. Rather, it would speak against our judging the deliberative system and its decisions to be meaningfully democratic.

My aim in this book has not been to sketch out a path to true democracy. Instead, I have used deliberative democracy and the normative standards it supplies to judge existing practices and the outcomes they produce. I rely on deliberative democratic theory less as an absolute ideal toward which to aim than as a critical tool with which to assess existing practices. Therefore, this normative standard can still be of practical use when it is not achieved.[38]

This book has tried to identify when and why our political practice falls short of our normative standards of justice. The crucial next step is to consider how best to proceed when we find that the normative conditions for meaningfully democratic deliberation are out of our reach. What recourse do citizens have when they experience failures of democratic listening? And how do we proceed if and when we are denied fair consideration? Are citizens expected to keep speaking up and sharing their perspectives, even as others refuse to listen or otherwise ignore their concerns?

People who are consistently denied uptake—either because their fellow citizens refuse to listen or they do not listen with the right disposition—have been denied participation in the lawmaking authority. The deliberative system and its laws thus would necessarily lack democratic legitimacy. Accordingly, in a non-ideal world, the ideal of fair consideration can support oppositional action. If people are consistently denied a fair hearing, they can appeal to the standard of fair consideration when lodging a complaint against the polity or even when engaging in civil disobedience.

Interpreting failures of listening as evidence of failed democracy can change the way we understand political protest. According to the view of democratic deliberation presented in this book, we might come to see protests and demonstrations more as a means of calling attention to the

---

[38] As Selen Ercan explains, even when unmet, normative conditions can "serve as a benchmark against which the democratic quality" of our deliberative practices "can be evaluated and improved." Selen A. Ercan, "From Polarisation to Pluralisation: A Deliberative Approach to Illiberal Cultures," *International Political Science Review* 38, no. 1 (2017): 124.

failure of listening itself rather than an attempt to secure uptake for a particular message.

Consider, for example, the public discourse around former San Francisco 49ers quarterback Colin Kaepernick's decision to protest the oppression of people of color in the United States. Kaepernick brought attention to this injustice by kneeling during the national anthem played before his football games. A common refrain among white moderates can be summed up in the following opening line from an editorial piece published in the *San Francisco Chronicle*, "Oh, Colin. . . . It was a noble thought. But not the right place for it."[39] These would-be supporters claim to agree with the message, but disagree with how the message was communicated. The speaker would be more effective in getting people to listen, they argue, if the message were delivered in a more civil or respectful way. To be sure, this criticism seems particularly absurd in the case of Kaepernick's kneeling. It's unclear, for example, how this act of kneeling could be interpreted as uncivil.

All the same, my theory would suggest that some demonstrations and acts of protest may not be aimed primarily at securing uptake for a particular message or input, but designed instead to call attention to the fact that members of this group have been left out of or ignored in political discourse. According to this view, the success or efficacy of protest and direct action in the face of failed listening should be judged according to whether it achieves disruption, not whether a particular message or proposal is taken up.

Importantly, however, such a disruptive protest or demonstration would not let citizens off the hook with respect to listening. When it comes to the question of fair consideration, the responsibility to listen and consider our fellow citizens' perspectives is not contingent on the packaging of the message. Instead, the responsibility to listen comes from the moral equality of each citizens' voice. As such, for the sake of democracy, we must continually remind citizens of the need to listen, even and especially when they find the speaker to be antagonistic or disruptive.

Citizens who are consistently denied democratic listening and, thus, fair consideration can appeal to this standard when making claims against the democratic legitimacy of particular decisions or when calling into question

---

[39] These white moderates seem to be taking a cue from Birmingham, Alabama's, white ministers who criticized Martin Luther King Jr. in 1963. See Martin Luther King, "Letter from Birmingham Jail," April 16, 1963, https://swap.stanford.edu/20141218230016/http://mlk-kpp01.stanford.edu/kingweb/popular_requests/frequentdocs/birmingham.pdf. Al Saracevic, "Kaepernick Anthem Protest: Wrong Place for a Noble Cause," *San Francisco Chronicle*, August 27, 2016.

the democratic nature of the polity itself. And as I have shown, citizens denied listening can appeal to the standard of fair consideration when engaging in oppositional politics. Regardless of any practical limitations and even in the case of real-world failures, fair consideration achieved through performative democratic listening remains a powerful deliberative ideal and an appropriate expectation of democratic citizens.

References

Albertson, Bethany and Shana Gadarian. *Anxious Politics: Democratic Citizenship in a Threatening World*. Cambridge: Cambridge University Press, 2015.

Allen, Danielle. *Talking to Strangers: Anxieties of Citizenship since Brown v. Board of Education*. Chicago: University of Chicago Press, 2009.

Aristotle. *The Politics*. New York: Penguin, 1981.

"ASL Sign for: Listen." *Handspeak*, https://www.handspeak.com/word/search/index.php?id=1285, accessed June 1, 2018.

Austin, J. L. *How to Do Things with Words*. Cambridge, MA: Harvard University Press, 1962.

Bächtiger, André, Simon Niemeyer, Michael Neblo, Marco R. Steenbergen, and Jürg Steiner. "Disentangling Diversity in Deliberative Democracy: Competing Theories, Their Blind Spots and Complementarities." *Journal of Political Philosophy* 18, no. 1 (2010): 32–63.

Bächtiger, André, and John Parkinson. *Mapping and Measuring Deliberation: Towards a New Deliberative Quality*. Oxford: Oxford University Press, 2019.

Bamford, James. "Big Brother Is Listening." *Atlantic Monthly*, April 2006. https://www.theatlantic.com/magazine/archive/2006/04/big-brother-is-listening/304711/.

Barber, Benjamin. *Strong Democracy: Participatory Politics for a New Age*. Berkeley: University of California Press, 1984.

Beausoleil, Emily. "Responsibility as Responsiveness: Enacting a Dispositional Ethics of Encounter." *Political Theory* 45, no. 3 (2017): 291–318.

Beck, Glenn. "Empathy for Black Lives Matter." *New York Times*. September 7, 2016.

Bejan, Teresa M. *Mere Civility: Disagreement and the Limits of Toleration*. Cambridge, MA: Harvard University Press, 2017.

Benhabib, Seyla. "The Democratic Moment and the Problem of Difference." In *Democracy and Difference: Contesting the Boundaries of the Political*, edited by Seyla Benhabib, 3–18. Princeton, NJ: Princeton University Press, 1996.

Benhabib, Seyla. *Situating the Self: Gender, Community, and Postmodernism in Contemporary Ethics*. New York: Routledge, 1992.

Bickford, Susan. *The Dissonance of Democracy: Listening, Conflict, and Citizenship*. Ithaca, NY: Cornell University Press, 1996.

Bird, Alexander. "Illocutionary Silencing." *Pacific Philosophical Quarterly* 83, no. 1 (2002): 1–15.

Bloom, Paul. *Against Empathy: The Case for Rational Compassion*. New York: HarperCollins, 2016.

Bodie, Graham D. "What Is Listening?" *Listen First Project*, 2018, accessed July 1, 2018 http://www.listenfirstproject.org/listen-first-academy/.

Bohman, James. *Public Deliberation: Pluralism, Complexity, and Democracy*. Cambridge, MA: MIT Press, 1996.

Bohman, James. "Public Reason and Cultural Pluralism: Political Liberalism and the Problem of Moral Conflict." *Political Theory* 23, no. 2 (1995): 253–79.

Bohman, James. "Realizing Deliberative Democracy as a Mode of Inquiry: Pragmatism, Social Facts, and Normative Theory." *Journal of Speculative Philosophy* 18, no. 1 (2004): 23–43.

Boros, Diana. *Creative Rebellion for the Twenty-First Century: The Importance of Public and Interactive Art to Political Life in America.* New York: Palgrave Macmillan, 2012.

Boswell, John, Carolyn M. Hendriks, and Selen A. Ercan. "Message Received? Examining Transmission in Deliberative Systems." *Critical Policy Studies* 10, no. 3 (2016): 263–83.

Bruneau, Emile G., and Rebecca Saxe. "The Power of Being Heard: The Benefits of 'Perspective-Giving' in the Context of Intergroup Conflict." *Journal of Experimental Social Psychology* 48, no. 4 (2012): 855–66.

Button, Mark E. "A Monkish Kind of Virtue? For and against Humility." *Political Theory* 33, no. 6 (2005): 840–68.

Button, Mark E. *Political Vices.* Oxford: Oxford University Press, 2016.

Button, Mark E., and Jacob Garrett. "Impartiality in Political Judgment: Deliberative Not Philosophical." *Political Studies* 64, no. 15 (2016): 35–52.

Chambers, Simone. "Balancing Epistemic Quality and Equal Participation in a System Approach to Deliberative Democracy." *Social Epistemology* 31, no. 3 (2017): 266–76.

Chambers, Simone. "Deliberative Democratic Theory." *Annual Review of Political Science* 6, no. 1 (2003): 307–26.

Chambers, Simone. "Making Referendums Safe for Democracy: A Call for More and Better Deliberation." *Swiss Political Science Review* 24, no. 3 (2018): 305–11.

Chambers, Simone. "The Many Faces of Good Citizenship." *Critical Review* 25, no. 2 (2013): 199–209.

Chambers, Simone. "The Philosophic Origins of Deliberative Ideals." In *The Oxford Handbook of Deliberative Democracy*, edited by André Bächtiger, John S. Dryzek, Jane Mansbridge, and Mark Warren, 55–69. Oxford: Oxford University Press, 2018.

Chambers, Simone. *Reasonable Democracy: Jürgen Habermas and the Politics of Discourse.* Ithaca, NY: Cornell University Press, 1996.

Cheon, Jongpil, and Michael Grant. "Active Listening: Web-Based Assessment Tool for Communication and Active Listening Skill Development." *TechTrends* 53, no. 6 (2009): 24–34.

Chun, Wendy Hui Kyong. "Unbearable Witness." *Differences: A Journal of Feminist Cultural Studies* 11, no. 1 (1999): 112–49.

Clinton, Hillary Rodham. *What Happened.* New York: Simon & Schuster, 2017.

Coles, Romand. *Rethinking Generosity: Critical Theory and the Politics of Caritas.* Ithaca, NY: Cornell University Press, 1997.

Collins, Eliza. "Trump: I Consult Myself on Foreign Policy." *Politico*, March 16, 2016. https://www.politico.com/blogs/2016-gop-primary-live-updates-and-results/2016/03/trump-foreign-policy-adviser-220853.

Connolly, William. *The Ethos of Pluralization.* Minneapolis: University of Minnesota, 1995.

Connolly, William E. *Identity\Difference: Democratic Negotiations of Political Paradox.* Minneapolis: University of Minnesota Press, 2002.

Coplan, Amy, and Peter Goldie, eds. *Empathy: Philosophical and Psychological Perspectives.* Oxford: Oxford University Press, 2011.

Dahlberg, Lincoln. "The Habermasian Public Sphere: Taking Difference Seriously?" *Theory and Society* 34, no. 2 (2005): 111–36.

Davis, Mark H. *Empathy: A Social Psychological Approach*. Madison, WI: Brown & Benchmark, 1994.

Dewey, John. *The Public and Its Problems*. Chicago: Swallow Press, 1954.

Dobson, Andrew. "Listening: The New Democratic Deficit." *Political Studies* 60, no. 4 (2012): 843–59.

Dobson, Andrew. *Listening for Democracy: Recognition, Representation, Reconciliation*. Oxford: Oxford University Press, 2014.

Dovi, Suzanne. "In Praise of Exclusion." *Journal of Politics* 71, no. 3 (2009): 1172–86.

Dreher, Tanja. "Listening across Difference: Media and Multiculturalism beyond the Politics of Voice." *Continuum* 23, no. 4 (2009): 445–58.

Dreher, Tanja, and Poppy De Souza. "Locating Listening." In *Ethical Responsiveness and the Politics of Difference*, edited by Tanja Dreher and Anshuman Mondal, 21–39. New York: Palgrave Macmillan, 2018.

Dryzek, John S. *Deliberative Democracy and Beyond: Liberals, Critics, Contestations*. Oxford: Oxford University Press, 2000.

Dryzek, John S. "The Forum, the System, and the Polity: Three Varieties of Democratic Theory." *Political Theory* 45, no. 5 (2017): 610–36.

Dryzek, John S. "Theory, Evidence, and the Tasks of Deliberation." In *Deliberation, Participation and Democracy: Can the People Govern?*, edited by Shawn W. Rosenberg, 237–50. New York: Palgrave Macmillan, 2007.

Dryzek, John S., and Simon Niemeyer. "Reconciling Pluralism and Consensus as Political Ideals." *American Journal of Political Science* 50, no. 3 (2006): 634–49.

Easley, Jonathan. "Poll: 57 Percent Have Negative View of Black Lives Matter Movement." *The Hill*, August 2, 2017, https://thehill.com/homenews/campaign/344985-poll-57-percent-have-negative-view-of-black-lives-matter-movement.

Elliott, Terri. "Making Strange What Had Appeared Familiar." *The Monist* 77, no. 4 (1994): 424–33.

Elster, Jon. "Deliberation and Constitution Making." In *Deliberative Democracy*, edited by Jon Elster, 97–122. Cambridge: Cambridge University Press, 1998.

Ercan, Selen A. "From Polarisation to Pluralisation: A Deliberative Approach to Illiberal Cultures." *International Political Science Review* 38, no. 1 (2017): 114–27.

Ercan, Selen A., Carolyn M. Hendriks, and John S. Dryzek. "Public Deliberation in an Era of Communicative Plenty." *Policy & Politics* 47, no. 1 (2019): 19–36.

Fedesco, Heather Noel. "The Impact of (In)Effective Listening on Interpersonal Interactions." *International Journal of Listening* 29, no. 2 (2015): 103–6.

Feola, Michael. "Speaking Subjects and Democratic Space: Rancière and the Politics of Speech." *Polity* 46, no. 4 (2014): 498–519.

Fishkin, James S. *When the People Speak: Deliberative Democracy and Public Consultation*. Oxford: Oxford University Press, 2009.

Fleming, James E., ed. *Passions and Emotions: Nomos LIII*. New York: NYU Press, 2012.

Foa, Roberto Stefan, and Yascha Mounk. "The Democratic Disconnect." *Journal of Democracy* 27, no. 3 (2016): 5–17.

Foa, Roberto Stefan, and Yascha Mounk. "The Signs of Deconsolidation." *Journal of Democracy* 28, no. 1 (2017): 5–15.

Fontana, Peter C., Steven D. Cohen, and Andrew D. Wolvin. "Understanding Listening Competency: A Systematic Review of Research Scales." *International Journal of Listening* 29, no. 3 (2015): 148–76.

Frazer, Michael. *The Enlightenment of Sympathy: Justice and the Moral Sentiments in the Eighteenth Century and Today*. New York: Oxford University Press, 2010.

"Frequently Asked Questions." *Listen First Project*, accessed July 1, 2018 http://www. listenfirstproject.org/faqs/.

Fricker, Miranda. *Epistemic Injustice: Power and the Ethics of Knowing*. Oxford: Oxford University Press, 2007.

Fultner, Barbara. "Gender, Discourse and Non-Essentialism." In *Dialogue, Politics and Gender*, edited by Jude Browne, 52–80. Cambridge: Cambridge University Press, 2013.

Galston, William A. *Anti-Pluralism: The Populist Threat to Liberal Democracy*. New Haven, CT: Yale University Press, 2018.

Gerace, Adam, Andrew Day, Sharon Casey, and Philip Mohr. "Perspective Taking and Empathy: Does Having Similar Past Experience to Another Person Make It Easier to Take Their Perspective?" *Journal of Relationships Research* 6, e10 (2015), 1–14.

Giroux, Henry A. "White Nationalism, Armed Culture and State Violence in the Age of Donald Trump." *Philosophy & Social Criticism* 43, no. 9 (2017): 887–910.

Goodin, Robert E. "Democratic Deliberation Within." *Philosophy and Public Affairs* 29, no. 1 (2000): 81–109.

Goodin, Robert E. *Reflective Democracy*. Oxford: Oxford University Press, 2003.

Goodin, Robert E., and John S. Dryzek. "Deliberative Impacts: The Macro-Political Uptake of Mini-Publics." *Politics & Society* 34, no. 2 (2006): 219–44.

Grillos, Tara. "Women's Participation in Environmental Decision-Making: Quasi-Experimental Evidence from Northern Kenya." *World Development* 108 (2018): 115–30.

Groenendyk, Eric. "Current Emotion Research in Political Science: How Emotions Help Democracy Overcome Its Collective Action Problem." *Emotion Review* 3, no. 4 (2011): 455–63.

Gutmann, Amy, and Dennis F. Thompson. *Democracy and Disagreement*. Cambridge, MA: Harvard University Press, 1996.

Habermas, Jürgen. "Popular Sovereignty as Procedure." In *Deliberative Democracy: Essays on Reason and Politics*, edited by James Bohman and William Rehg, 35–66. Cambridge, MA: MIT Press, 1997.

Habermas, Jürgen. *Between Facts and Norms: Contributions to a Discourse Theory of Law and Democracy*. Cambridge, MA: MIT Press, 1996.

Habermas, Jürgen. *The Theory of Communicative Action*. Volumes 1 and 2. Boston: Beacon Press, 1984.

Habermas, Jürgen. "Three Normative Models of Democracy." *Constellations* 1, no. 1 (1994): 1–10.

Hall, Cheryl. "Recognizing the Passion in Deliberation: Toward a More Democratic Theory of Deliberative Democracy." *Hypatia* 22, no. 4 (2007): 81–95.

Hauslohner, Abigail. "Southern Poverty Law Center Says American Hate Groups Are on the Rise." *Washington Post*, February 15, 2017.

Hendriks, Carolyn M., Selen A. Ercan, and Sonya Duus. "Listening in Polarised Controversies: A Study of Listening Practices in the Public Sphere." *Policy Sciences* 52, no. 1 (2019): 137–51.

Hibbing, John R., and Elizabeth Theiss-Morse. *Stealth Democracy: Americans' Beliefs about How Government Should Work*. Cambridge: Cambridge University Press, 2002.

Hoffman, Martin L. "Empathy, Justice, and the Law." In *Empathy: Philosophical and Psychological Perspectives*, edited by Amy Coplan and Peter Goldie. Oxford: Oxford University Press, 2011.

Honig, Bonnie. *Political Theory and the Displacement of Politics*. Ithaca, NY: Cornell University Press, 1993.

Houck, Curtis. "Networks Laud 'Artfully Painted,' 'Remarkable' Michelle Obama Speech; Touts People Crying." *NewsBusters*, July 2016, https://www.newsbusters.org/video/networks-laud-artfully-painted-remarkable-michelle-obama-speech-touts-people-crying.

Itkowitz, Colby. "What Is This Election Missing? Empathy for Trump Voters." *Washington Post*, November 2, 2016.

Iyengar, Shanto, and Sean J. Westwood. "Fear and Loathing across Party Lines: New Evidence on Group Polarization." *American Journal of Political Science* 59, no. 3 (2015): 690–707.

Jackson, Jeff. "Dividing Deliberative and Participatory Democracy through John Dewey." *Democratic Theory* 2, no. 1 (2015): 63–84.

Jilani, Zaid. "Video: Students at Elite Wharton Business School Mock 99 Percent Movement: 'Get a Job! Get a Job!'" *Think Progress*, October 21, 2011, https://thinkprogress.org/video-students-at-elite-wharton-business-school-mock-99-percent-movement-get-a-job-get-a-job-1e0ed111fbd/.

Johnston, Steven. *American Dionysia: Violence, Tragedy, and Democratic Politics*. Cambridge: Cambridge University Press, 2015.

Kang, Okim, and Donald L. Rubin. "Reverse Linguistic Stereotyping: Measuring the Effect of Listener Expectations on Speech Evaluation." *Journal of Language and Social Psychology* 28, no. 4 (2009): 441–56.

Khalid, Asma, "Tech Creates our Political Echo Chambers. It Might Also be a Solution," *All Things Considered*. NPR, April 12, 2017, https://www.npr.org/sections/alltechconsidered/2017/04/12/522760479/tech-creates-our-political-echo-chambers-it-might-also-be-a-solution.

King, Martin Luther, Jr. "Letter from Birmingham Jail." April 16, 1963, https://swap.stanford.edu/20141218230016/http://mlk-kpp01.stanford.edu/kingweb/popular_requests/frequentdocs/birmingham.pdf.

Komeda, Hidetsugu, Kohei Tsunemi, Keisuke Inohara, Takashi Kusumi, and David N. Rapp. "Beyond Disposition: The Processing Consequences of Explicit and Implicit Invocations of Empathy." *Acta Psychologica* 142, no. 3 (2013): 349–55.

Krause, Sharon R. *Civil Passions: Moral Sentiment and Democratic Deliberation*. Princeton, NJ: Princeton University Press, 2008.

Krause, Sharon R. "Empathy, Democratic Politics, and the Impartial Juror." *Law, Culture and the Humanities* 7, no. 1 (2011): 81–100.

Krauthammer, Charles. "Is Gay Marriage a Matter of Empathy or of Rights?" *Washington Post*, May 17, 2012.

Krznaric, Roman. "The One Thing That Could Save the World: Why We Need Empathy Now More Than Ever." *Salon*, November 9, 2014, https://www.salon.com/2014/11/08/the_one_thing_that_could_save_the_world_why_we_need_empathy_now_more_than_ever/.

Landemore, Hélène, and Scott E. Page. "Deliberation and Disagreement: Problem Solving, Prediction, and Positive Dissensus." *Politics, Philosophy & Economics* 14, no. 3 (2015): 229–54.

"Listen First Charlottesville." *Listen First Project*, 2018, accessed April 20, 2018 http://www.listenfirstproject.org/listen-first-in-charlottesville-event/.

Lebron, Christopher J. *The Making of Black Lives Matter: A Brief History of an Idea*. Oxford: Oxford University Press, 2017.

Lithwick, Dahlia. "It's about the Empathy, Stupid." *Slate*, May 10, 2012, https://slate.com/news-and-politics/2012/05/barack-obamas-decision-to-support-gay-marriage-was-a-rare-act-of-empathy-in-this-presidential-election.html.

MacKuen, Michael, Jennifer Wolak, Luke Keele, and George E. Marcus. "Civic Engagements: Resolute Partisanship or Reflective Deliberation." *American Journal of Political Science* 54, no. 2 (2010): 440–58.

Mansbridge, Jane. "Everyday Talk in the Deliberative System." In *Deliberative Politics: Essays on Democracy and Disagreement*, edited by Stephen Macedo, 211–40. Oxford: Oxford University Press, 1999.

Mansbridge, Jane, James Bohman, Simone Chambers, Thomas Christiano, Archon Fung, John R. Parkinson, Dennis F. Thompson, and Mark Warren. "A Systemic Approach to Deliberative Democracy." In *Deliberative Systems : Deliberative Democracy at the Large Scale. Theories of Institutional Design*, edited by John Parkinson and Jane Mansbridge, 1–26. Cambridge: Cambridge University Press, 2012.

Mansbridge, Jane, and Audrey Latura. "The Polarization Crisis in the US and the Future of Listening." In *Strong Democracy in Crisis: Promise or Peril?*, edited by Trevor Norris, 29–54. Lanham, MD: Lexington Books, 2017.

Marcus, George. "Reason, Passion, and Democratic Politics." In *Passions and Emotions: Nomos LIII*, edited by James E. Fleming. New York: NYU Press, 2012.

Markell, Patchen. "Contesting Consensus: Rereading Habermas on the Public Sphere." *Constellations* 3, no. 3 (1997): 377–400.

Martin, Robert W. T. "Between Consensus and Conflict: Habermas, Post-Modern Agonism and the Early American Public Sphere." *Polity* 37, no. 3 (2005): 365–88.

Maxwell, Lida, Cristina Beltrán, Shatema Threadcraft, Stephen K. White, Miriam Leonard, and Bonnie Honig. "The 'Agonistic Turn': *Political Theory and the Displacement of Politics* in New Contexts." *Contemporary Political Theory* 18, no. 4 (2019): 640–72.

McCarthy, Justin. "U.S. Support for Gay Marriage Stable after High Court Ruling." *Gallup*, July 17, 2015, http://www.gallup.com/poll/184217/support-gay-marriage-stable-high-court-ruling.aspx.

McPhail, Will, "These smug pilots have lost touch with regular passengers like us . . . " *New Yorker*, January 9, 2017.

Mills, Charles W. *The Racial Contract*. Ithaca, NY: Cornell University Press, 1997.

Mills, Charles W. "White Ignorance." In *Race and Epistemologies of Ignorance*, edited by Shannon Sullivan and Nancy Tuana, 13–38. Albany, NY: SUNY Press, 2007.

Morales, Lymari. "Knowing Someone Gay/Lesbian Affects Views of Gay Issues." *Gallup*, May 29, 2009, http://www.gallup.com/poll/118931/knowing-someone-gay-lesbian-affects-views-gay-issues.aspx.

Morrell, Michael E. *Empathy and Democracy: Feeling, Thinking, and Deliberation*. University Park: Pennsylvania State University Press, 2010.

Morrell, Michael. "Listening and Deliberation." In *The Oxford Handbook of Deliberative Democracy*, edited by André Bächtiger, John S. Dryzek, Jane Mansbridge, and Mark Warren, 236–50. Oxford: Oxford University Press, 2018.

Mouffe, Chantal. "Deliberative Democracy or Agonistic Pluralism?" *Social Research* 66, no. 3 (1999): 745–58.

Mouffe, Chantal. "Democracy, Power, and the 'Political.'" In *Democracy and Difference*, edited by Seyla Benhabib. Princeton, NJ: Princeton University Press, 1996.

Mouffe, Chantal. *The Democratic Paradox*. New York: Verso, 2000.

Mutz, Diana C. "The Consequences of Cross-Cutting Networks for Political Participation." *American Journal of Political Science* 46, no. 4 (2002): 838–55.

Mutz, Diana C. "Cross-Cutting Social Networks: Testing Democratic Theory in Practice." *American Political Science Review* 96, no. 1 (2002): 111–26.

Mutz, Diana C. *Hearing the Other Side*. Cambridge: Cambridge University Press, 2006.

Mutz, Diana C. "Reflections on Hearing the Other Side, in Theory and in Practice." *Critical Review* 25, no. 2 (2013): 260–76.

Narayan, Uma. "Working Together across Difference: Some Considerations on Emotions and Political Practice." *Hypatia* 3, no. 2 (1988): 31–48.

Neblo, Michael. "Thinking through Democracy: Between the Theory and Practice of Deliberative Politics." *Acta Politica* 40, no. 2 (2005): 169–81.

Neblo, Michael A., Kevin M. Esterling, Ryan P. Kennedy, David M. J. Lazer, and Anand E. Sokhey. "Who Wants to Deliberate—and Why?" *American Political Science Review* 104, no. 03 (2010): 566–83.

Neblo, Michael A., Kevin M. Esterling, and David Lazer. *Politics with the People: Building a Directly Representative Democracy*. Cambridge: Cambridge University Press, 2018.

Nichols, Michael P. *The Lost Art of Listening*. New York: Guilford Press, 2009.

Nussbaum, Martha. *Poetic Justice: The Literary Imagination and Public Life*. Boston: Beacon Press, 1995.

Obama, Barack. Interview with Robin Roberts. "Transcript: Robin Roberts ABC News Interview with President Obama—ABC News." *Good Morning America*, ABC, May 9, 2012, http://abcnews.go.com/Politics/transcript-robin-roberts-abc-news-interview-president-obama/story?id=16316043.

Obama, Michelle. "Democratic National Convention Speech." July 25, 2016. https://www.youtube.com/watch?v=4ZNWYqDU948.

O'Reilly, Bill. *The O'Reilly Factor*. Fox News. July 26, 2016.

Owen, David, and Graham Smith. "Deliberation, Democracy, and the Systemic Turn." *Journal of Political Philosophy* 23, no. 2 (2015): 213–34.

Parkinson, John. *Deliberating in the Real World: Problems of Legitimacy in Deliberative Democracy*. Oxford: Oxford University Press, 2006.

Pasupathi, Monisha, and Jacob Billitteri. "Being and Becoming through Being Heard: Listener Effects on Stories and Selves." *International Journal of Listening* 29, no. 2 (2015): 1–18.

Pedrini, Seraina, André Bächtiger, and Marco R. Steenbergen. "Deliberative Inclusion of Minorities: Patterns of Reciprocity among Linguistic Groups in Switzerland." *European Political Science Review* 5, no. 3 (2013): 483–512.

Plato. "Apology." In *The Trial and Death of Socrates*, edited by G. M. A. Grube. Indianapolis, IN: Hackett, 2000.

Plato. "Crito." In *The Trial and Death of Socrates*, edited by G. M. A. Grube. Indianapolis, IN: Hackett, 2000.

Plato. "Republic." In *The Collected Dialogues of Plato Including the Letters*, edited by Edith Hamilton and Huntington Cairns. Princeton, NJ: Princeton University Press, 1969.

Prinz, Jesse. "Against Empathy." *Southern Journal of Philosophy* 49 (2011): 214–33.

Quicksey, Angel. "Breaking Bread and Bridging Differences." *Civicist Civic Tech News & Analysis*, July 25, 2017, https://civichall.org/civicist/breaking-bread-and-bridging-differences/.

Rawls, John. *Political Liberalism*. New York: Columbia University Press, 2005.

Rorty, Richard. *Contingency, Irony, and Solidarity*. Cambridge: Cambridge University Press, 1989.

Rousseau, Jean-Jacques. *The Social Contract and Other Later Political Writings*, edited by Victor Gourevitch. Cambridge: Cambridge University Press, 1997.

Sanders, Lynn. "Against Deliberation." *Political Theory* 25, no. 3 (1997): 347–76.

Saracevic, Al. "Kaepernick Anthem Protest: Wrong Place for a Noble Cause." *San Francisco Chronicle*, August 27, 2016.

Schiappa, Edward, Peter B. Gregg, and Dean E. Hewes. "Can One TV Show Make a Difference." *Journal of Homosexuality* 51, no. 4 (2006): 15–37.

Scudder, Mary F. "Beyond Empathy : Strategies and Ideals of Democratic Deliberation." *Polity* 48, no. 4 (2016): 524–50.

Scudder, Mary F. "The Ideal of Uptake in Democratic Deliberation." *Political Studies* 68, no. 2 (2020): 504–22.

Setälä, Maija. "The Public Sphere as a Site of Deliberation: An Analysis of Problems of Inclusion." In *Deliberative Democracy: Issues and Cases*, edited by Stephen Elstub and Peter McLaverty, 149–65. Edinburgh: Edinburgh University Press, 2014.

Shapiro, Ian. *The State of Democratic Theory*. Princeton, NJ: Princeton University Press, 2003.

Shauk, Zain, and Todd Ackerman. "Sonograms Evoke Strong Reactions as Mandate Takes Effect." *Houston Chronicle*, February 8, 2012.

Silvers, Anita. "'Defective' Agents: Equality, Difference, and the Tyranny of the Normal." *Journal of Social Philosophy* 25, no. 1 (1994): 154–75.

Simas, Elizabeth N., Scott Clifford, and Justin H. Kirkland. "How Empathic Concern Fuels Political Polarization." *American Political Science Review* 114, no. 1 (2020): 258–69.

Simpson, Lorenzo C. "Communication and the Politics of Difference: Reading Iris Young." *Constellations* 7, no. 3 (2000): 430–42.

Snyder, Greta Fowler. "Multivalent Recognition: Between Fixity and Fluidity in Identity Politics." *Journal of Politics* 74, no. 01 (2012): 249–61.

Solidarity Cville. "Listen First Is Coercive. Some Say 'Listen' When They Actually Mean 'Comply.'" *Medium*. April 19, 2018, https://medium.com/@solidaritycville/now-hear-this-listen-first-is-coercive-787312856114.

Srader, Doyle W. "Performative Listening." *International Journal of Listening* 29, no. 2 (May 4, 2015): 95–102.

Steenbergen, Marco R, André Bächtiger, Markus Spörndli, and Jürg Steiner. "Measuring Political Deliberation: A Discourse Quality Index." *Comparative European Politics* 1, no. 1 (2003): 21–48.

Steiner, Jürg. *The Foundations of Deliberative Democracy: Empirical Research and Normative Implications*. Cambridge: Cambridge University Press, 2012.

Stevenson, Hayley, and John S. Dryzek. *Democratizing Global Climate Governance*. Cambridge: Cambridge University Press, 2014.

Stockdale, Katie. "Losing Hope: Injustice and Moral Bitterness." *Hypatia* 32, no. 2 (2017): 363–79.

Sunstein, Cass R. "The Law of Group Polarization." *Debating Deliberative Democracy* 10, no. 2 (2002): 80–101.

Sydnor, Emily. *Disrespectful Democracy: The Psychology of Political Incivility*. New York: Columbia University Press, 2019.

Tharoor, Ishaan. "Black Lives Matter Is a Global Cause." *Washington Post*, July 12, 2016.

Thomassen, Lasse. "Within the Limits of Deliberative Reason Alone: Habermas, Civil Disobedience, and Constitutional Democracy." *European Journal of Political Theory* 6, no. 2 (2007): 200–18.

Thompson, Dennis F. "Deliberative Democratic Theory and Empirical Political Science." *Annual Review of Political Science* 11 (2008): 497–520.

Valentino, Nicholas A., Ted Brader, Eric W. Groenendyk, Krysha Gregorowicz, and Vincent L. Hutchings. "Election Night's Alright for Fighting: The Role of Emotions in Political Participation." *Journal of Politics* 73, no. 01 (2011): 156–70.

Von Boven, Leaf, and George Loewenstein. "Empathy Gaps in Emotional Perspective Taking." In *Other Minds: How Humans Bridge the Divide between Self and Others*, edited by Betram Malle and Sara Hodges, 284–97. New York: Guilford Press, 2005.

Vozzella, Laura. "White Nationalist Richard Spencer Leads Torch-Bearing Protesters Defending Lee Statue." *Washington Post*, May 14, 2017.

Wahl, Rachel, and Stephen K. White. "Deliberation, Accountability, and Legitimacy: A Case Study of Police-Community Forums." *Polity* 49, no. 4 (2017): 489–517.

Warren, Mark E. "A Problem-Based Approach to Democratic Theory." *American Political Science Review* 111, no. 01 (2017): 39–53.

Wasil, Akash. "On Trump, Empathy, and Discourse." *Harvard Political Review*, November 11, 2016, https://harvardpolitics.com/united-states/trump-empathy-discourse/.

West Savali, Kristen. "#SandySpeaks: 'I'm Here to Change History.'" *The Root*, July 22, 2015, https://www.theroot.com/sandyspeaks-i-m-here-to-change-history-1790860601.

White, Stephen K. *A Democratic Bearing: Admirable Citizens, Uneven Justice, and Critical Theory*. Cambridge: Cambridge University Press, 2017.

White, Stephen K. *The Recent Work of Jürgen Habermas: Reason, Justice, and Modernity*. Cambridge: Cambridge University Press, 1988.

White, Stephen K. "The Very Idea of a Critical Social Science: A Pragmatist Turn." In *The Cambridge Companion to Critical Theory*, edited by Fred Rush, 310–35. Cambridge: Cambridge University Press, 2004.

White, Stephen K. "Varieties of Agonism" in critical exchange "The 'Agonistic Turn': Political Theory and the Displacement of Politics in New Contexts," *Contemporary Political Theory* 18, no. 4 (2019): 655–57.

White, Stephen K., and Evan Robert Farr. "'No-Saying' in Habermas." *Political Theory* 40, no. 1 (2012): 32–57.

"Who We Are: Listen First Coalition." *Listen First Project*, http://www.listenfirstproject.org/listen-first-coalition/, accessed April 25, 2018.

Young, Iris Marion. "Asymmetrical Reciprocity: On Moral Respect, Wonder, and Enlarged Thought." *Constellations* 3, no. 3 (1997): 340–63.

Young, Iris Marion. "De-Centering Deliberative Democracy." In *Democratizing Deliberation: A Political Theory Anthology*, edited by Derek W.M. Barker, Noëlle McAfee, and David W. McIvor, 113–28. Dayton, OH: Kettering Foundation Press, 2012.

Young, Iris Marion. "Difference as a Resource for Democratic Communication." In *Deliberative Democracy: Essays on Reason and Politics*, edited by James Bohman and William Rehg, 383–406. Cambridge, MA: MIT Press, 1997.

Young, Iris Marion. *Inclusion and Democracy*. Oxford: Oxford University Press, 2000.

Index

Note: Page numbers followed by *t* indicate a table on the corresponding page.

For the benefit of digital users, indexed terms that span two pages (e.g., 52–53) may, on occasion, appear on only one of those pages.